The Riddle

Where Ideas Come From and How to Have Better Ones

Andrew Razeghi

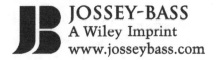

JOSSEY-BASS
A Wiley Imprint
www.josseybass.com

Published by Jossey-Bass
A Wiley Imprint
989 Market Street, San Francisco, CA 94103-1741—www.josseybass.com

Jossey-Bass books and products are available through most bookstores. To contact Jossey-Bass directly call our Customer Care Department within the U.S. at 800-956-7739, outside the U.S. at 317-572-3986, or fax 317-572-4002.

Jossey-Bass also publishes its books in a variety of electronic formats. Some content that appears in print may not be available in electronic books.

Library of Congress Cataloging-in-Publication Data
Razeghi, Andrew.
    The riddle : where ideas come from and how to have better ones / Andrew Razeghi.—1st ed.
    p. cm.
    Includes bibliographical references and index.
    ISBN-13: 978-0-7879-9632-1 (cloth)
    1. Creative ability.   2. Creative ability in business.   I. Title.   II. Title: Where ideas come from and how to have better ones.
  BF408.R244 2008
  153.3'5—dc22

                                      2007038036

Printed in the United States of America
FIRST EDITION
HB Printing   10 9 8 7 6 5 4

To the problem solvers

Contents

INTRODUCTION:
THE INNOVATION LAMENT

Have you ever had a problem you couldn't figure out no matter how hard you tried? Someone likely advised you, now clearly stumped, "Take a break. Don't think so hard." And so you did. And then, on waking up, while in the shower, or while stuck in traffic, it happened: you had a great idea. "Aha!" you said. "I've got it! I've figured it out!" This book is about that moment: why it happens, how it happens, and what you can do to make it happen more often. Welcome to *The Riddle*.

The riddle I am referring to is the conundrum that is the creative process: how we go about the journey into the origins of the so-called Eureka! moment: that magical split second in which a great idea holds a surprise party for your brain. It is during this mysterious adrenalin-charged moment that problems are solved, ideas are born, and inspiration soars. This blinding glimpse of unexpected brilliance is the siren's song of artists, designers, entrepreneurs, inventors, marketers, product developers, songwriters, and all those charged with the nearly impossible task of creating novel solutions to existing problems on an ongoing basis. By isolating and understanding what leads up to this ephemeral event, you will be better equipped to generate creative ideas deliberately rather than accidentally.

Isolating the eureka moment is not easy to do for a few key reasons. First, we do not actively screen people for creativity; rather, we tend to subjectively discriminate between those who are creative and those who are not. It is widely believed that those who are considered creative are somehow cosmically gifted versus deliberate about their success. Therefore, this categorization—"you've got it or you don't"—assumes that creativity cannot be learned and stymies attempts at understanding the creative process, including the origin of ideas. However, could it be that creative acts are not as random as they appear? Is underlying logic involved? Second, although almost everyone has experienced a eureka moment, we often do not recognize the underlying cognitive processes at work just prior to the moment; rather, we tend to recall only the moment itself. Our fascination with and enthusiasm about the ideas that are the outcomes of the creative process overshadows our understanding of why we had the big ideas in the first place and how to replicate what seems to be a random event. However, what if you were to replicate the events that precede the exact moment you had your last big idea? Could you learn to become deliberately, rather than accidentally, creative? And third, because of its mythical status, creativity is largely misunderstood, so we tend to excuse away our lack of success rather than attempt to understand and apply the logic that governs the creative process. This misunderstanding is compounded by the multitude of definitions of creativity. However, what if you were to learn to be more deliberate about creativity rather than waiting for divine inspiration? Could you increase your odds of success at innovation?

First, let's explore screening for creativity. Since writing my last book, I have been revisited occasionally by a remark that the financial services innovator Charles Schwab made to me. While he and I were discussing the topic of how to improve schools in order to better prepare our future leaders, he shared with me a conversation he had had with the dean of a Bay Area business school. The dean asked Schwab how the school might improve business education, and Schwab responded with something along the lines of, "The problem with you business school guys is that it is all about scores and boxes." By "scores and boxes," Schwab was referring to standardized tests, grade point averages, and other assorted clinical academic examinations. And by "you guys," he was referring to teachers and school administrators of the world.

Although standardized tests certainly play a vital role in our education system, the fundamental problem with scores and boxes from a creativity standpoint is relatively simple: the business of creativity is largely the business of thinking outside boxes, not filling them in. Even with changes to standardized tests, including the addition of written essays, they still do not account for or measure creativity, and herein is the great irony of standardized tests, particularly those used to assess business world aptitude: the business world revolves around creativity. New wealth flows to those who successfully introduce new products, new services, and new business models. Although those who design and administer standardized tests make no claims to test for creativity (in fact, they advertise that they do *not* test for creativity or motivation, for that matter), neither do most of the other measures used to assess a student's potential performance, including grade point average. Incidentally, it's not that there aren't tests available for measuring creativity because there are; rather, we don't use them as widely as we do tests for intelligence. Some would argue that a student's creative capacity can be gleaned by virtue of his or her extracurricular involvement, although I would contend that these activities are more often a better measure of a student's leadership aptitudes than creative skills. Nonetheless, I don't mean to harp on standardized tests alone because they are not the only contributors to the creativity crisis.

The responsibility for mitigating this crisis falls squarely on the shoulders of the field in which I work: innovation. Like all other fields, ours would benefit from a shared understanding or practical framework for comprehending and teaching creativity. This includes a rigorous understanding of the psychology of creative genius, as well as a comprehensive examination into the origin of ideas. However, this presents a challenge: even those of us who study creativity and innovation do not entirely understand the psychology of creative genius, although we do have informed opinions and a litany of academic studies to confirm those opinions. In fact, the greatest advantage within our field is that innovation is really not much of a field at all. Quite the contrary: we are a bit of a motley crew of artists, architects, behavioral psychologists, cognitive neuroscientists, inventors, musicians, mechanical engineers, product designers, social scientists, software engineers, and the occasional lunatic. Our diversity is our calling card. As creativity scholar Edward de Bono theorized decades ago, lateral thinking (the ability to think across conventionally drawn boundaries) is the foundation of creative insight. However, the challenge associated with our unique advantage is that we have no real operating models for managing the fuzzy front end that is creative insight, that is, the source of great ideas, and this is as true of individuals as it is of organizations. Lacking a framework for logically organizing creativity, individuals resort to all sorts of rituals in order to conjure up big ideas. From long walks to hot baths, we attempt to conjure up inspiration like clairvoyants channeling dead relatives. We'd like to believe it works, although we can't explain it.

Individuals are not the only ones in pursuit of a meaningful point of difference. Organizations invest heavily in the pursuit of new ideas, although they tend to be a bit more organized in their effort. Once they've identified ideas, many organizations have structured processes for moving ideas toward the desired reality of sales. Among these processes are a variety of innovation funnels and endless variations on the popular and pragmatic Stage-Gate process for managing new product development. However, in the light of such processes, random or deliberate, the innovation lament remains the same: Where will the next big idea come from? In order to answer this question, we must first understand how individuals are inspired before we can help organizations become inspired. In order to fashion a brave new world of creative problem solvers, we need to start a new conversation about creativity. We need to rethink *thinking differently*.

Beyond the profession of innovation, creativity is at best an afterthought in schools. Outside of business curriculums, it is taught as an artistic endeavor. And even within business curriculums, it is often taught as an elective course. I believe this is because applied creativity, or innovation, has not yet matured as a business discipline on par with, say, accounting or marketing. Innovation is spread across disciplines: marketing, manufacturing, organizational development, leadership, and so on. Yet there is no connective tissue. There are those like myself who teach individuals and organizations how to incubate and introduce new ideas to the world by virtue of new products, new services, and entirely new businesses, but there really is no such thing as a certified innovation expert or a master's degree in conceptual creativity; at least there are no such designations recognized as broadly as a Certified Public Accountant or even a certified Real Estate Agent. The field of innovation is not alone in this regard. All fields that have yet to mature to discipline status often suffer from a similar identity challenge. Because of the immaturity of our discipline, promulgated by a lack of a cohesive framework, organizations suffer the result: students graduate ill prepared in the concepts, methods, and logic of creative problem solving. I believe that by understanding how to teach, test, and manage creativity more systematically, we will be better equipped to solve many of the world's most challenging problems.

The innovation "profession" and our education system are responsible for mitigating the creativity crisis, but so too are our organizations. I halfheartedly joke with clients that innovation as a discipline inside organizations is somewhere like a student between his sophomore and junior years in college: he's relatively homeless and still spending his parents' money. Within the context of corporate innovation efforts, funding often comes from any number of sources: the research and development budget, the marketing budget, or some amorphous discretionary budget set up to fund interesting ideas. Innovation often does not have its own piggybank or its own internal metrics (for example, there is no innovation internal rate of return) or any common requirements for what the teams that propose new ideas must "prove" or "disprove" in order to receive further funding.

As far as who owns the innovation agenda inside organizations, if you want to know where innovation lives inside any company, follow the money. Whoever funds it, owns it—both its success and failure.

Given the vagabond lifestyle that innovation leads in our world today, is it any wonder that a large majority of new ideas fail in the marketplace? What else would you expect from something that is not taught, tested, organized, owned, or funded? A child born into a family of wolves would have a better chance of survival. However, I believe that failure is not required. This myth must be laid to rest. The reason that failure is often broached as a topic when people begin discussing innovation is that we are not organized about creativity. We believe it must be the result of a series of random and happy accidents. Herein is the crisis: there are sound reasons that new ideas fail, but the mantra about the need to "be willing to fail in order to succeed at innovation" has caused some significant problems.

First, no one wants to fail; more important, no one wants to be caught failing. Therefore, the lip-service paid to failure is rarely effective in actually creating behavioral changes in people. It sounds good from the podium but falls flat on its face in the boardroom.

Second, the failure myth has caused us to overlook the logic of creativity. Because "fail in order to win" has been preached so heavily, I believe we've given up before we've started. From my perspective, you do not need to fail in order to win at innovation. Individuals and organizations get lost only when they fail to travel with a compass and a map. The same is true in the search for new ideas. In the field of innovation, there are signposts, mile markers, and shortcuts to creative insight. You need to know how to recognize them in order to generate relevant solutions to problems on a more consistent basis. Among the tools explored throughout this book are precursors to creative insight: the behaviors and thought processes that often precede the birth of a big idea. By understanding how to apply these tools, you will be able to mitigate failure from your innovation efforts.

The third reason failure seems to be so prevalent in the field of innovation is the wholesale adoption of meaningless mantras, such as, "Think differently.""Think differently" is as helpful to would-be innovators as "swing differently" is to golfers. Imagine if Tiger Woods were having a tough time on the golf course and his coach simply looked at him and said, "Tiger, you may want to try swinging differently." The advice is virtually useless. If Tiger didn't know better, how would he know whether he should swing more slowly, swing backward, or swing while standing on his head? The useful advice is *how* he should swing differently. We see this same thing occur with innovation. Organizations that are encouraged to "think differently" often follow the same path: they introduce a litany of new products and services that are unique, new to the world, headline grabbing—and absolutely useless. Although they delivered on the initial mandate to think differently, ultimately they failed. Thinking creatively does not require thinking differently; rather it requires thinking deliberately, that is, in specific ways, about a given situation, problem, or opportunity. At times it even requires paying attention to thoughts that seem unrelated to the task at hand. This involves cognitive skills that most people possess yet rarely exercise.

My ambition of this book is to help you learn to become more conceptually creative by illustrating how the events that lead up to the eureka moment can be replicated in order to innovate continuously. Contrary to popular opinion, creativity does not have to be a random process. There is logic to it. By considering the evidence and techniques that often give rise to great ideas, I believe that we can begin to mitigate the creativity crisis facing most organizations today.

Crisis may sound a bit alarmist. In fact, it is, although I am not the one sounding the alarm. The clanging sound you hear is that of an increasingly loud, crowded, and homogeneous marketplace in which we are forced to compete. According to a productivity study conducted by the Dallas Federal Reserve, product categories have exploded since 1970. Today we live in a world with over 64 different types of dental floss (up from 12 in 1970), 141 different over-the-counter pain relievers (up from 17), 43 different McDonald's menu items (up from 13), and 285 brands of running shoes (167 men's and 118 women's, up from only 5 unisex models). You likely are able to name all 5 brands of running shoes that were on the market in 1970 (Adidas, Converse, New Balance, Nike, and Puma). Now try naming the 280 other brands on the market. Because of the glut of new products that are relentlessly introduced week after week, there isn't an organization on the planet that is not desperately seeking solutions to unmet needs or attempting to find that next big idea in search of relevance.

In corporate conversations, the phrase "finding a meaningful point of difference" is as common as a falafel stand in Tel Aviv. The challenge is to find the right ideas, great ideas, ideas that create value. What inspires creative genius? One way in which to answer these questions is to ask people who have conjured up big ideas where those ideas came from. However, I have discovered that this approach is somewhat futile because most innovators are unable to recall exactly why they had the big idea. They can typically recall what they were doing just prior to the eureka moment as well as the moment they reached an impasse in search of a solution. However, rarely can they explain why it happened. By way of example, in response to my question about the source of his company's creative inspiration, a client of mine once observed, "That's a bit like asking, *What is love?* I don't know where it comes from, but you can feel it when it's right."

Much like relationships, there are laws of attraction in the field of innovation. Those who study innovation (academics) and those who succeed in the introduction of new ideas (entrepreneurs, venture capitalists, corporate innovators) can often predict with a relative degree of accuracy why an idea will likely fail, as well as the conditions under which it will likely succeed. One of the reasons that we are able to predict these sorts of things is that we have access to a large sample size of unsuccessful ideas and therefore have learned much from the mistakes of others. In fact, in order to teach my students how to use clues in order to predict the likelihood of success or failure of a given idea, the first thing I have my students do in the course I teach on innovation at Northwestern University is fail. Imagine: you've worked your entire life to succeed. You've been admitted to one of the leading business schools on the planet, and the first thing your professor has you do is fail. Specifically, I give my students a failed product—one that they are to imagine they conjured up and launched. I then ask them to explain why they introduced it, why it failed, and what they would have done differently to relaunch, resurrect, or otherwise fix the idea. By the way, "kill the product" is an option, but it is rarely exercised. We cover the classics of failed products: Gerber's Singles (baby food for adults), Motorola's Iridium (satellite phones), Kleenex's Avert Virucidal Tissues (tissues with germ-fighting power that conjured up unfortunate images of suicidal and homicidal germs), Ford Motor Company's Edsel, and one of my personal favorites: Hey! There's a Monster in My Room (monster spray for kids).

Why did Hey! fail? Think about it. It's night. It's dark outside. You've just given your child a bath, read him a book, and tucked him snuggly under the covers. Then just when the child thought he was safe and cozy in his room, you hand him a bottle and tell him to spray it. "Why?" he asks, and you respond, "Because, *Hey! There's a monster in your room!*" Thanks for reinforcing the fear. Similar logic was at work in the case of Gerber Singles. Imagine: you're single. It's Saturday night, and you are home alone eating baby food out of a jar. How would this product make you feel? It deserved to fail, as did each of the other ideas.

If you are willing to listen, failure is the greatest teacher—although I suggest learning from someone else's failure rather than your own. For example, by resurrecting an old, broken idea, Kleenex, twenty years after the failed launch of its Avert tissues, re-launched it with new technology and under a new name: Kleenex Anti-Viral Tissues. It has thus far succeeded in meeting the unmet needs of its customers by telling a more relevant story about the benefits of the product: do more than capture the germs expelled from a sneeze that travels at a rate of 320 kilometers per hour; kill them. The tissues claim to kill "99% of cold and flu viruses in the tissue before they spread." Considering that a sneeze or cough can land viruses up to three feet away from the person who produced them and live on surfaces for up to twenty-four hours, the idea sells. But why did its predecessor, Avert, bomb? It could have been the name. What does *virucidal* mean anyway? Or perhaps it was the fact that the tissues were impregnated with a Vitamin C derivative, leaving consumers wondering how "citrus" may feel when wiped onto one's eyes. Either way, the fundamental problem remained: how to stop the spread of colds.

As Kleenex's Avert and endless other cases have taught us, although the execution of the solution was problematic, the need remained. When Avert failed, the need remained unmet for at least two decades. Why? Imagine if you worked for the Kleenex brand between the years of 1985 (when Avert was launched) and 2005 (when Kleenex Anti-Viral was launched). Who would dare suggest the resurrection of a failed idea?

The reasons we often miss the big idea is not necessarily that we are afraid to fail; rather, we are not prepared to see that idea in the first place or have forgotten that someone, somewhere, and at some other point in time attempted to solve the very same problem and failed in the execution of the idea. If you want to succeed with creating the future, study the past, both success and failure: What went wrong? or Why did it work? What can you glean from that experience that may help you innovate once again? Otherwise, in lieu of a disciplined approach to eureka moments, you will stand in wonderment when in the presence of a great idea and ask that perennial question: "Why didn't I think of that?"

The good news is that thinking creatively is a choice. You have control over it. And although the field of innovation has a long row to hoe before it takes its place alongside more established disciplines and although this book by no means attempts to solve the creativity crisis on its own, I view this is a starting point. In order to do so, it is first important to define creativity (as we'll explore in detail in Chapter One). One of the fundamental problems I have recognized in my work in this field is that *creativity* and *applied creativity* (or innovation) mean many different things to many different people. From creating unique things to thinking outside the proverbial box, *innovation* is at best loosely defined.

In order to help advance this conversation and subsequently the field of applied creativity, this book begins by distinguishing three fundamentally different forms of creativity: artistic creativity, scientific discovery, and conceptual creativity. As you'll soon learn, *The Riddle* is largely concerned with the most overlooked and often most misunderstood type of creativity: conceptual creativity, the creativity of business.

In addition, like divergent semantics, innovation is surrounded by a number of wildly popular myths, including these: innovation is about creating things that do not exist; you are either a right-brained or a left-brained thinker; first movers have a sustainable advantage; and failure is required. These myths, all red herrings promulgated as half-truths in the blogosphere, compound our misunderstanding of innovation. Having spent my career researching, teaching, and advising organizations around the globe on innovation, I believe that these myths hinder our capacity to solve problems. I seek to debunk these myths throughout the book, but for now, a few thoughts. First, there is no such thing as a new idea. There are only those that have not been combined in the right way and those for which the time was not appropriate. Heed the advice of Carlos Pellicer, one of the early Mexican modernist poets, who once observed, "I am time between two eternities. Before me, eternity and after me, eternity. Fire; a solitary shadow amid immense clarities." If you want to win at the business of innovation, study the past. It's all been done before—often in a different form or in a different place. Those who succeed at innovation often do so by reinterpreting the past and reconfiguring the present in order to create the future.

A second myth worth debunking is the belief that people are either right-brained (creative) or left-brained (logical). Although the idea would make for good science fiction, there is no such thing as a half-brained person. Diagnosing people as either right-brained or left-brained is as helpful to innovation as suggesting that a zebra has either black stripes or white stripes. As we'll explore later, your entire brain is involved in the creative process.

Third, and contrary to popular opinion, in many categories first movers do not maintain sustainable advantage. With the exception of some highly regulated industries such as pharmaceuticals or defense contracts where manufacturers design to specification, it is not unusual for an organization to follow a first mover and ultimately create greater value and sustain success over a longer period of time. In today's hypercompetitive, open-sourced world, if you want to create sustainable value, develop the capacity to *find* the first movers, and either do what they do better or figure out some way to work with them. The idea of connecting with ideas (versus inventing them) is not only a recent trend in innovation circles; it was at the heart of the unrivaled success of the world's most recognized inventor, Thomas Edison. Edison was more of a broker than an inventor. His talent was in attracting the best and the brightest inventors to his laboratory, knowing how to manage them in a collaborative effort, and promoting their work vigorously under the Edison name. Edison understood the value of a brand long before it became a buzzword.

Finally, the most pervasive myth in the field of innovation is that failure is required. Failure is *not* required. By learning to think appropriately, versus differently, you can mitigate failure from the creative process. Sure, there will always be those who fail; however, wouldn't you rather learn on someone else's dime than spend your own repeating their mistakes?

The Riddle seeks to dispel these myths; however, the ultimate goal of this book is to illustrate techniques for fostering conceptual creativity—to help you think deliberately, not just differently. This is based on my belief that creativity can be taught, and it can be learned. I believe that learning to think creatively is no different from learning to do math. There are rules, there is logic, there are right answers, and there are wrong answers. The only difference between creativity and mathematics is that applied creativity as a discipline has not had the deliberate focus given to mathematics.

The content of this book represents informed opinions, observations, and an occasional timeless truth that I have encountered in my work as an educator and adviser to individuals and organizations of all shapes and sizes on creativity, innovation, and growth. It is my intention with this book—and I invite you to join me—to help develop the field of applied creativity (innovation) not as a failure-induced happy accident but rather as a discipline. I believe the best place to start this conversation is not by thinking differently but by thinking deliberately about the common yet elusive precursors to creative insight.

Like most other riddles, the answer can often be found in the question. Clues exist. So too is the case of the creativity riddle. The answer to the creativity riddle—where ideas come from—can be found by studying the outcomes of inspiration (ideas) and the individuals responsible for creating them. If you look closely at ideas and the experiences of their creators just prior to the conception of these ideas, the ideas themselves offer clues as to their origins. In my research, I have identified five distinct clues—precursors to creative insight—that are often present at the conception of an idea. I have designed and written this book to explore each of these precursors in consecutive chapters—curiosity, constraints, conventions, connections, and codes—in order to help you learn to conjure up aha moments at will.

The ideas and concepts I propose here are by no means definitive. I do not profess to have discovered the Holy Grail that governs epiphany and would never attempt to guarantee that everything in this book will work in a particular case. However, what I can promise is this: if you approach the principles and suggestions in this book with an open mind and in the spirit of intellectual curiosity, you will be rewarded.

1

THE INNOVATION INTENT

The word *innovator* conjures up a plethora of personalities, among them the usual suspects: Leonardo da Vinci, Albert Einstein, Richard Branson. We have a tendency to lump all innovators into a single category: creative geniuses. However in order to understand where ideas come from, it is first important to distinguish the different forms of creative expression and the different types of innovators—artistic creativity (for example, Pablo Picasso), scientific creativity (for example, Marie Curie), and conceptual creativity (for example, James Dyson, the inventor of the Dyson vacuum cleaner, the cleaner that "doesn't lose suction")—since these three forms require different skills and have very different goals. By understanding these differences, you can avoid the predictable fender benders often associated with innovation: botched business ventures, failed product launches, and disastrous investment decisions. In order to put the innovation intent into context, I will share a personal experience with you that led to my own eureka moment about the field in which I work: innovation. If you have ever attended a creativity seminar, this experience may sound familiar.

Karaoke is a dodgy affair and ought to be heavily regulated. Care and use requirements should read as follows: *Karaoke is to be used only while intoxicated or while in the presence of a heavily sedated audience. Furthermore, karaoke is designed for entertainment purposes only and should not be used for practical applications. Break the rules, and face stiff fines.* There I was, minding my own business, when I was suddenly launched into the midst of a dozen complete strangers singing Gloria Gaynor's "I Will Survive." If you could have seen us: howling like caged animals with heads thrown back in ecstasy and fists pumping wildly. Survival was certainly on my mind, but so too was spontaneous combustion. You might conclude that I was involved in some sort of premarital ritual, but this was not the case. Quite the contrary, I was attending a creativity seminar: a day-long event designed to help participants "think differently." The room had a romper room feel to it: games, toys, beanbags. You get the picture. At one point, we even paused for an ice cream break. The session facilitator had arranged for the Good Humor man to swing by in his ice cream truck just in time to inspire our palates. I had a Bomb Pop, the original cherry-, lime-, and blue-raspberry-flavored frozen treat.

And then it happened. Aha! I was indeed beginning to think differently. While licking the remains of my cherry-, lime-, and blue-raspberry-stained fingers, I suddenly realized the extent to which creativity and innovation are profoundly misunderstood.

In an attempt to reduce inhibitions, a hallmark of creativity, many purveyors of innovation employ games such as these to promote new ways of thinking. Their belief is that divergent thinking (thinking outside the box) will increase as inhibitions retreat. This is absolutely true; however, where they run into trouble is how they go about promoting creativity. Promoting *artistic* creativity (the creation of unique objects) by virtue of song and dance may be temporarily entertaining, but it is not necessarily the most effective method for encouraging *conceptual* creativity (the art of problem solving). It does include an element of fun and when used in moderation can be effective. However, one could argue that public displays of artistic expression may heighten inhibitions for many people, particularly when done in the company of strangers or even coworkers.

Since creativity is a function of both cognition and emotion, the feeling of anxiety that these stunts often produce works to narrow our attention (cognitively) and motivates us (emotionally) to withdraw from creative collaboration ("I've got to get out of here!" may be the overwhelming thought). Anxiety and creativity are strange bedfellows. Robert Sternberg, a leading researcher in intelligence and creativity, has found that "a creative person is willing to tolerate this anxiety [of trying to reach a solution] long enough to reach an optimal or near-optimal solution." For others, however, crawling into the nearest box (versus thinking outside it) is a more likely response. These techniques often fail to surface relevant ideas not because they are silly but because they are designed on the premise that all creativity is art. The goal is to create something unique versus creating something that serves a relevant purpose or solves an existing problem.

This myth is deeply rooted in a shared misunderstanding of applied creativity, that is, innovation. It is so widely misunderstood that many of us even have an image in our mind of what innovators should look like. By way of example, during a Webcast interview in Monterrey, Mexico, at Tecnológico de Monterrey, one of Mexico's leading universities, I was once asked by Carlos Cruz, the president of innovation and institutional development at the university, whether I could identify an innovator based on that person's physical appearance. He then went on to say that when we met, he expected me to be wearing jeans and to be a bit disheveled in my appearance—the romantic vision of an artist—and was surprised to see me wearing a suit and tie. This image of "the innovator" that we carry around in our minds is not necessarily a mythological image; it simply reflects our shared misunderstanding of the difference between artistic creativity and conceptual creativity. After I had responded to his question, which I will share with you shortly, Cruz then shared with me why he asked me the question: he too wears a suit and tie and is often asked the same question. After all, the word *innovation* is in his job title. This collective misunderstanding of innovation is so widespread that we even have a stereotypical image for what an innovator should look like: a hybrid of Albert Einstein and Andy Warhol. Herein is the problem.

Although all art involves creativity, not all creativity involves art. For example, surgeons get creative once they discover an unanticipated problem during a procedure. So too do entrepreneurs once they've burned through their seed funding. As far as I know, there have been no documented cases of karaoke-inspired heart surgery, and although many entrepreneurs may not be able to paint, they are certainly no strangers to bootstrapping. The creativity employed by entrepreneurs, new product developers, physicians, parents, and all those others charged with finding innovative solutions to existing problems is not artistic creativity; rather, it is conceptual creativity. These two forms of creativity are vastly different.

Art includes all unique objects, including music, that are admired for their aesthetic principles. Artistic creativity consists of the ability to render things that attract attention for their inherent beauty or simply because of their mere existence, as Michelangelo's *David* does. Artistic creations may be unique, but are they relevant to solving any particular problem? It really doesn't matter. Artistic creations do not have to be relevant to anything or anyone. The *Mona Lisa* is to be admired, but it doesn't have to solve a problem. It is art—and great art at that. But conceptual creativity has a goal: to solve a problem or fill an unmet need, want, or desire. For example, figuring out how to get potable water to those living in sub-Saharan Africa is a problem. Ethos Water has in part figured it out. For every bottle of Ethos designer water that a person buys at Starbuck's or elsewhere, five cents goes directly to support water programs throughout the world. Ethos is a uniquely relevant solution to an unmet need and a conceptual innovation. It is not art. An example of a technological solution to this same problem is the LifeStraw, a ten-inch drinking straw with a charcoal filter that filters out bacteria and parasites. A person can use it to drink safely from a possibly contaminated water source. It's the same problem with two creative solutions.

This common misunderstanding between artistic creativity (inventing unique things) and conceptual creativity (solving problems) is one of the primary reasons that so many new ideas fail in the marketplace. The reason so many people and organizations fail at innovation is that they focus too much on artistic creativity when attempting to introduce new ideas. They end up introducing novelty, not solutions. Ideas that fail are often unique and therefore succeed as art; however, they are rarely relevant and therefore fail as concepts. Ultimately they are admired but not consumed.

Ford Motor Company's famous $400 million flop, the 1958 Edsel, was admired for its novelty but rejected for its concept. In fact, it didn't have one. Consumers did not understand what it was, how it was different from existing products including Ford's own Mercury brand, or why they should buy it. It did not solve a problem or create a relevant opportunity for its intended audience. It was not a concept. It was art (and dangerous art at that, as Ralph Nader's *Unsafe at Any Speed* revealed). Although most organizations, including Ford, certainly do not intend to create art when developing and introducing new products, new services, and new ventures, they often do because they confuse artistic creativity with conceptual creativity. This goes well beyond semantics to the heart of what people believe about creativity.

As an educator and adviser to organizations on creativity and innovation, I often hear the phrase, "I'm just not creative." From Chicago to Shanghai, this declaration knows no cultural boundaries. However, it is not true. Just because you may not be able to sing, dance, or play an instrument does not mean you are not creative. You may not be *artistically* creative, but you are likely *conceptually* creative. Think about it this way. When was the last time you had a problem and solved it? Perhaps you ran out of a key ingredient while cooking and had to make do. Or you were forced to jury-rig your car door with duct tape. Or during the Q&A portion of the presentation of your life, you had to improvise almost all of the answers. Regardless of the problem you had, how you solved it was an act of creativity. If you have ever solved a problem, you are conceptually creative. So give yourself credit: you have the capacity to create.

My definition of conceptual creativity is simple: creativity is what makes a dog paddle. Once the barking stops, the swimming begins. When we have to figure things out, we do.

The difference between successful innovators and would-be innovators begins with their intent. In order to succeed at innovation, do not focus on being creative; rather, focus on solving problems. Committing to innovation in the absence of a well-defined problem is like a surgeon committing to surgery in the absence of a diagnosis. Bloody failure is imminent. Therefore, the application of conceptual creativity as a tool must always begin by identifying and defining a problem. This encompasses nurturing curiosity about the problem, identifying constraints associated with solving the problem, challenging prevailing conventions about what solutions are possible, and making unorthodox connections between disparate domains. In turn, conceptually creative thinking gives rise to new ideas. Given this distinction, *thinking differently* is a distraction inasmuch that it simply suggests that you must think "in some other way" from how you are currently thinking. This cliché does nothing to help you learn how to think more creatively. And therefore my focus is not so much on getting you to think differently as it is getting you to thinking more deliberately and in specific ways about the mind-set and the methods of creative problem solving. For example, one such way of thinking involves making unorthodox connections between seemingly disparate pieces of information—what I call *thinking sideways*. This type of information processing is a hallmark of creative thinking. All humans have the capacity to think sideways; you need only be deliberate about how you go about it.

For example, contrary to popular opinion, Henry Ford did not invent the assembly line; rather, he borrowed it from Chicago's meatpacking industry. He then combined it with the concept of interchangeable parts, an idea that Eli Whitney introduced in 1801 when he suggested that the U.S. Army could assemble new pistols from the parts of broken ones. And he subsequently combined both of these ideas with yet a third idea: continuous-flow production, an idea first used in the tobacco industry in 1882 to make cigarettes. In blending these disparate ideas together, a great idea was born:

modern manufacturing. Andrew Hargadon, assistant professor of technology management at the University of California, Davis, deftly illuminates Henry Ford's real creative genius: "Ford's system was revolutionary in its impact on the automobile industry, on manufacturing, and on society . . . *because* its origins drew on existing technologies." The future is happening all around you. But if you look only straight ahead, in the direction that conventional wisdom and "futurists" suggest you look, you'll never see it coming. But if you look around you (sideways) and behind you (historically), the future will become increasingly apparent.

Why study history? Because there is no such thing as a new idea. For example, the disposable camera is a one-hundred-year-old idea with a twist. At the turn of the nineteenth century, photographers would send off the entire camera for their film to be developed and receive the camera back along with the developed photographs. Today they simply throw away the camera.

Although there is no such thing as a new idea, there are such things as new concepts. You can think of concepts as idea systems. Although the individual components of the concept may not be new, the combination of ideas—what you cannot see—is where the money is. For example, Henry Ford envisioned the invisible (the assembly line). It was not the assembly line per se; rather it was the concept of manufacturing. It was not the greasy mechanical parts moving across the shop floor; rather, it was the manifestation of many existing and disparate microconcepts. Ford arrived at his aha moment not just by thinking differently, but rather by thinking deliberately. Specifically, he thought sideways: outside his category of cars but not outside his competency of manufacturing. By combining three very different ideas he had observed in other industries and throughout history, Ford created a concept that was both unique and relevant: the modern automobile manufacturing plant. Most important, the pursuit of novelty was not the motivating factor driving Ford's process innovation; rather, it was the pursuit of an answer to his problem: to make cars better, faster, and cheaper. Henry Ford was not an artist. He was a conceptually creative thinker.

Conceptual creativity demands that an idea perform on three levels. First, the idea must be directly aligned with a well-defined problem. For example, making cars in large quantities was not cost-effective; this was an internal constraint for Ford the entrepreneur and his company. Second, the idea must be unique in its response to the problem. Continuous work flow and interchangeable parts were unconventional methods in automobile manufacturing. It is important to note here that an idea does not necessarily have to be new to the world to be innovative; it must be unique only to the situation. In this case, how Ford applied these two ideas to automobiles was in fact new. And third, for an idea to be conceptually creative, it must be relevant to its intended audience. In this case, the intended audience was an internal audience: Ford's employees. By having the work come to them, labor became more productive, and thus the plants became more efficient.

In hindsight, Ford's concept seems sophomorically straightforward. That's because it was. It was not new. It was simply an idea that no one else could see, comprising three disparate ideas that were brought together to solve a problem. In practice, individuals and organizations often fail to "get creative" when they fail to align these three requirements: a *unique* and *relevant* solution to an existing *problem*. More often than not, in the pursuit of innovation, individuals are distracted by the romantic vision of the purely new-to-the-world idea. In pursuit of the creatively romantic, we ultimately put far too much effort behind identifying the unique character of an idea versus solving a problem. Subsequently we introduce artwork instead of concepts.

Ironically, although Henry Ford was a brilliant concept creator, among the most famous "artists" in the world is the very company he founded, Ford Motor Company. You may be wondering how a company that bears Henry Ford's name produced one of the most spectacular new product failures in history. It is worth noting that Henry Ford passed away a decade prior to the launch of the Edsel. In fairness, although many factors contributed to the Edsel's demise, it is safe to say that Ford the company got lost in the art of innovation (versus the concept of innovation). Over time, the company became infatuated with the products it sold and appeared to have forgotten the problems it should have solved. In fact, in the case of the Edsel, there was no problem, and therefore the Edsel became a very, very expensive piece of art. Unfortunately, Ford is not alone. This confusion between artistic and conceptual creativity is often blurred. If your intent is to create for creation's sake, then by all means, strike up the band and sing! But if your goal is to meet an unmet need, solve an unsolved problem, or create an opportunity where one does not exist, different questions must be asked and different puzzles solved.

This brings us to the third form of creativity: the process of scientific discovery. Although scientific discovery is often discussed in the context of creativity, science is very different from both art and concept. In science, there are definitive answers. Unlike Picasso's *Guernica* (art) and Apple's iPhone (concept), the double-helix, electricity, and benzene are not things that people engineered. These things existed long before we had the maturity of mind to discover them. Furthermore, unlike art and concept, scientific discovery involves absolute truths. And unless Congress repeals the laws of physics, truth is not going to change anytime in the near future. In the simplest terms, scientific creativity involves discovery (truth), whereas conceptual creativity involves bringing something into being (ideas). With this distinction in mind, although I cannot promise to make you the next Thomas Edison, Mary Kay Ash, or Aaron Spelling (America's most prolific television producer, who could have held master classes on both conceptual and artistic creativity), the following chapters will improve your creative capacity.

In order to attempt to solve this riddle, let's begin by taking a step back in time. History is our most forgotten teacher.

Summary Points and Creative Exercises

- Not all creativity has the same objectives or uses the same thought processes. In order to mitigate failure with innovation, try not to confuse artistic creativity (the ability to render things revered for their aesthetic beauty) with scientific discovery (the uncovering of things that already exist) with conceptual creativity (creating uniquely relevant solutions to existing and emerging problems).

- There is no such thing as a new idea. It has all been done before. Look for ways in which to apply existing and preexisting ideas from other places, industries, or categories to your situation.

- Innovation is not the result of thinking differently. It is the result of thinking deliberately (in specific ways) about existing problems and unmet needs. These specific ways are discussed throughout this book in the context of precursors to creative insight.

2

THE GODS MUST BE CRAZY
(OR IS IT JUST ME?)

Since antiquity, scholars—among them Socrates, Plato, and Aristotle—have been enchanted by the origin of ideas. The Greeks did not see much mystery in creativity. From their perspective, ideas came from a single source: the gods, or more specifically, the goddesses. Each of Zeus's nine daughters, the Muses, held court over different aspects of creative expression: poetry, song, dance, and so on. Plato observed, "A poet is holy, and never able to compose until he has become inspired, and is beside himself and reason is no longer in him . . . for not by art does he utter these, but by power divine." Not only were the goddesses responsible for inspiring creativity; they were a discriminatory bunch insofar as they chose *who* was to be inspired ("breathed into"). It was commonplace for the inspired to maintain a unique relationship with some otherworldly being. Such was the case of Socrates, who attributed most of his knowledge to his "demon."

The Socratic conception of demonic possession was a divine gift granted to a select few. Once you were chosen by a Muse to be inspired, you had only one job to do: transport the idea from the heavens to humans. To the Greeks, we humans were the humble messengers of heavenly messages, and therefore the only way to "be creative" was through particular states of mind such as demonic possession or while in some sort of trancelike state like sleep in which you could possibly communicate with the gods. In this regard, creativity was thought to be an act outside our control. In fact, the expression "you must be out of your mind" did not equate to insanity; rather, it referred to the notion that creative ideas are originally conceived outside the human body (literally) and subsequently transferred to us in an act of divine inspiration.

Inspired madness was a desired state of mind. Eventually Aristotle, perhaps in an act of intellectual liberation from his mentor Plato, later suggested that mental illness might play a role in creativity. Nevertheless, in regard to mental illness, the creatively gifted Greek philosophers were quick to distinguish between "divine disturbance" and "clinical insanity." But, of course! The *gods* must be crazy. Not me! Plato postulated, "Madness, provided it comes as a gift of heaven, is the channel by which we received the greatest blessings. . . . [It] is a nobler thing sober sense. . . . Madness comes from God, whereas sober sense is merely human." Although Aristotle concurred that there was a difference between a person of distinction and a complete nut, his greater contribution was his suggestion that the capacity to create is not only above us; it is within us. Apart from Aristotle's gentle nod in the direction of willful creativity, the belief that creativity was the product of divine inspiration continued to dominate our thoughts through the Middle Ages and well into the sixteenth century.

During the Italian Renaissance, the term *genio* began to be used; at that time, creative genius was largely measured by a person's ability to imitate others (master artists) or to imitate life (nature). It is worth noting that artists such as Leonardo da Vinci and Giorgio Vasari were admired and revered examples of the "imitation-ideal"; however, both fought the notion that creativity was measured by how best one could imitate and suggested instead that creativity must also include the creation of novelty.

Like the Greeks, the Italians also clung to the possibility of madness (*pazzia*) as a precursor to creativity. *Pazzia* was not insanity; it shared attributes with a melancholic temperament: solitariness, moodiness, eccentricity, and sensitivity. Like the Greeks, this state of mind was highly desired. In fact, in sixteenth-century Europe (and 1950s America), this temperament became a fad. As Joyce Johnson wrote in her *Minor Characters* memoir of 1950s America, "*Beat Generation* sold books, sold black turtleneck sweaters and bongos, berets and dark glasses, sold a way of life that seemed like dangerous fun—thus to be either condemned or imitated." Although creativity was admired, it was also something to be feared as a sort of dangerous fun. And therefore we held the Beat Generation in check with parody. Legendary journalist Herb Caen coined the term *beatnik* in 1958 in an article he wrote for the *San Francisco Chronicle* in order to portray members of the Beat Generation as "un-American." *Beatnik* was a spin on the Russian space icon *Sputnik I*.

Just as we held 1950s Beat poets in check with parody, we held eighteenth-century imagination in check by reason. In fact, both imagination and reason are required in the conception of great ideas. As we'll explore in the book, the Enlightenment, the Age of Reason, revered scientific explanation and fostered an intellectual climate and lifestyle that largely paved the way for the innovation feast that ensued during the Industrial Revolution of the nineteenth century. However, prior to our infatuation with scientific discovery, Western scholars continued to explain creativity from an Aristotelian position. And therefore, since antiquity, those who have made the most significant contributions to the field of creativity have been those who study the mind: psychologists.

Eventually the study of creativity moved "from above" to "from within," although it is worth noting that long after the Enlightenment, some continued to attribute their creativity to divine inspiration, among them, writer Harriet Beecher Stowe who once commented on the source of her inspiration for *Uncle Tom's Cabin* saying: "I did not write it; God wrote it. I merely did his dictation!" Independent of divine inspiration and assuming that some people are inspired from within, the mystery remains: Where do great ideas come from? Although we today are enlightened thinkers who believe in the notion of willful creativity, this question remains largely unanswered. Some contemporary scholars suggest that creativity is a cognitive exercise whereby creative insight is the result of conventional thinking versus some other type of out-of-the-box thinking. However, this begs yet another question: Is creativity a result of conscious or unconscious thinking? After all, although you may not need to be "out of your mind" to be creative, this does not necessarily mean you are in control of creativity.

Among those who most famously promoted the role of the unconscious was Freud, and so it should come as no surprise that he would apply his ideas to creativity as well. Freud believed that creative acts are informed and shaped by the unfulfilled needs of the creator. Childhood experiences and unresolved conflicts were central to Freud's thesis on creativity. Why does Leonardo da Vinci's *Mona Lisa* look so distant? Because, according to Freud, the orphaned Leonardo longed for his absent mother's affection.

An alternate view of the role of the unconscious in creativity was also proposed by nineteenth-century scientist and mathematician Henri Poincaré. For subject matter, Poincaré chose himself. By examining his own creative accomplishments, he concluded that his aha moments, while not necessarily divinely inspired, indeed came from somewhere outside his normal conscious processing. Poincaré's concept became known as *illumination* or *incubation*: the sudden appearance of solutions to problems. *Incubation*, which involves the parallel processing of information, suggests that aha moments arise as a result of unconsciously thinking about a problem (for example, how to decipher the volume of an irregular object) while consciously thinking about something entirely different (perhaps while taking a bath).

Poincaré's incubation concept was later expanded in the 1920s by theorist Graham Wallas, who suggested stages of creativity: preparation, incubation, intimation, illumination, and verification. Preparation involves focusing on the problem and its dimensions. Incubation is the process of internalizing the problem into the unconscious mind. Intimation is associated with the feeling that often precedes creative insight. Illumination is the experience itself—the aha moment. And verification is when the idea is consciously confirmed and applied. Wallas considered creativity to be a natural extension of the evolutionary process: allowing humans to adapt to a changing environment. The human brain can move through these stages in a matter of seconds. These leaps of insight were the focus of the Gestalt psychologists of the early twentieth century who, unlike the Italians, dismissed the imitation ideal in favor of the creation of novelty.

Intelligence expert J. P. Guilford later promoted the notion of divergent thinking, when, in his 1950 presidential address to the American Psychological Association, he surprised the audience by suggesting that the profession he led spent an inordinate amount of time studying intelligence at the expense of the study of creativity, a set of skills not captured by IQ tests. In the field of creativity, divergent thinking holds two definitions: a break from the past and a special kind of thinking. Although the products of creative thinking often diverge (make a significant break) from "the way things are done" (an example is the electric light versus candles), divergent thinking is also a means to an end, that is, a way of thinking. Guilford's work eventually led to the creation of a battery of psychometric tests designed to measure a person's creative capacity. His three-factor model of creativity was based on *fluency* (the quantity of ideas generated), *flexibility* (the capacity to think in many different directions), and *originality* (the ability to generate statistically rare ideas as defined by those appearing in less than 5 percent of the population). However, Guilford left out one important factor: *relevance*, the key differentiator between what I refer to as artistic creativity and conceptual creativity. Conceptually creative thinkers must not only be fluent, flexible, and original, but must also have the capacity to identify and produce a relevant solution to an existing problem. Otherwise they are not creators of concepts; they are artists.

Guilford's work led to the development of confluence models of creativity, which suggest that moments of creative insight are the result of the confluence ("coming together") of several factors, including how a person thinks (divergent or convergent), what a person knows (expertise inside and outside of a domain), personality (flexible or inflexible), and environment (fostering or interfering). This "coming together" is often attributed to creativity scholar and Harvard Business School professor Teresa

Amabile, who suggested a relationship among domain-relevant skills (knowledge about a subject), creativity-relevant skills (knowledge of heuristics for generating novel ideas), and task motivation (attitude). Her findings on motivation and creativity have widespread implications for the way in which organizations foster creativity among their employees. For example, there is evidence, both scientific and anecdotal, to suggest that people are more creative when intrinsically motivated ("I'm working on the project because I love it!") versus extrinsically motivated ("I'm doing it because my company offers cash bonuses for new ideas"). Soichiro Honda, founder of Honda Motor Company, understood this intuitively. As Honda put it, "Generally speaking, people work harder and are more innovative if working voluntarily, compared to a case when people are being told to do something." In keeping with his beliefs, Honda took things to the extreme. In fact, he believed so strongly in the role of intrinsic motivation as fodder for creative inspiration that he promoted free-rein experimentation and banned organizational hierarchies in his businesses.

In the field of creativity, intrinsic motivation is required. A premium is placed on passion. You must want to find a solution to the problem. You must care. Psychologists, among them Amabile, have since confirmed Honda's intuition. However, "free rein experimentation" does not suggest that creativity is without rules. Quite the contrary, there are very specific rules, many of them examined in this book, that work to inspire creative insight.

Of note, the leadership and employees of the world's leading product, service, and environmental design company, IDEO, put rules on only a single aspect of the organization: the creative brainstorm. At IDEO, a conversation about office rules and regulations follows something along the lines of: "What's that? You would like to bring your dog to work? No problem. You say you want to install a redwood deck in your work space, fully equipped with outdoor furniture? Sure. And I suppose if you really believe that installing a DC-3 aircraft wing above your work station will inspire your creativity, then by all means, have at it! However, if you, your dog, your redwood decking, or your aerospace gadgets prematurely judge (positively or negatively) an idea in a creative brainstorm, watch your back!" IDEO repeatedly wins in the marketplace for a single reason: it understands that creativity is not an entirely random process. It just looks that way. Logic is part of it.

In addition to the logic of creativity and various findings linking motivation to creative insight, others have developed creativity theories based on economic principles. The general thinking is that creative thinkers "buy low," proposing ideas that are unpopular but have high potential for growth, and sell high, giving up work on an idea once it has become popular. This is often the case of serial entrepreneurs who introduce one business after another in the practice of empire building. And others, perhaps in the spirit of divergence themselves, have used Darwin's theory of evolution to explain creativity by suggesting that ideas, like species, evolve into being through chance and selection.

As much as we have studied, theorized, and postulated on the origins of ideas, two questions remain unanswered: Where do great ideas come from? and How can you have better ones on a more consistent basis? In order to begin to solve this riddle, let's take a step inside that magical moment of creative insight: the eureka moment.

Summary Points and Creative Exercises

- The origins of creative inspiration have been debated for more than three thousand years. However, with advances in brain science, we have learned that existing knowledge may be as important as rule breaking in the context of innovation. Therefore, work to deepen your knowledge of the problem.

- Like knowledge, ignorance is also a key ingredient to fostering creative insight. When organizing a creative team, invite both domain experts and novices.

- Creative thinking and aha experiences are often the result of both conscious and unconscious information processing: your brain goes on thinking even when you are not attempting to be creative. Therefore, when you are attempting to solve complex problems, take breaks. Let your mind wander. Read something entirely unrelated to the problem. Then come back to it from a new perspective.

- Recall psychologist J. P. Guilford's three-factor model of creativity: fluency, flexibility, and originality. In order to increase your creative fluency, write down a problem, and generate as many solutions as you can imagine. In order to practice creative flexibility, put yourself in the shoes of another person (perhaps even a child) who you believe thinks much differently than you do, and ask how he or she might solve the same problem. In order to practice creative originality, identify as many existing solutions to your problem as possible (you can search the Internet for this). Once you have compiled the list, try to think of ways not on that list to solve the problem.

- In the pursuit of new ideas, intrinsic motivation (I care to solve this problem) is more effective than extrinsic motivation (you want me to solve this problem). If you are assigned a problem to solve, try to find ways to align it with your personal interests (for example, What excites me about this opportunity?). If you are not intrinsically motivated to figure it out, find someone who is. You and your boss will be much happier. As a team leader responsible for generating new ideas, allow people to sign up for or interview for the task, project, or venture chartered to solve the problem. Motivation matters.

- Creativity is more than rule breaking. It is also governed by rules. There is logic to it. Put parameters on your brainstorming sessions. Give them structure. Use more than a flip chart and a marker. Employ provocative questions—for example, What if our company was on the brink of bankruptcy and the only way to save it was to introduce a revolutionary new product? What would that new product be? What problem would it solve? And how would we sell it?

3

THE EUREKA MOMENT

What would cause a mathematician to streak naked in public? According to a twenty-five-hundred-year-old legend, it takes nothing more than a great idea.

As the story goes, Archimedes had a problem: how to compute the volume of an irregular object, namely, the king's crown. The king wanted to know whether his royal helmet was made of pure gold or was of the fool's variety, a mixture of silver and gold. His question was whether the maker of the crown had cheated him. Archimedes was stumped. Not until he stepped into his bath, thereby causing the water to overflow, did he realize that he could use water displacement to compute volume. At this point he famously shouted *Eureka!* ("I have found it") and subsequently ran through the streets of Syracuse naked with excitement (or so the story goes). The question is, Where did the idea come from? (And why didn't he get dressed first?) Even more puzzling, why did the idea appear to Archimedes at a time when he was likely not focused on attempting to solve the problem (or was he?). Could it be that we are more creatively insightful when we are less deliberately thoughtful about the very problem we are attempting to solve? Do we create more by thinking less? The anecdotal evidence does make one wonder. It appears that great ideas are like in-laws: they show up unexpectedly. But are big ideas really that random? Archimedes, like many other innovators, actually knew much more than one would be led to believe. For example, as the king's ship designer, he knew a lot about measuring volume with water displacement. At his eureka moment, he likely had unconsciously combined his knowledge of volume and mass. He knew the mass of gold, so a certain volume should have a specific weight.

If the weight was less than it should be, then the crown was not pure gold (as he discovered). Knowledge is as useful to creative insight as novelty.

In 1666, due to the plague, the University of Cambridge closed, thereby sending one of its promising young physicists, twenty-three-year-old Sir Isaac Newton, to seek refuge at his family's estate in Lincolnshire. It was in Lincolnshire, not in the clinical setting of a Cambridge laboratory, that the sight of an apple falling to the ground inspired Newton to develop his theory of universal gravitation. Of course, apples had been falling from trees for centuries. What was it about *that* apple and *that* man at *that* moment that led to one of the most significant breakthroughs in scientific history? As you'll soon learn, these and other aha moments, while seemingly random, are actually quite predictable. The challenge we have is in increasing our awareness to what our brain is doing while we are not paying attention to it. Although we would like to believe that we are able to control when we think and when we choose to "give our brain a rest," as Freud suggested, the brain has a mind of its own.

In order to illustrate the enormous processing power of your brain, try reading the following passage:

> Aoccdrnig to rscheearch at Cmabrigde Uinervtisy, it deosn't mttaer
> in wihc oder the ltteers in a wrod are, the olny iprmoatnt thnig is
> taht the frist and lsat ltteer be at the rghit pclae. The rset can be a
> total mses and you can raed it wouthit a porbelm. Tihs is bcuseae
> the hmaun mind deos not raed ervey lteter by istlef, but the wrod
> as a wlohe.

Although research scientists at the Cognition and Brain Scientists Unit in Cambridge, England, have no idea who (if anyone) conducted this research, this mind game spread like wildfire throughout the virtual world in September 2003. Nonetheless, even as legend, scientists agree that it contains some truth about the brain's massive parallel processing capabilities. The most obvious bit of truth is that it is readable. However, the anonymous author's claim that "the olny iprmoetnt thnig is taht the frist and lsat ltteer be at the rghit pclae" is not entirely accurate. While the scrambled letters between the first and last may not seem useful to you, in fact, they are. Try reading this:

A • • • • • • g to r • • • • • • h at C • • • • • • • e U • • • • • • • • y, it d • • • • • 't m • • • • r in w • • t o • • • r t • e l • • • • • s in a w • • d a • e, t • e o • • y i • • • • • • t t • • • g is t • • t t • e f • • • t a • d l • • t l • • • • r be at t • e r • • • t p • • • e. T • e r • • t c • n be a t • • • l m • • s a • d y • u c • n s • • • l r • • d it w • • • • • t a p • • • • • m. T • • s is b • • • • • e t • e h • • • n m • • d d • • s n • t r • • d e • • • y l • • • • r by i • • • • f, b • t t • e w • • d as a w • • • e.

With the letters removed, this passage was likely much more difficult for you to read—and would be nearly impossible had you not read the same paragraph only moments ago. Here is the passage in full:

According to research at Cambridge University, it doesn't matter in which order the letters in a word are, the only important thing is that the first and last letter be at the right place. The rest can be a total mess and you can still read it without a problem. This is because the human mind does not read every letter by itself, but the word as a whole.

This phenomenon reflects biases we maintain based on memory—in this case, our memory of language. In the scrambled passage, your brain rearranged the letters in order to meet your expectations of what you believed the words should say. However, in the second passage, where the scrambled letters were replaced by dots, you were likely unable, or at least were significantly more challenged, to figure it out. All the letters are relevant. You need them to understand the passage (by limiting the possible words). This illustrates the contributions of both top-down and bottom-up processing. Knowledge of grammar, syntax, and context, for example, is a top-down process. It creates expectations for what should be there: for example, certain words cannot appear in just any position in a grammatically correct sentence. The letters themselves provide bottom-up information and limit the possible words. For example, how many different words can you create with the letters F-I-R-S-T if the F must come first and the T must come last? Neither of these processes, top down or bottom up, is necessarily occurring in consciousness, and so we are surprised by our ability to read the scrambled sentences.

Any act of cognition involves the interaction and combination of many processes, including memory, perception, and attentional processes. Information can come from the external world (objective reality) or can be retrieved from internal representations (imagination). Moreover, information can be consciousness (working memory) or, at least for the moment, unconscious (long-term memory). Like reading the scrambled passage above, as you read the words and sentences on this page, you are simultaneously aware of other things: the pressure of the chair on your legs, the feel of this book in your hands, and so on. Even as you read, you allow your attention to shift to other things so that you can monitor what is going on around you. If the phone rings or someone comes into the room, you are likely to notice. At the same time, there are many things that your brain is doing that are going on outside your awareness and will not normally attract your attention. For example, you are breathing, your heart is beating, and your eyes are moving across the page. You can become aware of these things and control them indirectly, but you are not normally paying attention to them or consciously controlling them. In fact, even now that you are paying attention to your eye movements, you probably are not aware of how your eyes really move across the page. And although it may seem that your eyes move smoothly across this sentence, they are actually moving in quick jerky motions known as saccadic eye movement. These are examples of your brain engaged in parallel processing, that is, your brain doing several things at the same time—aware of some things while blissfully ignorant of others. This is an important starting point for improving your ability to be creative and innovative. Here's why.

When you are faced with a problem, your brain does not focus all of its efforts on solving it. Your brain continues to do many different things at the same time. Most of these things are unrelated to solving the problem, yet there are things going on outside your awareness that may be helpful to solving the problem or, just the opposite, they may hinder reaching a solution.

The Stroop task was designed to investigate attention, but it also illustrates how the automatic parallel processing of information can hinder your performance at creative tasks. My adaptation of the Stroop task in Exhibit 3.1 illustrates how information is in constant competition for your attention. In order to illustrate this, try to complete the task presented in Exhibit 3.1. Then determine which of these tasks was most difficult for you to complete. If tasks 3 and 5 were more difficult to process than the others, you are not alone. The words themselves have a strong influence over your ability to say the shape. Because the words and the corresponding shapes do not match, this interference causes a problem. In fact, even when the task is to ignore the names of the words, they are automatically activated by practiced readers. You can't help but focus unconsciously on them. A few theories help explain this phenomenon.

The first is the speed of processing theory. This theory contends that the interference occurs because words are read faster than shapes are named (and therefore the second task was likely easier for you to complete even though the shapes and words do not match). In order to say the name of the shape, you must first recognize the shape and then translate the shape into a word so that you can articulate it. If you speak a second language, you likely are familiar with this notion. In order to speak in a second language, you must first identify the word you wish to say (*hello*), then translate it in your mind into its equivalent (*bonjour*), and then speak the translated word. This takes much longer than in simply saying *hello*.

Exhibit 3.1. Thinking Without Thinking: The Stroop Effect

Task 1: Read these words.

CIRCLE   SQUARE   TRIANGLE   RECTANGLE

Task 2: Read these words.

Task 3: Now, say the *shape* NOT the name of the word.

Task 4: Again, say the *shape* NOT the name of the word.

Task 5: And finally, say the *shape* NOT the name of the word.

The second theory that may help to explain why we have difficulty processing conflicting information is selective attention theory. This theory proposes that the interference occurs because naming shapes requires more attention than reading words. Because of the need to convert the shape, which is a symbol, into a word, you go through the unconscious routine of interpreting things such as the number of corners of the shape or the relative angles in the shape, and so on in order to ascertain what it is. This requires more attention to the task.

In the exercise in Exhibit 3.1, you were asked to ignore the information that is automatically processed, that is, the words, and to pay attention to a normally irrelevant aspect of the stimulus, the shape. The challenge associated with this task explains why we turn down the radio in the car when traffic gets heavy. The more relevant task of driving the car, much like reading the word, becomes divided by the task of listening to people (the radio, a child screaming in the back seat, and so on). To reconcile, you split your attention between the two tasks of driving and listening. Although this is related to the Stroop task, the difference is that in the Stroop task, you are asked to try to direct your attention away from an automatic task, reading the word, and toward another task that requires conscious effort, saying the shape.

When we are selectively paying attention to anything, our attention is never really allocated to one task or the other. In the driving example, your attention is split between the two tasks (divided attention), and you physically turn off one of the tasks so you can focus all of your attention on the other. Some people suggest that the problem with mobile phones or listening to talk radio while driving is that we can't physically see the other people we are speaking to, so we imagine the other people. This requires some of our processing capacity, taking some capacity away from other tasks such as paying attention to traffic, stopping at red lights, and heeding the recommended speed limit. Because of our unconscious division of attention, hands-free devices aren't necessarily the answer. After all, we've been driving while eating in the car since the 1950s. It's the image in our minds that is distracting.

In the case of driving (divided attention), we have the challenge of trying to stop the unconscious dividing of attention in order to focus on the more important task at hand. In the Stroop task (selective attention), we have the challenge of shifting attention from one task to another. Both selective attention and divided attention are important for creativity.

Divided attention requires more diffuse attention. By spreading your attention over more possible fields of information, you are more likely to activate a creative solution. This is one argument for why today's digitally tethered, split-screen young people theoretically should be adept and creative problem solvers. For them, multitasking is a way of life. However, multitasking requires some conscious thinking about the information received into long-term and short-term memory, but selective attention is necessary for focusing on one of the possible solutions to test it. This is one argument for why multitaskers could have difficulties in making their creative solutions practical. At some point, you must focus in order to translate big ideas into even bigger realities.

The third theory that helps explain the Stroop effect is response competition theory. It contends that the interference between the words and the shapes occurs because the normal, that is, more dominant, response to a word is to say its name. It is difficult to inhibit the more dominant response. When attempting to solve a problem or generate a unique idea, we often miss the great idea because of more accessible or conventional responses to a question. These often take the form of conventions or beliefs we maintain about what works and what doesn't.

In addition to these prevailing theories, current theories on the Stroop effect emphasize the interference that automatic processing has over more effortful tasks, for example, the impact of naming words on the more effortful task of just naming the shapes. The task of selecting an appropriate response when given two conflicting (if not diametrically opposed) conditions has tentatively been located in the anterior cingulate cortex (ACC) in the brain. This region lies between the right and left halves of the frontal portion of the brain, and is involved in a wide range of thought processes and emotional responses. Although the functions of the ACC are complex, broadly speaking it acts as a conduit between lower, more impulse-driven brain regions and higher, more rationally driven behaviors. Because reading, that is, the practice of decoding strings of letters into words, is a highly practiced skill, it has become automatic and normally requires virtually no conscious effort. However, much attention is required to *not* read the word and say the shape instead. This is less difficult if the words match the shapes in which they are written because the responses are not competing. This phenomenon of conflicting information may help to explain why it is that some individuals seem to be able to experience aha moments more readily than others. As is often the case, creative individuals are able to suspend or ignore information that may hinder finding a solution to a problem or help in the creation of a new idea. This skill may explain why they are able to see beyond existing norms and rules and challenge prevailing assumptions in the pursuit of a solution.

The practical import from these insights is to consider information that at first may seem irrelevant to solving your problem or coming up with a new idea. As you'll learn later in the book, encounters with extraneous and apparently irrelevant bits of information appear to be common precursors to moments of creative insight. Your brain is more aware (unconsciously) of its surroundings than you are (consciously). This in part helps to explain why aha moments seem to occur when we are least deliberate about being creative, a notion that flies in the face of conventional brainstorming techniques. This also helps explain the feeling often associated with aha moments. For example, after reading the scrambled passage earlier, or perhaps even while reading it, you were likely impressed with your mind's ability to read it. After all, once you noticed that the letters were mixed around, you weren't likely expecting to be able to comprehend it, and so you felt good when you could figure it out. This is a common phenomenon associated with epiphany: it feels good when a connection is made, a problem is solved, and a great idea is born. And therefore, in response, your heart must race to catch up with your sudden brilliance.

There is no question that Archimedes felt good. After all, not only did his heart run, so did he. While Archimedes' encounter with creative inspiration is perhaps history's most famous, it is certainly not the only one. Throughout history, sudden bursts of unexpected creative insight have been reported by scores of artists, entrepreneurs, inventors, scientists, and writers, among them one of the world's living literary legends, Carlos Fuentes.

Carlos Fuentes is an institution. Not only is he Mexico's most celebrated living writer, he is one of the world's creative treasures. Fuentes' literary accomplishments would make even the most prolific artists blush with envy. Given his prolific nature, one wonders whether he has ever feared losing his creative capacity. After all, it seems that writer's block has everyone's address at her fingertips (although it appears she's lost Fuentes'). A reporter once asked Fuentes, "Have you ever feared losing your love of writing?" Fuentes responded, "No . . . I've come too far for that. I've never been afraid of the blank page. Every day I get up . . . or should I say, every night I go to sleep anxious to get up and write again the next day, already knowing more or less what I'm going to say." Although his confidence in confronting the blank page might help explain his work ethic, it still does not explain the basis of his abundant imagination. Where do his great ideas come from? To the observer, his ideas seem to materialize out of thin air. However, to Fuentes, fostering creativity is a bit more pragmatic. Like most other great innovators, Fuentes has a trick—one that he borrowed from another creative genius, Ernest Hemingway. As Fuentes explained, "Hemingway said you should always leave your last sentence unfinished: 'He opened the door and saw . . . ' What? Leave it there, go to bed . . . don't end the sentence, so you'll know where to pick up again. Then there's the dream factor: You know in your head what you're going to write the next day, but then a dream comes along and changes everything in a way that's impossible to control."

Fuentes, like many other creative geniuses throughout history, appreciates that sleep is more than just a way to rest the body; it is a way to exercise the mind. Sleep is a time to think without consciously controlling the direction of the thinking. As it turns out, sleep and the subconscious play more than supporting roles in the drama of creative inspiration. Like Fuentes, many innovators throughout history attribute their creativity to trancelike states of mind. "It came to me in a dream" is a common explanation for the origin of ideas.

In 1905, a widowed black washerwoman invented a method for straightening African American hair while she was sleeping. After waking from her inspired slumber and as a result of dedicating the next ten years of her life to her inspired dream, Sarah Breedlove Walker (later Mme. C. J. Walker) became the wealthiest black woman in America through the introduction of the Walker method of hair care.

Like Walker, in 1864, while dreaming of an Ouroborus (a mythological symbol of a snake swallowing its own tail), the thirty-five-year-old chemist Friedrich August Kekulé von Stradonitz awoke with the solution to a perplexing question: What is the structure of the benzene molecule? Kekulé recounted his dream: "But look! What was that? One of the snakes had seized hold of its own tail, and the form whirled mockingly before my eyes. Then, as if by a flash of lightning I awoke." The ringlike structure of the snake was that of the benzene molecule. Could the metaphorical image of dancing reptiles, rather than scientific drawings of molecules, have inspired chemistry's most famous aha moment?

While Kekulé's story is circumspect, the notion of trancelike creative experiences seems to be quite common among those who have reported aha moments, among them, Albert Einstein. In 1907, while working in the patent office in Bern, Switzerland, the twenty-eight-year-old Einstein recalled "a breakthrough came suddenly one day." Lost in a daydream, Einstein's mind wandered as he pondered, "If a man falls freely he would not feel his weight." As Einstein recounted, "I was taken aback. This simple thought experiment made a deep impression on me." In that moment, Einstein made the connection between gravity and accelerated motion, which, after nearly a decade years of hammering out the math, led to his magnum opus: Einstein's general theory of relativity.

This phenomenon of trancelike inspiration seems to apply not only to scientific discovery but also to artistic creativity. In fact, the simple act of waking up seems to be at least partially responsible for the conception of the world's most widely recorded song, "Scrambled Eggs."

In 1964, the Beatles front man, Paul McCartney, awoke with his most successful melody squatting in his mind like a toad. As McCartney recalls in *The Beatles Anthology*, "I woke up one morning with a tune in my head and thought, 'Hey, I don't know this tune—or do I?'" For weeks, McCartney was convinced that he must have heard the melody somewhere and was simply unable to place it. He thought he may have been suffering from cryptomnesia ("concealed recollection"), a theoretical phenomenon in which a person believes he or she has invented or created something new, when in fact the idea is actually something the person encountered at some point yet has forgotten it. McCartney was certain that he was under its spell. In fact, he believed that the melody of "Scrambled Eggs" was a widely known jazz tune, although his friends eventually convinced him otherwise, concluding that his musical wakeup call was in fact a novel melody in search of lyrics. Therefore, in lieu of a better title and for several weeks, McCartney used "Scrambled Eggs" as the song's working title along with the placeholder lyrics: "Scrambled eggs, oh, my baby, how I love your legs—diddle diddle—I believe in scrambled eggs." "Scrambled Eggs" has since become the most-recorded song in history, performed over 7 million times in the twentieth century alone. Much to the chagrin of the Egg Farmers Association, McCartney eventually changed the title and lyrics from "Scrambled Eggs" to "Yesterday."

Like Einstein and McCartney, you have likely shared a similar experience of waking up with a great idea. Those moments may not have garnered you a Nobel Prize or a Grammy, but nonetheless, you are familiar with the rush of clarity associated with solving a problem or creating something new (at least, new to you). The question remains: What is going on while we sleep? and Why does it appear to make us more creative? To these questions we turn in the following chapter.

Summary Points and Creative Exercises

- Your memory of experiences, information, and language affects your creativity. Be aware of how your past experiences may hinder your ability to see things anew.

- When you are attempting to solve a problem, at first some information may seem to be irrelevant. However, it may be exactly the key to figuring things out. Try not to discount tangential information too early in the creative process.

- As Fuentes and Hemingway did, practice leaving questions unanswered and sentences unfinished. You don't have to solve everything all at once. Write down the problem or question you have. Then do something else for a while. When you come back to it, see what new ideas may have emerged.

4

IT CAME TO ME IN A DREAM

Several studies have examined the connection between sleep and creativity. Using technology in the place of historical anecdote, one of them provides evidence that neuronal activity in the human brain during wakeful hours is reactivated during sleep; that is, we replay activities during sleep that we experienced while awake. More important, we rehearse variations of those activities. In other words, we are not beholden to what actually happened; rather, we use the information we have and reorganize it during sleep to create all sorts of unique combinations. During sleep, disparate, seemingly unrelated experiences and information are rearranged, thus forming connections that otherwise might not be made while awake. This may help explain the waking genius phenomenon.

The confluence of disparate information that transpires as a result of the information consolidation during sleep gives rise to a new point of view that has the potential to produce a novel thought. Specifically, this is observed by increased activation in the hippocampus, which is thought to be critical for information consolidation and memory formation. As someone who has done a lot of sleeping over the years, you are likely very familiar with the phenomenon of your mind's rearranging the experiences you've had during your waking hours. The dreams you can remember are often a mishmash of the people, places, and activities you've encountered during that day. For example, let's say that during your waking hours, you got stuck in traffic while taking your cat to the veterinarian; you stopped for ice cream on the way home; and later that day, you ran on a treadmill at your health club. That night while you slept, these experiences were rearranged in your mind and translated into something else—for example, you were being chased by an oversized cat while desperately attempting to run up a mountain of ice cream. And then you woke up thinking: *Aha! I've got a great idea! They should make ice cream for cats.*

This phenomenon of waking creativity occurs for three reasons. First, sleep is the time when the experiences you've encountered during your waking hours are consolidated into memories. Second, sleep is a time when you tend to relax some of the constraints of reality. And third, sleep is a time when your attention becomes less focused. Because of these three factors, you are more likely to allow yourself to consider outlandish thoughts while you are unconscious and illogical than while you are conscious and logical. *Cats could eat ice cream. Why not? They drink milk.* Due to these factors, you may likely see things from different perspectives while you are asleep than while you are awake; connections between disparate information and experiences are made, creating the ideal conditions for sudden bursts of creative insight. In addition, because of the relaxed constraints, your mind is more open to new possibilities, yet another precursor to creative insight. In order to help solve this mystery, that is, beyond recording the firsthand accounts of expert sleepers, we turn to scientists' favorite crystal ball for all things unexplained: lab rats.

In one study, scientists explored how sleep interacts with learning. To test their hypotheses, they used two groups of rats learning to run a maze. One group practiced running the maze, followed by a period of sleep, and then ran the maze again when they woke up. The other group practiced running the maze but was not allowed to sleep before running the maze again. The scientists found that the sleepers learned more quickly. More revealing, even when the rats that were not allowed to sleep were given more time to practice running the maze, the sleepers still learned more quickly. Why did this occur even when one group was given more practice time? Not only does the mind consolidate information during sleep, it does it for a reason: to prepare and store that information in long-term memory. The learning process continues during sleep (although as an educator, I must insist that my students don't do it in class!). The performance of the wakeful rats with additional training on the maze did not improve because their experiences and knowledge of the maze did not have a chance to be moved into long-term memory.

To bolster these study's findings, another study looked at actual brain activity in rats as they ran mazes and while they slept after practicing running the mazes. The finding was that the brain activity recorded while the rats were running the maze was similar to that recorded while they slept. In other words, they were likely practicing the mazes in their sleep. Therefore, although the sleeping rats had less time practicing running the maze, they were not disadvantaged in their learning process because they practiced in their sleep. If you do not have the opportunity to work through these mental routines (that is, if you do not sleep), your chances of storing information in long-term memory may decrease. Hence, learning does not occur, and you (and the rats) get lost. As a result, you will not likely come up with that next big idea, pass that exam, or do well on that presentation if you do not get a good night's rest. More important, you will likely tend to forget almost everything you had learned that day since you are not allowing that information to be consolidated and stored in long-term memory.

Given these findings, one thing is certain: in the field of creativity and innovation, pulling an all-nighter is the worst thing you can do. If you have a choice between staying up all night versus getting three hours of sleep, by all means, go to bed. While you sleep, particularly during rapid eye movement sleep, your spatial and procedural memories are consolidated. Spatial memory involves recording your environment and your relationship within that environment. For example, gray squirrels exhibit phenomenal spatial memory in hoarding and making numerous small caches of nuts and subsequently returning to those caches months later. Birds use spatial memory to migrate south for the winter. You and I use spatial memory to remember how to get to work. Recall Einstein's thought while working in the patent office in Bern about "a falling man" and the connection between gravity and accelerated motion.

This thought was likely tagged and stored as spatial memory in Einstein's brain and later called on in a unique combination of apparently unrelated thoughts. Procedural memory involves the long-term memory of skills—how to do things, such as remembering how to swim, ride a bike, or drive a car. Recall Archimedes. He knew how to measure weight, a procedure that had been logged into his long-term memory, where it became knowledge.

It is worth noting that the benefit of sleep is not necessarily that you feel rested the next day; rather, the benefit is the process of information consolidation that takes place in your brain while you sleep. This creates the conditions for creative insight the next morning while you are in the shower or sitting stuck in rush-hour traffic. This is why you should not dismiss existing knowledge prematurely as an obstruction to innovation. If our experiences become dogmatic, then we run the risk of being unable to see new or unorthodox opportunities. Knowledge, that is, known procedures or domain expertise, is also required for generating novel thoughts, as was the case with Archimedes: there was information that Archimedes knew that in its absence would have obstructed his ability to solve his problem.

Contrary to popular opinion, knowledge is a critical component to creativity, even when creating things that are new to the world. In lay terms, thinking about the box is as important as thinking outside it. The combination is what matters. The confluence of domain knowledge and seemingly irrelevant information creates the ideal conditions for epiphany; therefore, scores of people have experienced waking brilliance. Unfortunately, sleep alone won't get anyone to the big idea. It is what occurs during sleep—the recombination of information—that enables creative insight. It is my belief that by mimicking, or at least attempting to recreate, the conditions that occur naturally while sleeping—the recombination of information and the juxtaposition of domain expertise with seemingly irrelevant information—you may be able to deliberately inspire creativity. You can learn to make these connections while you are awake, although you must work a bit harder to make sense of apparently nonsensical relationships. One technique illustrated later in this book is to create connections between what you know (your proverbial mental "box") and what on the surface may appear to be random information (things outside your area of expertise, interest, and daily routine).

Like rats in mazes, studies also provide similar findings in humans. The study illustrated in Figure 4.1 concludes that sleep inspires insight in problem solving. Insight is the act of finding a hidden (not obvious) solution to a problem, a highly sought-after skill when in search of a new idea.

In this study, groups of participants were asked to complete a common problem-solving task; some groups were allowed sleep, and others were not. They were instructed to find the "final solution": the number that would come last in a series of numbers. Referring to Figure 4.1, this could be accomplished by processing the digits 1, 4, and 9 in pairs from left to right using two rules. The first rule was referred to as the "same rule": where you see a like pair, "1 and 1," the response would be the same: "1."

Figure 4.1. Effect of Sleep on the Number Reduction Task

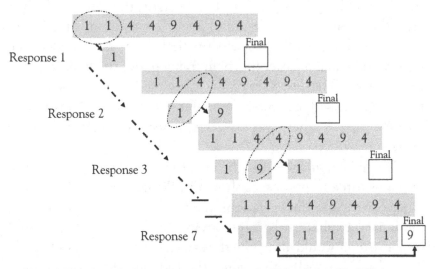

Source: U. Wagner and others, "Sleep Inspires Insight," *Nature*, Jan. 22, 2004, pp. 352–354.

The second rule was referred to as the "different rule": where you see a different pair, "1 and 4," the result would be the remaining digit, "9." After the first response, participants moved to the right and compared the next pair of numbers in search of the third, and so on, until they finished the task and arrived at the final solution. Once they figured out the final solution, they were asked to press a key to confirm their answer. So, for example, beginning on the far left side, the pair "1" and "1" would invoke the "same rule," and therefore the response would be "1." Moving to the right, the next pair, "4" and "1," would invoke the "different rule" and therefore the response would be "9," and so on to the end. The figure here illustrates only one string of numbers: 1–1–4–4–9–4–9–4. Once participants completed this string, an additional string of numbers would appear and they'd repeat the instructions. However, finding the final digit is not all that interesting. There is more to this study than meets the eye.

Although participants were told to "find the final solution," the researchers weren't actually all that interested in whether the respondents found the final answer. Rather, they were interested in ascertaining whether participants experienced insight in solving the problem. In order to test for insight, the researchers had embedded a secret (a hidden rule) in each of the numbered series, but they did not tell the participants that there was a hidden rule that would make it easier for them to figure out the final solution more quickly. The discovery of this rule served to signal the precise moment of insight: the eureka moment. Once the participants discovered the rule, there was no longer a need to walk through the series step by step.

The hidden rule was that the final three responses mirrored the previous three responses: as shown in Figure 4.1, 9–1–1–1–1–9. Once participants discovered this hidden rule and it had gone from implicit to explicit, it became obvious to them that the second response digit would always be the same as the final solution digit. Therefore, those who discovered the hidden rule recorded their final solution as soon as they figured out the second answer from the left. Subsequently, respondents who discovered this hidden rule reduced their average solution time by 70 percent. Moreover, 59 percent of the subjects who slept for a night between initial training of the task and retesting discovered the short-cut the following morning. By contrast, only 25 percent of the subjects who did not sleep found the hidden rule.

Ultimately, as shown in Figure 4.2, a night of sleep more than doubled the likelihood of solving the problem. "Wake-day" in the figure represents participants who remained awake between initial testing in the morning and retesting that evening. "Wake-night" represents participants who did initial training in the evening, stayed awake that night, and then retested in the morning. And "Sleep" indicates those who did initial testing training in the evening, slept that night, and then retested in the following morning. What is interesting to note are the two hatched boxes on the far-right labeled "After Sleep" and "After Awake." These represent groups that tested directly after nocturnal sleep or daytime

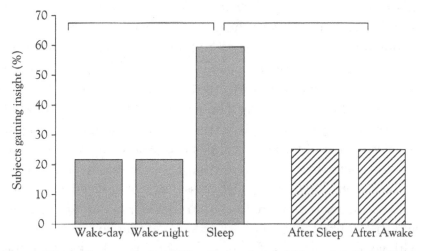

Figure 4.2. Effects of Sleep and Wakefulness on Creative Insight

Source: Ullrich Wagner and others, "Sleep Inspires Insight," *Nature*, Jan. 22, 2004, pp. 352–354.

wakefulness without initial training. It is worth noting that they performed the same as those who were allowed to train first (the groups represented by gray-shaded boxes on the left side), although they still underperformed those who worked on the problem, went to bed, and then figured it out in the morning. In other words, the effect of training prior to the testing improved the chances of only those who had the opportunity to sleep. Training did virtually nothing for those who remained awake.

Given these findings, I suggest that the next time your boss asks you to solve a problem or to come up with a big idea on the spot you do one of two things. Option one is to heed the advice of 1970s rock legend Meat Loaf and tell your boss: "Let me sleep on it and I'll give you my answer in the morning." Option two is to try a few of the techniques introduced in this book. We'll explore several cognitive tricks and creative methods throughout the book, but in the interim, try this: tonight when you go to bed, take a piece of paper and a pen with you. Just before you lie down, write down a problem (in the form of a question) that you may be dealing with, and, as Fuentes and Hemingway suggested, leave it unanswered. Keep the problem statement simple. One sentence is preferred. For example, consider this problem: *Why does it take so long to check in and check out of a hotel, yet no time at all to rent a car?* Once you've written the question down, think about it for a minute or two, and then go to bed. Let your unconscious mind figure it out (or at least attempt to propose a solution). When you wake up, immediately start writing down whatever comes to mind: answers to the question. You'll be surprised at how much thinking goes on inside your mind while you sleep. For example, you might have wondered why you can't check in at a hotel like you check in as a club member of a rental car company or at the check-in kiosks at the airport. Then you could bypass the front desk, go directly to your room, insert your credit card in the door in order to open it, and then immediately get back to sleep so that you can come up with your next big idea. The next day when you check out, do the same in reverse: close the door, insert your credit card in the door lock to pay, and you're on your way. The bill will be sent to your e-mail account on file.

Sleep is a great time to think. I suggest not only that you take a single piece of paper to bed with you, but that you keep a journal on your nightstand to record questions, unsolved problems, and big ideas that you haven't yet figured out how to make work. As it turns out, we waste at least eight hours a day by overlooking the most obvious time in which to be creative: while in the arms of Morpheus.

Although there is still much to learn about the connection between sleep and creativity, these and other findings already provide ample evidence to underscore two important tenets of and precursors to creative insight. First, in order to solve a problem, you must have some understanding of the mechanics of the field in which you have the problem, for example, industry expertise, product knowledge, understanding the rules of the game, and so on. Second, you must work to nurture curiosity in areas that may be foreign to your area of expertise or even to your comfort zone. When knowledge interacts with novelty, either information or experiences, new ideas emerge. It is important not to dismiss what you know but rather to cherish what you know and introduce unknown and even unorthodox perspectives to your existing knowledge.

Developing deep domain knowledge does not imply that you must become an expert in a field to be creative in it. Quite the contrary, throughout history "new entrants" have contributed significantly to the creation of new wealth. Although the idea of new entrants creating new wealth is widely accepted, the more revealing question is how new entrants create new wealth. What do they do differently? Specifically, how do they think?

New entrants are often cited as rule breakers because they are all too familiar with and entirely dissatisfied with the rules, not because they were naive to the rules. You cannot think outside the proverbial box if you do not know what the box looks like to begin with. Innovation is the act of tearing apart boxes and rearranging them in ways that make more sense. Almost all visionaries throughout history seem to come in from nowhere and change the game. How do they do it? They knew the rules. That's how they were able to break them. The interaction of domain knowledge, that is, the rules, with novel insights begets inspired thought. While this happens to occur naturally during sleep, it can be recreated during waking hours.

This brings me to the second practical lesson from what we know about sleep and creativity. In addition to building domain knowledge, you must be deliberate about engaging in activities outside your regular routine, such as reading magazines you ordinarily don't read or visiting places you've never been before, so that you can increase your odds of acquiring information that you may not otherwise encounter. This unrelated information may be just the thing you need to solve your problem or generate that next big idea. We will discuss how you can go about doing this in Chapter Eight on creating unorthodox connections. In the interim, what is most promising about inspired thought is that it is very much within your conscious control, even though it may not seem like it when it occurs. In addition to sleep or trancelike states of mind as common precursors to creative insight is the notion that experiencing epiphany feels good. Figuring things out evokes a sense of self-pride. Emotion seems to play an important role. This begs the question: Which mood is most conducive to creativity? To this we turn in the following chapter.

Summary Points and Creative Exercises

- Sleep fosters creative insight. When you face the choice of pulling an all-nighter or getting a few hours of sleep, go to bed.

- While you sleep, information is reorganized in your brain, and novel relationships are formed. In order to increase the likelihood of the convergence of disparate ideas while you are sleeping, do something new: take a new route to work; watch a television show you've never watched before; read a section of the newspaper you've always put aside. This new experience, combined with your previous knowledge, may inspire novel thoughts.

- Keep a journal on your nightstand. Just before you go to bed, think about a problem you are trying to solve (activate it) and write it down. When you wake up, write down as many solutions to the problem that you can imagine. Sure, you'll write down a lot of nonsense, but you may also find the right idea to help solve the problem.

5

IN THE MOOD FOR INNOVATION

Particular emotional states (anger, depression, joy) seem to have played a role or were at least present at the moment of inspired thought in a number of cases. One is that of famed television producer Aaron Spelling and his origination of the idea for the hit TV show *Fantasy Island,* a show set on a fictional island in the Pacific Ocean where guests would pay fifty thousand dollars to come and live out their fantasies. As Spelling recalls, "*Fantasy Island* began as an argument. Leonard Goldberg [Spelling's production partner] and I were at ABC pitching TV movie ideas, but all of our best ones were getting shot down. The executives kept telling us that they didn't want sob stories, but ones with heat. Finally, I kinda' went crazy. I said, *You guys don't really want a show! You don't want something with characters or plot or a story! You just want to have some sort of an island where you can go and act out all of your dumb fantasies!* And that is when they started jumping up and down shouting—*Do it! Do it!* Believe it or not, that's the truth."

On a much more somber note is the case of classical composer Robert Schumann. Robert Weisberg, a leading creativity scholar, professor of psychology, and director of the Brain, Behavior and Cognition Cluster at Temple University, sought to test a hypothesis that "being in a manic state can increase the creativity of the thought processes." He chose Schumann since the composer was known to have suffered from bipolar disorder, making him an appealing subject for understanding the effect of mood (depression and mania) on creativity. Psychologists who studied Schumann prior to Weisberg's analysis derived their findings from doctors' records and letters written by Schumann and his acquaintances.

They discovered (as shown in Figure 5.1) that Schumann was five times more productive during his manic years (designated in Figure 5.1 by "H" for hypomania, that is, a mild state of mania).

However, here is where Weisberg's analysis of Schumann is more appropriate for our discussion of conceptual creativity: not just art revered for its novelty but unique solutions with some commercial value. While Figure 5.2 underscores Schumann's prolific creativity while manic (he certainly produced more during these periods), it says nothing about whether he was producing relevant pieces—those that others viewed as important. In order to determine whether his manic work was relevant, Weisberg used a wonderfully simple metric: "the number of recordings available for a musical composition, with more recordings indicating a better work. This measure is based on the opinions of critics, musicians, and the record-buying public. It should also be noted that this measure of quality correlates highly with other measures, such as

Figure 5.1. Number of Compositions Robert Schumann Produced over His Career

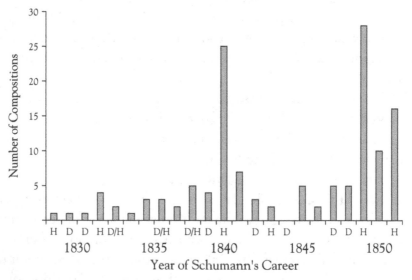

Note: H = hypomania. D = depression. D/H = depression/hypomania.

Source: Robert Weisberg, *Creativity*, Copyright 2006 John Wiley & Sons.

Figure 5.2. Number of Compositions Schumann Produced over His Career as a Function of Mood

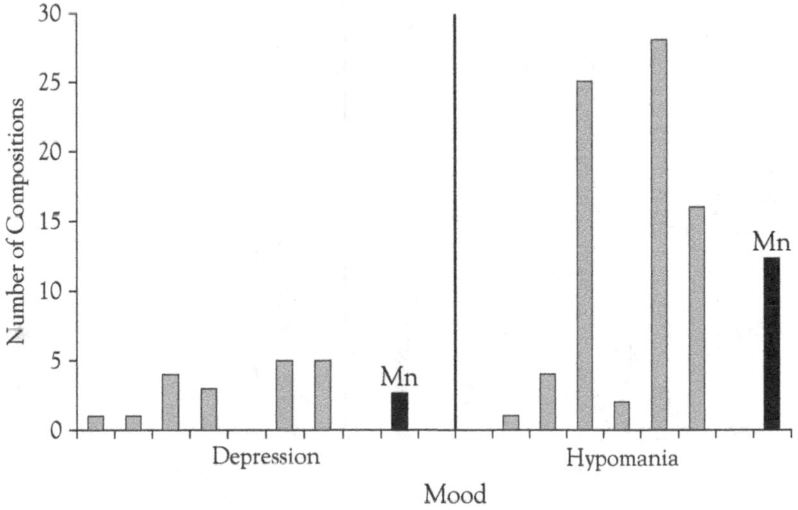

Note: MN = mania.

Source: Robert Weisberg, *Creativity*, Copyright 2006 John Wiley & Sons.

how often a composition is discussed in critical analyses of music. Thus, the number of recordings is more than simply a measure of the popularity of compositions." Weisberg used this logic: "If Schumann's periods of mania improved his thought processes, then compositions produced during his manic years should be recorded more frequently, on average, than compositions produced during the depressive years." The findings are illustrated in Figure 5.3.

As Weisberg's analysis illustrates, relative to the totality of his compositions over his lifetime, Schumann's manic years did not produce more "relevant" compositions than did his depressive years. In at least the case of Robert Schumann, "madness" (depression or mania) was not a prerequisite to creative productivity. However, Weisberg also conducted a study of poet Emily Dickinson, who suffered from bipolar disorder. He found some evidence that the poems produced during her manic years were more conceptually creative; they were unique, relevant, and met the needs of her audience as measured by the number of publications

Figure 5.3. Average Number of Recordings of Compositions from Schumann's Periods of Depression and Hypomania

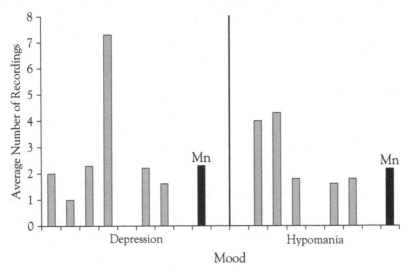

Note: MN = mania.

Source: Robert Weisberg, *Creativity*, Copyright 2006 John Wiley & Sons.

in which they appeared. As I explored in my previous book, *Hope*, we know that a generally positive outlook is highly correlated with the capacity to be open to new ideas, although the scientific jury is still out on establishing a direct biological link between emotion and creativity.

Cognitive neuroscientists generally believe that being relaxed and in a good mood (what they refer to as "positive affect") is better for creativity insofar that it facilitates broader attention for accessing more distantly related ideas. Passion and motivation are clearly important as well, since strong emotions are needed to focus attention on the task at hand. After all, a great idea holds little value if you cannot make it happen. However, tread cautiously in the area of intense focus. There are diminishing returns associated with too much focus because it can lead to anxiety, which may not only hinder creativity but encourage action in the wrong direction, for example, sending that nasty e-mail to your boss before you have had a chance to sleep on it. And so, particularly as a leader—a manager, a coach, a parent—be mindful of this delicate balance between positive outlook and focused anxiety in order to encourage creativity among your team. As the body of research on emotion and creativity expands, the precise nature of this relationship, correlation or causation, will likely be determined.

In the interim, heed the advice of a colleague of mine, cognitive neuroscientist Edward Bowden, who has dedicated his career to the study of creative problem solving:

> In my opinion the jury is still out on the connection between mood, emotion, and creativity. So far most of the evidence suggests that creativity is enhanced by being in a positive mood. However, I tend to think that any emotion that *changes* how you are thinking can contribute to a creative solution. For example, when you have a great idea (at least when you think it's a great idea), it is likely that at least *one* person will tell you how stupid it is. Subsequently, you get angry which activates many other thoughts related to your past experiences of anger including *these people are idiots!* It is from this change in your thought process, the change in the information you are now retrieving from memory and the new connections that arise, that a creative idea can be born. Therefore, if you are normally laid back it might help to get angry. If you are normally angry it might help to mellow out a bit. Any change in the way you approach a problem increases the probability of a new solution idea.

The research that Bowden is referring to stems from the question: How does context, including emotional context and a change in context, affect memory, problem solving, and creativity?

In experiments, participants were given learning tasks in different environments and subsequently asked to recall what they had learned inside and outside those contexts. *Context* refers to both physical and mental contexts. For example, in a study of physical context, scuba divers were asked to learn lists of words on dry land and while under water. Later they were asked to recall the words in either the environment in which they had learned them or in the other environment. The researchers found that recall was higher in the context in which the words were originally learned. If the scuba divers learned the words under water, their under-water recall of the words was higher than their on-land recall of the words, and vice versa.

In practice, these findings support what most detectives have come to realize through years of experience: take victims back to the scene of the crime in order to conjure up memories. Inciden-tally, if you are a student, this is a compelling argument for why you should try your best not to miss an exam on the day it is given versus making it up in the professor's office at a later date. More-over, it is best not to miss class either since it is better to have learned the information in the same room as you will be asked to remember it. In fact, if you are able, sit in the same seat in the classroom for the exam that you sat in during the quarter. Or if you are a parent, encourage your children to prepare for that upcom-ing standardized test at the actual test facility. This phenomenon is related not only to physical context but also to mental context. An additional study compared memory performance when learn-ing and testing occurred while the person was in the same or a dif-ferent mood. It turned out that the specific mood state was not as important as being in the same mood that the person was in during the learning.

Context serves as a cue for memory, and since you are more likely to remember things you learned while you are in that con-text, changing the context changes the memory cues, making it more likely that you will recall different things. And since chang-ing your interpretation of a problem is often a precursor to creative insight, it follows that changing physical or mental context would also be helpful in creating the conditions for creativity to flourish. You "get more creative" when memory doesn't "get in the way." As Pablo Picasso is reported to have said, "It took me a lifetime to think like a child." Although we have much to learn from the past, learning to forget now and then can inspire alternative ways to solve problems.

The challenge with the past is in learning how to use it. What can we learn from it that is helpful, and what should we learn to forget that is a hindrance? What you believe can adversely or positively affect how you think. For example, for decades, banks believed that they were in the "security business" and therefore installed large vaults within view of their customers in order to send the message that "your money is safe with us." Over time, as banking customers' needs changed, driven by trends they had experienced in other retail outlets such as grocery and clothing stores, banking customers came to value features not typically offered by banks, such as convenience, but convenience was not a competitive feature of banks until the market demanded it. Once banks learned to forget that security had become "table stakes" (the lowest and most common cost of entry) in the banking business, convenience features became more prevalent in the form of automated teller machines, weekend hours, and online banking services. These and other product innovations required that banks challenge their prevailing beliefs about what they believed was historically meaningful to their customers. Identifying and challenging beliefs is one of the cornerstones of innovation and is also a common precursor to creative insight.

As we continue to learn more about the mystery of creative insight, one thing is certain: from artists to scientists to entrepreneurs, the chorus is often the same: *the idea just came to me* (or at least it felt that way). This makes the riddle that much more puzzling. Those highly desired moments of creative insight often leave those who experienced them dumbfounded by their origins. They don't necessarily know why the idea happened or where it came from, they simply know that it happened, and it happened in a flash. So asking, "Where did the idea come from?" is often futile. With the exception of those who study ideas, most of us are at a loss to explain the origins of our ideas. What is most intriguing about those who study the origin of ideas and are more aware of the creative process at work is that they may be better able to recall how they conjured up the solutions. For example, as Bowden recalls his own experiences,

> As one who spends his time researching creativity, I often deliberately trace my thinking back to find what inspired the thought. For example, I once solved a puzzle that got me on the NPR show with Will Shortz. The puzzle was to rearrange the letters in "shout danger" so that they formed new words that could be considered opposites. The solution was "son daughter." The idea came to me while I was at the opera *Don Giovanni* (which was supertitled). I had actually been thinking about the puzzle during the opera when I suddenly got the solution. Tracing my thoughts backward, I realized that seeing the word *daughter* in the supertitle had led to the solution.

Bowden's account offers hope to those interested in learning to become deliberately creative: when we remain aware of a problem and hold it in the forefront of our minds, solutions are more readily available. Without this activation of thought, it may be that the information required to solve the problem is available but unable to connect with the problem itself, and so the problem goes unsolved. If this is true, then perhaps one way in which to solve this riddle of where great ideas come from is to understand the events and experiences that typically give rise to moments of insight. Do precursors exist? And if so, what can we do to be more deliberate about using them to our advantage?

Although I do not believe in silver bullets (at least, I do not propose to have discovered any), it does appear that isolating epiphany might provide some useful clues that we can use to improve our creative capacity. That said, for those who are in search of a quick fix to creativity, the age of "smart foods" and "smart drugs" is dawning. Both of these social inventions illustrate just how far people will go to control emotional states and interfere with the brain's normal processing in order to conjure up creative inspiration at will.

The emerging smart foods category (products that promise to enhance creativity, memory, and attention) is becoming an increasingly popular area of opportunity for food and pharmaceutical manufacturers as well as the occasional extreme inventor. One such extreme product in this category came from Japanese inventor Dr. Yoshiro Nakamatsu (commonly known as Dr. NakaMats). His Yummy Nutri Brain Food snack crackers are a mixture of eel, eggs, seaweed, yogurt, dried shrimp, beef, and chicken livers. NakaMats claims "they are very helpful to the brain's thinking process." For his work, NakaMats was awarded the *Ig* Nobel Prize in the Nutrition category in 2005 for "photographing and then analyzing every meal he has eaten over 34 years and counting." *Ig* Nobel Prizes are a parody on the real Nobel prizes and are given out each year at a ceremony at Harvard University for ten achievements that "at first make people laugh, and then make them think."

In addition to NakaMats's smart foods, scientists around the globe are working on the smart pill, a new category that includes a product named HT-0712 (a memory enhancer), modafinil (used to treat narcolepsy, but also seems to enhance certain mental powers such as memory), donepezil (marketed under the name Aricept, which boosts electrical transmissions between brain cells), and, a staple, Ritalin (designed to treat attention deficit disorder but also used by college students without this disorder or a prescription to get an "edge"). At least one wealthy investor is very interested in the emerging smart pills category: the U.S. military. In fact, in 2005, the Pentagon spent $20 million researching ways to "expand available memory" and build "sleep-resistant circuitry" in the brain. Of course critics abound due to the presence of potential negative side effects associated with smart pills, including the notion that "knowing too much" in the way of detail could lead to knowing nothing at all. For that matter, aren't there some things in life that you'd rather forget? Nonetheless, with the rise of cosmetic neurology, the future may ultimately crown the 1960s counterculture icon Timothy Leary, a creative genius born long before his time. As a proponent of mind-enhancing drugs, most notably LSD, Leary would have been the ideal spokesperson for companies launching products into the smart pills category.

Although these tactics are extreme, they illustrate just how far humans are willing to go to conjure up creative inspiration. However, you need not consume eel crackers or cosmeceuticals in order to enhance your creativity. Cognitive tricks exist in the form of precursors to creative insight. From drawing metaphors to challenging prevailing assumptions, you can think of these precursors as fingerprints at the scene of a crime: always present yet sometimes overlooked. I believe the reason that these precursors to creative insight are often ignored is not that we find no value in them; rather, when we "have a great idea," we are often so emotionally moved by the idea itself that we seldom stop and ask, "Where did *that* idea come from?" or "How did I think of that?"

Recall Archimedes. I'm quite certain that once he had his big idea, he didn't care that much about its origins. However, this is precisely why understanding the origin of creative insight matters. Epiphany is the greatest gift bestowed on would-be innovators insofar that if we can understand why it happens and how it happens, we may be able to recreate when it happens. Once we have come down from the initial emotional high of having a great idea, we could learn a lot by dispassionately reviewing the thoughts and activities we were engaged in shortly prior to the idea. I can't imagine a greater thing for an aspiring innovator than self-inflicted epiphany. Wouldn't you rather be able to control your creative inspiration rather than leaving it to chance? It would certainly help the cause of creativity for a single reason: the greatest challenge to applied creativity is that great ideas are never lonely. Once you have a great idea and that idea becomes known to others, you are then challenged to come up with the next big idea. Innovation is not a destination or an event. In its ideal state, innovation is a capability. In order for one to be considered "innovative" (versus lucky), repeated acts of applied creativity are required. And for our purposes, the outcomes of this creativity must be relevant to an intended audience. With over a thousand patents and a litany of life-changing inventions, Thomas Edison and his team were innovative. With a single widely known composition, "Canon in D Major," Johann Pachelbel was a flash in the creativity skillet—a one-hit wonder.

Conceptual creativity is not a product of thinking differently; rather, it is the product of thinking deliberately about unsolved problems, unmet needs, and unexplored opportunities in order to keep the innovation funnel rich in ideas. You may be familiar with the notion of the innovation funnel. You start with a thousand ideas and converge through a few hundred, then a few dozen, and ultimately to a handful of great ideas to be implemented. The innovation funnel sounds good in theory, but it doesn't work in practice. In reality, the innovation funnel is more like a tunnel. Most of us start with a single great idea (or so we think) and subsequently do everything in our power to ensure that the idea exits the funnel just as it entered. Thus, in practice, we have the innovation tunnel. However, like measuring performance in any field, success with creative tasks is largely a function of the work produced.

Consider baseball great Cy Young as an example. At 512 wins (surpassing his nearest rival by 150 games), he is indisputably the best pitcher ever to have played the game; however, at 313 *losses*, he also maintains the distinction as the worst pitcher ever to have lived. And Babe Ruth was not only the home run king, with 714 home runs, but also the strike-out king, with 1,330 in his at-bats. As Michael Covel of *Turtle Trader* writes, "Ruth understood full well that the hits help a whole lot more than the strikeouts hurt. He gave his philosophy in a nutshell with these words: Every strike brings me closer to the next home run. And when reporters asked him how he dealt with the occasional slump, he replied: I just keep goin' up there and keep swingin' at 'em." So swing for the fences to get that breakthrough idea. This is the same logic that governs innovation: win bigger than you lose. How do you know which ideas are the good ones and which are the bad? We'll explore this shortly, but for now, consider Chairman Mao Zedong's advice from his 1963 musings, *Where Do Correct Ideas Come From?* "Those that succeed are correct and those that fail are incorrect." Simplicity is elegant.

In the field of innovation, it's fine to lose now and then as long as your net score is positive. This implies that you must create on a continuous basis. And because of this need for ongoing inspiration, epiphany is a gift worth opening. The good news is that it appears that flashes of brilliance do not appear out of thin air after all. Quite the contrary, these inspired moments seem to be logical extensions of common cognitive processes.

Although many factors contribute to where great ideas come from, there are five precursors that appear to be the most effective at inspiring creative insight: curiosity, constraints, conventions, connections, and codes. Each of these concepts is explored in the subsequent chapters of this book. By becoming aware of these precursors and practicing the techniques I suggest, you will be able to inspire epiphany deliberately versus waiting for divine inspiration. Sure, that's an aggressive goal, but why not? After all, this is the business of creativity. Big ideas are expected.

What is most revealing, and as you'll learn later in the book, is that a large majority of innovators—artists, scientists, entrepreneurs—operate with unique formulas that enable their capacity to create on a continuous basis. This "creative code," which is unique to each person and his or her situation, is the ultimate prize of innovation. This creative code is not a code in the sense that it is a secret that only Leonardo da Vinci or Dan Brown could have dreamed up. Rather, they are codes in the form of logical frameworks from which to apply creativity, simplify complex situations, and ultimately create novel and relevant solutions to existing problems. These codes are the invisible logic of creativity. You will learn how creative codes are constructed as well as how to create one for yourself so that you may increase your creative performance.

Let's now turn to the precursors to eureka beginning with a single-word question that every three-year-old child on the planet has asked: *Why?*

Summary Points and Creative Exercises

- A positive affect (demeanor or outlook) may increase your likelihood of success with innovation.

- Changing emotional states appears to be highly corrected with increased creativity. If you tend to be pessimistic, try to approach a problem optimistically. Conversely, if you tend to be overly optimistic, try to approach the problem pessimistically.

- Like changing your emotional state, changing the context in which you are trying to solve the problem may help inspire new ideas. For example, if you always have your brainstorming sessions in the same place, try somewhere new. If you run ideation sessions during the day, try them at night.

- Theoretically the more ideas you can generate, the greater your likelihood is of finding an idea that will work. However, this also increases your likelihood of failure. Manage failure by thinking of failure not as a mistake but as a way in which to increase the probability that the next idea will work. Of course, it may not; in that case, see the first item in this list.

6

ENDLESSLY INTRIGUING

Curiosity

Some things in life just make sense: disposable diapers, cordless phones, Kevlar. Although these products are indisputably superior to those that existed prior to their introduction, like all other great ideas, they were initially met with an inkling of skepticism. Marion Donovan's "Boater" (the first disposable diaper) was dismissed as "too expensive to produce." Teri Pall's cordless phone was rejected because it was "too good." As Teri explains, "I invented the cordless phone in 1965, but I couldn't market it." The reason: "It had a two-mile radius and would interfere with aircraft." Pall's invention was later adapted (dialed back to a much smaller radius) and eventually made commercially viable. And although Stephanie Kwolek's magical synthetic material, Kevlar, became the main ingredient in bulletproof vests (its strength is five times that of steel), Kwolek registered the patent under *S. L. Kwolek* in fear that her invention would be dismissed by patent officers due to her gender. What do these three creators and their creations share in common? Apart from the fact that all three are among the often forgotten mothers of invention (women), on the surface, it appears that the products they introduced were inspired out of needs. Thus, we have the phrase, *necessity is the mother of invention* (or in these cases, it may have been the other way around). But the question here is whether necessity really is the mother of invention or just a clever phrase.

If necessity were the mother of invention, one would think that a person without access to electricity would have invented the hand-powered radio or that a blind person would have invented a method for reading without sight. However, it turns out that both of these great ideas were introduced not by those who needed them but rather by those who did not. Trevor Baylis, whom you'll meet later in this book, did not have an explicit need for a radio that could be powered by hand, just as Valentin Haüy did not have the need to read without the capability of seeing. This then begs the question: If necessity is not alone at the birth of invention then who, or what, else is present prior to epiphany? In order to answer this question, let's consider the events that preceded the inspiration of one of humanity's greatest innovations: reading without the ability to see.

As legend has it, in 1784, on departing church services at Saint Germain des Prés in Paris, linguist Valentin Haüy gave a coin to a young blind beggar. Surprised by the size of the coin, and thus Haüy's generosity, the blind boy immediately called out to Haüy, at which point—aha!—Haüy realized that the blind boy could decipher differences between denominations through touch. Some believe this story may be apocryphal, suggesting instead that the young blind boy knew of Haüy's interest in educating the blind and therefore threw himself in the path of opportunity. Regardless of how they met, the seventeen-year-old beggar, François Lesuer, became Haüy's first student. Haüy began to teach Lesuer to read using wooden letters to form words. And then one day, while "looking" for an object on Haüy's desk, Lesuer's hand brushed over a funeral card on which the letter "o" was raised (it had been struck unusually hard). This observation led to Haüy's second epiphany: raised letters on paper (versus wooden blocks) would be a much more efficient way to teach the blind to read insofar that books could be made. Subsequently, Haüy's improved method for reading without sight involved applying soaked paper over cursive letters leaving behind tactile shapes as the paper dried.

Once the paper dried, Haüy glued the pages together to create two-sided sheets and bundled the sheets into books. As you can imagine, this became a labor-intensive exercise because each letter had to be formed independently, and it made transporting the finished books nearly impossible due to weight. However crude the initial books were, within six months, Lesuer mastered most of the basic principles of primary education using Haüy's methods. Haüy eventually demonstrated Lesuer's progress to a stunned group of France's leading scholars at the Royal Academy, which subsequently paved the way for the opening of a school for the blind.

Haüy's curiosity, not necessity, was the mother of his invention. Necessity, in this case, was more of a distant uncle: related but not fully responsible. Without Haüy's curiosity, it is highly likely that necessity (the inability to read) would have remained. While it is certainly true that blind people could not read, reading was not an explicit need of blind people at that time. Therefore, Haüy innovated based not on needs but on his own curiosity.

Curiosity is the first of the five precursors to creative insight. Curiosity begets creativity. The challenge we humans have is that our curiosity seems to diminish as we grow older. At some point (typically, shortly after we leave school), our knowledge, experience, and infinite wisdom trump our ability to think like a child: to ask why, to get lost, to attempt to fit round pegs in square holes. But this is precisely the type of thinking that fosters creative insight. Alison Gopnik, one of the coauthors of *Scientist in the Crib: What Early Learning Tells Us About the Mind*, explains, "Babies are just plain smarter than we are, at least if being smart means being able to learn something new. . . . They think, draw conclusions, make predictions, look for explanations, and even do experiments. . . . In fact, scientists are successful precisely because they emulate what children do naturally." Gopnik's sentiment is shared by Silicon Valley venture capitalist Steve Jurvetson. When asked which value he most cherished, Jurvetson replied, "Playfulness. I cherish the child-like mind. . . . From what I can see the best scientists and engineers nurture a child-like mind. They are playful, open minded and unrestrained by the inner voice of reason, collective cynicism, or fear of failure." Haüy's childlike curiosity—both his ability and his willingness to temporarily part with "the inner voice of reason"—inspired his eureka moment.

It is important to clarify that the mantra "think like a child" does not necessarily mean to think simplistically. To be creative, it helps to maintain a childlike curiosity about the world, but one must also develop a complex (as opposed to simplistic, childlike) way of thinking about the world. Children may have greater curiosity about the world than adults do, but they have more limited knowledge. For example, people often say that children are better than adults at the game of Memory; however adults can usually outperform children by using a strategy: metacognitive knowledge not yet developed in children that could improve their performance. For example, children are notoriously overconfident in their ability to remember things because they have not yet developed the habit of rehearsing to-be-remembered information or creating retrieval cues. Thus, as was the case of reading without the ability to see, it is curiosity combined with knowledge that leads to the most meaningful innovation.

Although Haüy's contribution to humanity was significant, it was not sustainable. As is often the case with innovation, the first mover rarely maintains a sustainable advantage, yet another innovation myth. We'll explore who sustained the competitive advantage in "sightless learning" momentarily; however, first, we must address another first-mover myth.

The mantra *we must be first in order to win* is a romantic notion frequently batted around in innovation circles. It is not true. The belief that first matters is based largely on how most of us were taught to define "success": whoever crosses the line first wins. This is a part of our childhood best left in the past, at least in terms of innovation. Seldom do we really know, or even remember, the first movers in categories because first movers often fail at making their ideas commercially viable. We think we know who the first mover was, but it is often the result of hype (that is, who did the best job of promoting that he or she was first). Such was the case of the electric light bulb.

Contrary to popular opinion, Thomas Edison did not invent the electric light bulb. In fact, his original patent application for the bulb in 1880 was rejected in 1883 due to the existence of prior art (meaning that aspects of the idea had previously been conjured up by someone else for which a patent was filed, granted, and issued). Although the decision (that Edison's ideas conflicted with prior art) was later overturned, the original concept of an electric light was someone else's big idea. In fact, there are twenty-two different inventors credited with the invention of incandescent lamps, each of whom had worked on this idea over the course of decades prior to Edison's arrival in the lighting business. Most notable was the work of British inventor Joseph Swan, whom Edison eventually partnered with in 1883 to form the Edison & Swan United Electric Light Company. Ediswan sold lamps with a cellulose filament that Swan had invented in 1881. Thomas Edison continued using bamboo filaments until the 1892 merger that created General Electric, at which point they converted to cellulose filaments. Edison also acquired the rights for both the U.S. and Canadian patents on incandescent bulbs from a Toronto electrician, Henry Woodward, and his co-inventor, Mathew Evans. Edison later improved on all of these existing ideas in his attempt to make bulbs burn longer. It is worth noting that even the process itself for making the filament was a technology invented not by Thomas Edison but by Lewis Latimer, the unsung hero of the electric light bulb.

Lewis Howard Latimer (1848–1928) was born to fugitive slaves on September 4, 1848. At age sixteen, he enlisted in the Union Navy and served aboard the U.S.S. *Massasoit*. Upon receiving an honorable discharge, he was hired by the Boston-based patent firm Crosby and Gould, which was looking for an intern to help out around the office. While he was working for the firm, Latimer taught himself drawing skills, convinced his reluctant employer to allow him to draw, and eventually became the firm's head draftsman. Latimer was much more than a tradesman. He was an engineer, author, poet, expert witness, violinist, and inventor— what some would refer to as a Renaissance man. His greatest contribution was a process that enabled the manufacture of carbon filaments for the electric light bulb. Creating a filament that could burn longer than eight minutes was the unsolved problem that evaded not only Edison but also his competitors, among them Hiram Maxim and his United States Electric Lighting Company. Latimer's process fixed the problem, although he didn't originally fix it for Edison.

On September 13, 1881, while working for Hiram Maxim, not Edison, Latimer received a patent for producing "incandescence of a continuous strip of carbon secured to metallic wires." Six days prior to the issuance of the filament patent, which involved using an unorthodox material, cardboard, instead of the conventional tissue paper, Latimer filed the patent on the process for manufacturing the filaments. The patent was issued to Latimer's employer, Maxim's United States Electric Lighting Company, on January 17, 1882. Unfortunately, history is not necessarily written based on facts. Latimer's long-lasting filaments first appeared in Hiram Maxim's lamps and were later made popular by America's greatest inventor.

Edison was a master connector as much as a master inventor, and Latimer was a dilettante (back in the days when *dilettante* was an endearing term). Latimer eventually joined Edison, becoming the only African American member of Thomas Edison's "pioneers," the scientific team that worked for various Edison-owned companies, and contributed to his many breakthrough inventions. In addition to being a master connector, Edison was a master promoter. In fact, in order to promote the "Edison lighting system," Latimer authored a book in 1890, with Edison's encouragement, entitled *Incandescent Electric Lighting: A Practical Description of the Edison System*. (Who can argue with the guy for whom the book was written? Genius.) The title would lead one to believe that Latimer created the filament *for* Edison, when in fact he didn't even work for Edison when the patent was issued. In the spirit of Edison's idea-brokering approach, in a more contemporary example, is Procter & Gamble's "connect and develop" innovation strategy, but this too is not a new idea. This strategy is based on the simple premise that a single organization alone cannot outperform the collective capacity of the much larger creative community. Therefore, P&G reaches out to academics, entrepreneurs, inventors, and even competitors in order to develop new products and new business ventures. For example, the consumer products brand Glad (trash bags, plastic wrap, sandwich bags, plastic containers) is a joint venture between P&G and the Clorox Company. In many cases, P&G contributes its intellectual property while Clorox contributes other assets such as manufacturing equipment and personnel. A. G. Lafley, P&G's chief executive officer, sings the praises of the partnership: "We expect the combination of Clorox's well-established Glad business and P&G's R&D expertise would provide consumers with important new products and outstanding value." Like Lafley, connect and develop was the secret to Edison's success: connecting with Latimer and many others enabled electric lighting.

Latimer's contribution to the electric lighting industry is only a footnote in the career of this relatively unknown creative genius. Before joining the Thomas Alva Edison Electric Light Company, Alexander Graham Bell commissioned Latimer to draw up the plans for his telephone. In fact, Latimer issued the patent application and drawings for the telephone on Bell's behalf, literally minutes before Bell's competitors did, which subsequently led to the issuance of the patent on March 7, 1876. In addition to the electric light bulb and the telephone, Latimer created improvements for railroad car toilets and hat and coat racks, and he introduced an apparatus for cooling, deodorizing, and disinfecting rooms. Incidentally, in an ironic twist of fate, the firm that needed an intern to help out around the office became Latimer's attorneys.

Like most other great innovators, Edison stood on the shoulders of giants: Swan, Woodward, Evans, Latimer, and many others. However, even with his improvements to the existing bulb, Edison's unique genius was not in making the light last longer; it was in making the light commercially viable. He did this by bringing together the electric light's many disparate components into a system designed to produce light: the parallel circuit, an improved dynamo, an underground conductor network, devices for maintaining constant voltage, safety fuses and insulating materials, light sockets with on-off switches, and a long-lasting and durable bulb. As Hargadon writes, "The economic historian Nathan Rosenberg has argued that our persistent misconceptions about the innovation process are a product not only of our need for clean histories but also, at the moment, of the entrepreneur's need for ownership of ideas in the courts of law and of public opinion."

Hargadon then continues, "Worse than simply being incomplete and inaccurate accounts of what happened, however, these simple stories distort our ideas of how to pursue innovation, how to manage it, and even how to make sense of it when it happens again. Every 'modern-day Edison' who graces the cover of *Time* and *Newsweek* touting his or her invention, every business guru who insists upon demonstrating his or her individual genius takes us one step further away from understanding and emulating the successful innovations of the past." I couldn't agree more with both Rosenberg and Hargadon. Although all of human progress stands squarely on the shoulders of giants, it seems history would rather have us stand on their heads.

Like the twenty-two first movers who preceded Edison, there really is no such thing as a single owner of any idea. No one has a monopoly on curiosity. There are 6 billion people on the planet. To imagine any single person could maintain jurisdiction over an inspired thought is borderline naive. There are those to whom we award patents, but this does not mark the precise moment in time when the idea was conceived; it simply marks the precise moment when someone decided to complete a patent application. The future belongs not to those who create ideas but to those who make them viable. Such was the case with Thomas Edison. The myth became worth more than the man. Edison's brand, as much as his inventions, was invaluable. Reflecting on the power of the Edison name, Thomas Edison's wife, Mina, wrote in her diary on the day before the fiftieth anniversary of Edison's introduction of the light bulb: "I feel that dearie [Thomas] is so much more than the electric light and that the light jubilee is one grand advertisement for General Electric and the light companies, that [he] has just been made the excuse." Edison was branding while the rest of the world was still marketing. He understood the power of his name, his reputation, and especially the romantic notion of the inventor.

History has all but forgotten most first movers or at least forgotten that they were first. Among them are German manufacturer Leica, which created the 35 mm camera in 1925 but lost ground to Canon by 1934; Diner's Club, a viable ongoing enterprise that created the credit card in 1950 but succumbed to American Express by 1958; and Code-a-Phone Corporation, which created the telephone answering machine in 1958 yet yielded to Panasonic by 1970. History, not reality, crowns first movers. To test this bold declaration, in the context of "learning without the ability to see," which name is more familiar: Haüy or Braille? Although reality credits Valentin Haüy, history credits one of his students, Louis Braille.

Louis Braille was a student at Haüy's school thirty years after it opened its doors. Braille had been blind since age three; while he was playing with one of his father's awls, he accidentally poked one of his eyes, which subsequently became infected and eventually caused him to lose sight in both eyes. After he finished school, Braille became a teacher known for his generosity and support of his students with both his time and money. His empathy for his students led to an epiphany when he realized that although his students could read, thanks to Haüy, they could not write. Specifically, he observed that his students had no way of communicating with their families back home other than by dictating letters to sighted teachers. This disability created all sorts of complications for students: finding time with a sighted teacher to "take down a letter," sharing information with that teacher (likely *about* that teacher) in order to tell his parents, and so on.

Ironically, like Sir Isaac Newton's trip home to Lincolnshire, it was while visiting his parents' home on vacation that Braille had the flash of insight that led to his better idea. While sitting in his father's leather shop, Louis picked up one of his father's awls, and suddenly the idea came to him. The very tool that caused his blindness would go on to become the same tool that would enable his, and many others', ability to read and write efficiently without the ability to see. Within six days from his discovery, he created an alphabet made up of six dots, with the position of the different dots representing the letters of the alphabet.

In 1834, Louis Braille demonstrated his "code" at the Paris Exposition of Industry, which was attended by visitors from around the globe, as well as King Louis-Philippe of France, who, as history tells us, didn't understand what Braille had invented. In 1837, students at the school published the first braille textbook: a three-volume history of France. Unfortunately, like Haüy's system, Braille's improved methods remained labor intensive. Enter Pierre Foucault.

In 1841, on learning of Louis Braille's intention to help the blind communicate through writing, a blind inventor, Pierre Foucault, created a machine (a "piston board") to punch the entire letter at once, thus saving time and effort. In 1847, Foucault evolved his "piston board" into a "keyboard printer," much like a typewriter, so that blind people could write to sighted people in black type. In fact, Braille himself used Foucault's keyboard printer to write letters to his mother. Incidentally, like Braille's and Edison's ideas, Foucault's idea of a typewriter was not new: a similar machine had been invented in 1808 to help a blind countess write to sighted people. Nonetheless, Foucault's piston board became common. (Print typewriters did not gain scale in Europe until the 1870s.)

With Braille's help, blind students were finally able to read and write, often with greater speed and accuracy than sighted people. Unfortunately, the students' new history book was not a celebrated publication: the Académie française instead awarded its prestigious prize to assistant director P. Armand Dufau, a former geography teacher at the school, for his book: *The Blind: Considerations on Their Physical, Moral and Intellectual State, with a Complete Description of the Means to Improve Their Lot Using Instruction and Work.*

Ironically, Dufau opposed braille, which he believed made the blind "too independent." In fact, he was so vehemently opposed to the method that he didn't even bother to cite Louis Braille's work in his award-winning book. It didn't necessarily help matters that the school administrators didn't seem to care that Dufau ignored braille. Why? Dufau's sudden fame helped the school get a new building.

Dufau eventually became the director of the school, at which point he began eliminating what he viewed as "frivolous" subjects (for example, history and geometry) and adopted a new reading system to replace braille, one that he had discovered at the Asylum for the Blind in Glasgow. In order to ready the school for the new method, Dufau burned every book in the school's library (over fifty years of progress), including Haüy's original books, along with the braille-writing equipment (slates and styli). A mutiny ensued. In lieu of the equipment, students used knitting needles, forks, and nails to send messages to each other. In response, Dufau slapped and starved students who didn't submit to him. But the students would have none of it. Older students taught younger students braille in secret sessions (clearly text messaging is also nothing new), and then one day, Dufau suddenly changed his opinion of braille (the method and the man).

Persuaded by his assistant, himself fluent in braille, that the students' ingenuity could enhance the school's reputation (and, in turn, Dufau's), Dufau embraced Braille's teachings. Once the school moved into the new building, Dufau provided each student with a new braille slate, thereby winning back their support. He even went so far as to include a description of the braille system in the second edition of his book, published in 1850.

Braille died on January 6, 1852, a relatively unknown teacher. In fact, not a single newspaper reported his death. However, braille (the writing) survived Braille (the man). In 1854, France adopted braille as its official communication system for the blind. Braille soon spread throughout Europe, although it was met with opposition outside France for a number of reasons: sighted people couldn't read it, it was believed that blind people had no need to read (and thus were contained in asylums and such), and so on. Perhaps the most obtuse story of opposition to braille is that of the superintendent of the Missouri School for the Blind in St. Louis who resisted the use of braille at his school saying that it was "not pleasing on the eye." (Go figure.) However, when one of the school's board members, Dr. Simon Pollak, learned that French students were teaching each other a new system for communication (braille), he visited France and returned with the strong recommendation that braille be adopted even though it was not "pleasing." In 1860, the Missouri School for the Blind became the first American school to adopt braille.

Louis Braille touched the hearts of blind people not because he gave them a chance to learn but because he gave them a chance to teach. For the first time, blind people were given the opportunity to communicate their own ideas in writing, not only to consume those of the sighted world. In a debt of gratitude to Louis Braille, Helen Keller wrote, "Braille has been the most precious aid to me in many ways. It made my going to college possible—it was the only method by which I could take notes of lectures. All my examination papers were copied for me in this system. I use Braille as a spider uses its web—to catch thoughts that flit across my mind for speeches, messages and manuscripts." Braille has since been adapted to nearly every language. And due to the easy reproducibility of braille, the computer age has helped make it the standard medium of literacy for blind people.

As for whether necessity is the mother of invention, the answer is yes and no. Haüy, Edison, Latimer, Lafley, and most other innovators rarely possess the needs themselves; rather, they possess the intrinsic motivation—the curiosity to figure things out. Haüy did not have the need himself to "read without sight"; rather, he observed the need in others. He was curious. And so, you may be thinking: *Yes, that is true. Haüy was not blind. He did not have the need himself. But what about Louis Braille? He was not only curious but also had a need: he could not see.* Well, there is more to this story. As it turns out, the concept of dots on paper that Louis Braille used was inspired not only by Haüy's work but also by the work of one other system, which also was invented by a sighted person, although a sighted person who happened to be "occasionally blind."

Braille's inspiration was born out of the French army by soldiers who were unable to execute orders at night because they could not see them (in combat, striking a match for reading purposes could be fatal). Therefore, the military developed an alphabet code for sending messages between officers and field soldiers. The code used raised dots and dashes, a system that Louis Braille would soon adopt. In this case, was necessity the mother of invention? Sure. However, it was not only necessity but also the intellectual curiosity of those who solved the problem that served as precursors to creative insight.

It may appear that my distinction between necessity and curiosity is on par with splitting hairs; however, hair splitting is an important procedure in the field of innovation. How questions are phrased and how problems are positioned can radically change the ultimate solution or idea. When they are positioned appropriately, human ingenuity is without boundaries. When they are positioned poorly, human error is also without boundaries.

I have arrived at this distinction between necessity and curiosity based on a belief I have developed working in the field of innovation: most people do not really know what their needs are and are ill equipped to articulate them even when they do, so focusing on need states is often a futile exercise. But when curiosity is nurtured through observation and enlightened experimentation, uniquely relevant ideas become more apparent.

Curiosity is the mother of invention. It is only when an idea is "out in the world" (as was the case with braille, the electric light, and plastic wrap) that people suddenly realize what their needs are and how they can use it, how it may help them solve a problem, and how their life might change should they choose to adopt it. Here is the paradox of innovation. Before great ideas are introduced, we rarely see the need for them. However, once they are introduced, they become necessities. Yesterday's impossibility becomes tomorrow's expectation. We didn't need a theory of relativity, but once we had it, it was certainly useful. Nor did we really need a way of getting around faster, but riding horses sure beat walking. Apart from basic human needs, all others are luxuries in disguise.

This phenomenon of a new idea's "becoming necessary" is what made the blind students revolt. It was not braille itself that the students were longing for; it was what braille did for them: it gave them freedom. Taking it away was the equivalent of someone telling you that you could no longer use your cell phone, e-mail, or sticky notes. You'd revolt too. We all would! This logic is integral to all new ideas, at least to the great ones. Once we experience a new idea, we cannot imagine living without it. We didn't really need, say, electric lighting, indoor plumbing, and the automobile. We had candles, outhouses, and horses. However, each of these ideas came fully loaded with unfortunate side effects: candles drip, outhouses stink and are cold in winter, and horses require riding without protection in bad weather. Therefore, we innovated not out of necessity but out of curiosity. "What if?" not "we need," is responsible for innovation. *What if you could create light without candles? What if you didn't have to go outside to heed nature's call? What if you didn't need a horse to take a trip?*

As a result of our curiosity, our innovations that might have once seemed needless have made life a bit more comfortable, if not more entertaining. And thank goodness. Consider the beauty of a seventy-two-inch flat screen television. Do we need it? Absolutely! Or what about a candy-colored computer shaped like a gum drop. Do we need it? Are you kidding me? Gotta have it! And who could possibly make it through the day without a portable music player to lay down the soundtrack of life. Can't live without it! Do we need any of these things? Of course not, but people love them. In fact, our translucent love affair with candy-colored computers became so strong that everything from irons to toasters began to pop up in translucent multicolored plastics. The iMac design was popular without being necessary to anyone except Apple. It is worth noting, however, that ideas that are necessary to producers (versus users) are not as valuable as those that are integral to solving fundamental problems users have, like braille, toilet paper, and the Swiffer. Although necessity certainly plays an important role as a precursor to creative insight, it is not a direct precursor. Herein is the challenge to conceptual creativity: most people do not really know what they need. How then do you go about nurturing curiosity if needs are misleading? The simple answer is, Focus on what people are able to articulate, which is often what they are unable to do. Although most people have no idea what they need, nearly everyone knows what they are unable to do. We are all too familiar with the location of the roadblocks—the detours of life that we need help navigating.

For example, consider soldiers. If you were to focus on a question of needs—*What do soldiers need in a foxhole?*—you might get to things such as they need to eat, rest, and shoot guns. Based on these needs, you may then introduce products to help soldiers fulfill these needs: compact meal kits, lightweight blankets, and equipment to carry ammunition. Although all of these ideas are relevant to soldiers' needs, you would likely never arrive at the big idea of *reading with your fingers*. Why? Because of the way that you thought about and framed the question, What do soldiers need? Rather than focus on needs, focusing on constraints—*What can't soldiers do in a foxhole, and why can't they do it?*—would likely lead to a much more interesting set of answers, including *they can't execute orders at night because they can't read and they can't read because they can't see and they can't see because they can't use lights or they'll get shot*. The solution statement would then become: *create something that will allow soldiers to execute orders without visually reading them.*

At this point, the big idea (the solution) becomes more apparent: tactile reading methods. In hindsight, this seems obvious—and that's the point. Once introduced, all great ideas slip seamlessly into our lives.

The fundamental challenge with focusing on needs is that they become apparent only once people experience them and suddenly realize that they couldn't imagine life without a particular product or service. After all, new parents did not know they needed disposable diapers until they saw Marion Donovan's Boater. Only after its introduction did they say, *I gotta have it!* The same can be said of braille. Prior to the introduction of braille and other systems, blind people did not contemplate possibility. Not only did they not think it was possible to be able to read, write, or communicate with each other or with sighted people in any manner other than by speaking, they didn't deem it necessary. That's "just the way it was." Or, as Dufau put it, it was "their lot" in life. If you were to study the needs of a blind person in the mid- to late eighteenth century, you would have likely gotten responses such as, *We [or they] need food, shelter, and clothing.* In fact, most of the innovations for blind people prior to braille's widespread adoption were direct responses to these precise needs: asylums. The logic behind that was, *We just need to take care of these people.* Blind people were hemmed in by perceived needs. They were confined by their lot in life.

Now imagine an entirely different way to approach "their lot." If you were to consider the constraints placed on blind people at that time (their inability to see left them uneducated, which left them without work or the ability to make intellectual contributions to society) and you were to couple this insight with your own curiosity, you would have likely arrived at entirely different and much more compelling solutions. Rather than create more asylums, you would have arrived at precisely what both Haüy and Braille did: a learning system for blind people to help them become more independent.

Perhaps the greatest irony in the development of braille is who taught whom. If innovation involves the ability to "see what does not exist," I would argue that a blind person taught sighted people to "see." Lesuer taught Haüy—not what was needed but what was possible. In this regard, when seeking to create something new, the worst question you can ask is, What do you need? Just like blind people living in the eighteenth century, people today have no idea what they need, much less how to solve their problems. This is the innovator's job: to solve problems. By observing what others are unable to do (the behavioral constraints) and through the management of what is available to you (the resource constraints), your odds of identifying great ideas will increase. We'll delve into the role of constraints as a precursor to epiphany shortly, but first a brief comment on motivation.

A litany of academic studies have highlighted the relationship between intrinsic motivation (curiosity) and creativity. Among them are a 1926 genetic study of geniuses that cites "tenacity of purpose" as a common accompaniment to creative inspiration; a 1952 and a 1984 study of eminent scientists cites "driving absorption"; and a 1993 biographical study of seven creative geniuses (Einstein, Eliot, Freud, Gandhi, Graham, Picasso, and Stravinsky) cites "intense involvement in their work." On the surface, this notion that you must care in order to create makes sense. However, here is the challenge: How do you get others to care? As mentioned earlier, identifying the need is only part of the challenge. Without curiosity, needs would remain. For example, one could argue that if it weren't for Haüy's curiosity, blind people would have likely spent many more years in asylums, unable to read or write. His motivation played an instrumental role in his capacity to create a unique solution to an existing problem.

What role does motivation play in creativity? Motivation can be thought of as an act of focusing the mind on an activity. When motivation is too low, the person doesn't care about the outcome and therefore thinks about other things rather than the task at hand. Of course, this daydreaming may inadvertently create serendipitous connections between previously isolated information in our minds, therefore leading to a new idea; however, it is highly unlikely that a person would act on this new idea without the personal interest required to translate big ideas into practical and actionable solutions. Then we have the opposite question: Can motivation be too high? The answer here is, It depends. If the motivation is extrinsic (for example, your parents want you to go to medical school, but you would rather be a musician), motivation may be counterproductive to creativity. But if motivation is intrinsic (you derive some value from the task itself), you are more likely to "get creative" in how you solve problems because you care more and therefore keep on trying.

To get the most out of a creative team, a leader must work to create intrinsic motivation within each individual team member, using, for example, individual incentives versus group incentives, individual training and career development plans versus group programs, and individual brainstorming versus only team-based brainstorming. In regard to individual brainstorming, the next time you get together for an off-site innovation lab or discussion about new ideas, ask meeting participants to spend time alone prior to the meeting working on ideas of their own. This can be the most creative time of all. Then ask them to bring those ideas to the meeting and share them with the group. It is one thing to start a meeting by stating that "there is no such thing as a bad idea" and "let everyone speak"; however, this rarely works as the cynics chime in, and curiosity is often shelved in favor of those with the greatest political equity or largest share of voice in a given meeting.

As discussed, creativity is an inspired existence. Motivation matters. In order to avoid the risk of oversimplifying the very complex subject of employee motivation, I will refer you to my earlier book, *Hope: How Triumphant Leaders Create the Future*, which explores the role of belief systems in the context of leadership and innovation in more detail. Now let's turn to the second precursor to creative insight: constraints.

Summary Points and Creative Exercises

- Curiosity is the mother of invention. Observation can be more powerful than conversation in generating new ideas. In the context of the problem you are attempting to solve, observe what people are unable to do versus what they say they want.

- First-mover advantage is a myth. Being first is not as important as being relevant. Seek out first movers to learn from their mistakes. Use their experiences, weaknesses, and shortcomings to jump-start ideation.

- Recombining existing ideas in new ways can be as valuable as creating new-to-the-world ideas. Try to create novel relationships by joining existing ideas.

- Individual brainstorming is often overlooked in lieu of the popularity of group brainstorming, particularly inside organizations. However, group brainstorming can also lead to groupthink and thus overshadow some of the best ideas. Before entering a group brainstorming session, spend some time alone thinking, and encourage those on your team to do the same. Write down your own ideas, and share them with each other. Use the ensuing conversation to make the ideas better as opposed to generating entirely new ideas.

7

PAINFULLY OBVIOUS

Constraints

You can't squeeze blood from a turnip. This was a favorite saying of my undergraduate law professor. I was reminded of Professor Teeven's counsel when I discovered that although you cannot squeeze blood from a vegetable, you can squeeze water from a stone. If you are unfamiliar with this phenomenon, it is likely because you live in an area of the world where water is plentiful. However, if you lived in the middle of a desert, you would have to get creative or die of thirst. Watery stones may not be something you ponder often, but in Israel, it's virtually cocktail party conversation. As we'll explore in this chapter, creativity is a function of resourcefulness as much as a question of resources. How you perceive the environment in which you live, work, and play is as important as the reality of the environment itself. By way of example, consider Israel's capability at squeezing water from a stone.

No other country in the world is as knowledgeable as Israel is about how much water it has, where that water is at any given moment, and how it can get more of it. Nor is any other country in the world as deliberate about managing water consumption. Gardens can be watered only at night. Cars can be washed only from a small bucket, not a running hose. Supervisors on patrol help to reinforce desired behavior, and whenever water reservoirs run low, Israelis are encouraged to take efficient baths. Efficient bathing techniques were promoted as part of a government-sponsored water management campaign several years ago that encouraged bathers to turn off the shower while they lather up and then turn it on again to rinse. And you thought getting a parking ticket was invading your space.

Much like a cruise ship on the high seas, Israel's entire water system exists within closed pipes and lined canals, giving this tiny desert oasis the most sophisticated and complex water supply system in the world. This system depends on a small number of unreliable rivers, one average-sized lake, intermittent rainfall, underground aquifers, wells, cloud seeding, reclaimed sewage, and even the ability to harness the occasional flash flood. Today the Israeli National Water System derives a majority of its water resources from three primary sources: Lake Kinneret, the coastal aquifer, and the mountain (Yarkon-Taninim) aquifer. Even so, this small nation barely gets by, and therefore the system is designed on the premise that every drop literally counts.

Israel derives 600 to 800 million cubic meters per year from its sophisticated water system. However, current nonagricultural demand for things ranging from baths and drinking water to cappuccinos, has reached 600 to 700 million cubic meters. To make things a bit more complicated, when the League of Nations established the British Mandate in 1919, the Jordan River and Lake Tiberias were placed in Palestine. Add to this already challenging reality the fact that the most important long-term water source (the mountain aquifer) straddles the pre-1967 cease-fire lines (referred to as the "Green Line"), and you will realize that the next conflict in the Middle East probably will be over water, not oil. In fact, to some degree it already is. Water is a central issue every time peace talks are exhumed and examined, though the subject of water rarely makes the headlines in places like the United States and Europe. More troubling, Israel is not alone in the search to quench its thirst. By 2025, 67 percent of the world's population will face water shortages, and by 2030, a 54 percent increase in global food production will be required in order to keep up with population growth. Knowing how to squeeze water from a stone will be a highly sought-after skill in the coming decades. Water, after all, is the most basic human necessity: although you can live for weeks without food, you can live for only days without it.

Since 1943, Israeli's water engineers have accomplished nothing short of a miracle. Many of the advances in water technology—desalination, water-saving flush toilets, and drip irrigation—are testaments to Israeli (and human) ingenuity. In fact, the Israeli firm Netafim, which invented drip irrigation for agricultural applications in the late 1960s, is now the world's largest low-volume irrigation company. Today Netafim offers such innovative products as wireless sensors digitally tethered to radios, mobile phones, and the Internet in order to provide farmers with continuous information feeds on water levels, soil moisture, and pump status. Netafim even manages its own university where customers can learn about best practices in soil-water-plant ratios, crop rotation, and drip irrigation system design and maintenance.

In the case of squeezing water from a stone (and similar situations in which resources are limited), the presence of constraints is ironically one of the greatest contributors to creative insight. When we have no other choice, we somehow find a way. We get creative. However, there is a distinction to be made in how we get creative. For example, in the case of natural resource management, Israeli ingenuity is a bit different from the plain vanilla variety. Their achievements in water management can be attributed to a unique perspective Israelis have on problem solving. This perspective was best expressed decades ago by Aharon Wiener, once the director general of Tahal, the Israeli pioneer in planning, development, and management of water resources since the 1950s. According to Wiener, "Most water planners in developing countries consider the emphasis given to groundwater development and underground storage . . . to be a racket invented by hydrological eggheads in order to bring confusion to the straight-forward engineering programs of the hydraulic and civil engineering professions." He attributes this mentality to differences in how people solve problems.

As Wiener suggests, surface water is visible, measurable, and controllable: you can watch it flow and build dams. Groundwater, however, is invisible, evasive, and only indirectly controllable: you must manipulate resources to decipher source, flow, and so on. For example, in the mid-1950s, water planners used dyes to label water in order to track its flow. Put bluntly, Wiener explains, the use of groundwater requires "the substitution of brain for brawn."

Of course, to achieve what Israel's water magicians have achieved required both brains and brawn. One such application of both brains and brawn involves a near-legendary story in Israeli water circles about a dam built at Ein Kerem. Shortly after it was built, storms filled the reservoir behind the dam, but suddenly the water disappeared. An exhaustive search for the water determined that an extensive aquifer system happened to lie beneath the area in which the reservoir was constructed. It has since been put to use for water storage. Brawn (building the dam) gave way to brains (using the earth's natural response to store the water).

Because of the constraints placed on them, Israelis have figured out how to achieve the impossible: squeeze water from a stone. Curiosity is indeed the mother of invention; however, so too is necessity often present prior to epiphany. Alas, it is time to tell the story of "uncle inspiration": the role of constraints as a precursor to creative insight.

In a perfect world, we would have access to infinite resources to support an infinite number of ideas. In reality, we have six months, no budget, and two weeks of vacation. Resources are finite, but desire is infinite. However, creativity is more than a question of resources. It is a question of resourcefulness. "Make do" and "find a way" are frequent marching orders issued to those responsible for innovation. In this regard, focusing on constraints creates just the right conditions for epiphany.

Constraints come in two varieties: behavioral and resource. Behavioral constraints represent obstacles to desired behavior: someone has a problem with something, typically with the status quo (for example, although parents would rather not interact with a dirty diaper, they must). Resource constraints represent limitations placed on problem solvers, such as time, money, or knowledge. Another way to think about constraints is this: behavioral constraints are someone else's problem (say, a customer), while resource constraints are your problem if you are the problem solver, the innovator, the person who has to figure things out.

Although it may seem counterintuitive, focusing on constraints rather than strengths creates the conditions for creative insight. This will likely make more sense to you if you consider the logic in reverse. Take resources, for example. When there are no limits in terms of resources (time, money, people), the motivation to get creative is lost in abundance. We can do anything, and so we do nothing. Our inspiration to get creative is thwarted. But when things are tight, we are forced to make do with what we have, and so we find water in stones. In this way, constraints provide the perfect opportunity for conceptual creativity to flourish. We have no other choice than to figure things out. Duck Tape, the original brand of duct tape, has made a fortune off this very notion. In order to explore the role of constraints as a precursor to epiphany, let's consider both behavioral and resource constraints and how you can use them to create the conditions for creative insight beginning with the relationship between creativity and the world's third most precious natural resource (after water and food): time.

In the context of inspiring creativity within organizations, I am often asked, "What is the appropriate time to allocate to discovery, exploration, and ideation before making a decision about which ideas to implement?" Of course, what they really want to know is, "When can I expect to see results?" Like all other resources, time is limited, thereby making it a sticky subject. Some believe that having less time inspires creativity, while others believe that having more time is preferable. In a study of workplace inventiveness, creativity researcher Teresa Amabile, Constance N. Hadley, and Steven J. Kramer arrived at a more insightful answer: it depends. The relationship between time and creativity is largely dependent on three additional factors: environment, motivation, and the people charged with the task. For example, some people are contemplative, and others are impulsive. Both types of people can be creative, but time pressure affects each differently: some perform better under pressure, and others require more time to think. Before we review Amabile, Hadley, and Amabile's findings in this regard, let's revisit the unconventional methods of Yoshio Nakamatsu.

NakaMats artificially recreates time pressure by submerging himself under water, the final step in a three-step process designed to conjure up aha moments at will. The first step is achieving a state of calm. In order to help attain this state of mind, NakaMats has created what he refers to as the "static room." The room is all white and furnished only with natural objects: a rock garden, natural running water, plants, and a five-ton boulder from Kyoto. The physical description of the room may lead you to think that NakaMats goes into this room in order to meditate or to calm his mind. However, he does just the opposite: "I go into the room to free-associate. It's what you must do before meditating, before focusing on one thing. I let my mind wander where it will." From here, he goes directly into what he calls the "dynamic room," which is dark with black-and-white striped walls, leather furniture, and audiovisual equipment. In the dynamic room, he does not attempt to come up with ideas; rather, he meditates. Finally, he goes to his third and final room: the swimming pool. It is here that he does his best thinking. He submerges himself in water and holds his breath to the point of near-drowning in order to achieve inspiration. In order to facilitate his brainstorming, NakaMats invented an acrylic plastic pad to record his ideas. Although these techniques may be extreme, his philosophy and some of his unorthodox methods are illustrative of the relationship between time pressure and creativity.

Through their analysis of over nine thousand journal entries written by 177 employees working in seven U.S. companies, Amabile, Hadley, and Kramer found that time pressure is effective only when the individual feels that he or she is "on a mission." There are three prerequisites to creating a mission-based mentality: individuals must be able to focus on a single activity, they must believe that what they are working on is important, and they are working on identifying problems as much as generating solutions.

In the absence of this mission-based mentality, respondents claim to feel as if they are "on a treadmill": distracted, overextended, engaged in unimportant work, consumed with an abundance of meetings, and spending a large amount of their day fighting fires versus solving fundamental problems or generating novel solutions. Amabile, Hadley, and Kramer's findings also support the notion that low time pressure is effective only when an individual feels as if he or she is "on an expedition." The focus of the work is more on generating ideas than solving problems, and collaboration tends to occur with a single person versus a large group. In summary, time is largely dependent on intent. If you or your team have a focused charter (for example, identifying how your brand can extend into adjacent categories or developing new products for a specific customer need), there is a case to be made that shorter time lines may foster creativity. But if you or your team have a broad-based charter (for example, to create the future of fast food or come up with the next generation of mobile telephony), then allowing more time to explore will likely beget more uniquely relevant ideas. Beyond time is the equally scarce resource of money.

The evidence in support of the relationship between money and creativity is a bit counterintuitive. In a study of the Global Innovation 1000, management consulting firm Booz Allen Hamilton reports little if no correlation between increased R&D spending and subsequent increases in sales growth, gross profit, or total shareholder returns regardless of whether you consider R&D spending as a leading or lagging indicator. Nonetheless, the top one thousand R&D spenders spend approximately $400 billion in search of big ideas. So if money can't buy you a great idea, what does?

How you define a problem not only helps you find the most appropriate solution, but it also helps you find it relatively cheaply. The world's best creative problem solvers use capital more efficiently than others. Toyota, for example, is the fifth highest R&D spender in the world but only the third highest spender in the auto industry. However, consider what it has achieved even though it spends less than its competitors. First, it has the shortest development cycle time in the industry, allowing it to bring new products to market much more quickly than its competitors can. Second, it is the world's leader in hybrid technology, placing its foot squarely in the future of alternative fuels and building equity in the Toyota brand as environmentally conscious and innovative in the process. And third, and most compelling to those who count the beans, Toyota Motor Company maintains a market value that is greater than that of the next three largest vehicle manufacturers combined ($167 billion versus $160 billion). How does it create more with less? The answer is not only about the product but also about the process of creative insight. It's about how Toyota manages solving problems.

The history of creativity at Toyota has strong ties to its founder, Sakichi Toyoda, considered the father of the Japanese industrial revolution. Masaaki Immai, the grandfather of lean manufacturing, chairman of the Kaizen Institute, and a lifelong contributor to Toyota Motor Company's success, once shared a story with me about Sakichi Toyoda just prior to an event at which Immai and I were the scheduled keynote speakers. Immai was invited to speak on *kaizen*, the philosophy of continuous improvement, and I was invited to speak on innovation, the philosophy of continuous creation. Immai and I come from different schools of thought. Whereas variance is the enemy of quality, it is innovation's best friend. Innovators are the outliers. And so in one of life's poetic moments, Immai and I were seated directly opposite one another at breakfast: he on the side of improvement and I on the side of creativity. The fact of the matter is that you need to encourage both creativity and improvement in the pursuit of growth. Although we come from different worlds culturally, geographically, and philosophically, Immai and I share one thing in common: we are both enthusiastic supporters of great ideas and the people who have them.

Immai told me that Toyoda maintained a building with three hundred rooms. In each room were small groups of people dedicated to making his ideas a reality. One day, Toyoda went missing, and for the next three days, no one could find him. It turned out that Toyoda was locked inside a room in the building working on his ideas. For seventy-two hours, he barely slept or ate—not because he had no food or a place to rest his head but because he couldn't sleep and had no appetite. His ideas had literally gotten the best of him, as great ideas have a way of doing. Ultimately Toyoda emerged running out of his room with great excitement, only to discover that no one was to be found anywhere in the building. All three hundred rooms were empty. Toyoda had no idea that it was New Year's Day.

Toyoda was an incessant problem solver. Once he identified a problem, time became trivial to him. And the problems he solved were many. Through the introduction of new products (such as the automatic power loom for textile manufacturing) and the creation of new processes (such as the principle of *jidoka*, that is, machines that stop themselves from operating when a problem occurs, a hallmark of Toyota's legendary production system), Toyoda built an empire. Adequate funding for his new ventures was a recurring problem, yet he always seemed to find a way to get the financing together in order to make his dreams a reality. What kept Toyoda awake at night were questions, specifically five questions—the "five whys"—a method he employed to use constraints as innovation platforms.

Sakichi Toyoda's concept of the five whys is simple. When a problem is identified, ask *why* five times in order to find its source. The reason you must ask why more than once (in fact, five times) is to get to the root cause of the problem versus dealing with some fleeting symptom associated with the problem. Once the source is discovered, fix it. In order to illustrate Toyoda's five whys in action, let's consider one of our most pressing and most painful problems and how one British entrepreneur was inspired to help solve it. The problem is the AIDS epidemic in Africa. The solution is a hand-powered radio. The problem solver is Trevor Baylis.

Trevor Baylis spent the majority of his life as a professional stunt man. Most notably, in the early 1970s, he performed as Ramses II, an underwater escape act in a Berlin circus. In addition to his day job, Baylis has always maintained an interest in creative problem solving. He likes to invent things, if for no other reason than to make his life on Eel Pie Island in the midst of the River Thames in England much more enjoyable. It was here, on a rainy evening in autumn 1991, that Baylis had the breakthrough idea of his life while, of all things, watching television.

After polishing off a bottle of red wine and reading a few books, Baylis turned on his TV in order to enter the world of mind-less couch potatodom. He had no idea that the following ninety minutes would change his life. As he recalled, "The screen came to life and I dumbly watched what was offered. I just sat there, your standard couch potato. But I soon became absorbed. The program sent my mind racing, stretched like a spinnaker on a fair wind." The show was about the spreads of AIDS in Africa. Baylis became consumed by the show as its narrator presented the relative statistics of this contemporary human tragedy: the great plague of the fourteenth century killed 20 million people, a quarter of Europe's population, in just four years; the Spanish influenza of 1918–1919 killed another 20 million people. Tragic as those were, over 40 million people today live with AIDS, 20 million people have lost their lives to it, and an additional 3 million people die each year leaving millions more orphaned. As Baylis recalled,

> The program lowered my spirits. I had the zapper in my hand and could easily have switched to less harrowing fare. But I stayed with it. The narrator was telling me that the biggest problem was getting the health education message across to the population. A campaign to broadcast propaganda counseling safe sex was being hampered by a lack of cheap receivers. In remote villages there was no electricity, and the cost of batteries was prohibitive—as much as one-month's income for one set alone. Solar power wasn't the answer, the narrator intoned dismally, because most people did their listening after dark, when they

came home after spending a day working in the fields. I was sitting there, taking in this somber picture, when all at once my mind began to take flight. Maybe the red wine helped, but I was suddenly aware of a blindingly obvious way in which the problem could be solved.

At this point, Baylis, like most other people who become enchanted by the challenge of an unsolved problem, was knocking on the door of creative insight. With the problem clearly defined in his mind, he did what almost all others who experience leaps in creative insight do: he fell asleep.

Watching television frequently introduces me to that best friend of the discerning viewer, sleep. I sometimes wake up to a scene where Jeremy Paxman [an abrasive British journalist] is being beastly to William Hague [former leader of the British Conservative party] and wonder what on earth they're doing in the Clint Eastwood spaghetti Western I started watching a couple of hours earlier. Now, however, I was absorbing all the information coming from the screen, but at the same time I had been transported to the edge of the desert somewhere in the Sudan. In overpowering heat, sand-flies high-diving into my gin and tonic, my faithful bearer Hassan attending to my every whim, I was suddenly some sort of colonial wallah in tropical uniform, plotting gun-boat diplomacy or the outer edge of The Empire. As the civil servant sipped his drink, he listened, wrapped in the magic of Enrico Caruso, his ear close to the horn of an old-fashioned gramophone.

And now was the point, just prior to epiphany, at which the common precursors to creative insight came clashing together for Baylis: curiosity of the problem, constraints (in Baylis's case, the constraints placed on those fighting the AIDS epidemic in Africa), and seemingly random information (introduced by watching television). While basking in the teleglow, Baylis's curiosity blended with the unsolved problem in a sort of couch potato daydream puree. He continued,

I thought about the gramophone. Enrico's mighty top Cs shimmer in the heat because a needle followed the inscribed pattern of the aria on a piece of Bakelite. The vibrations of the needle in the groove of the disc made a noise which was amplified by the horn, and the whole glorious noise was driven by a simple spring that operated a gear that drove the turntable that dragged the disc past the needle. Instantly I had this glaring flash of something so obvious a child of six could have thought of it. If a clockwork gramophone can produce that volume of sound, then why not apply the principle to building a spring-driven radio?

As Baylis described the experience, "That was the Alka-Seltzer moment, the moment when the tablet hits the water and begins to fizz. I left the television set on, with the narrator still submerging viewers in a tidal wave of dismal statistics and, late as it was, went to my workshop. A good idea turns every cog in your mind, making you scared of bed in case the whole machine grinds to a halt." And then, he said, "I lit my pipe and had a think." Baylis attributes pipe smoking to every one of his two hundred inventions. As he puts it, "My pipe gives me something to do with my hands that is marginally more macho than knitting."

With pipe in hand, Baylis began to sift through the thousand "dead components" on his workbench—what he refers to as "a defeated army of mechanical carcasses, waiting to be bodged back into life." He eventually found what he was looking for: an old transistor radio. After removing its batteries, he turned his attention to cannibalizing an electric motor from an automatic guitar tuner and then introduced the motor into the cadaver of the radio. He needed one additional part: a hand drill. Why a hand drill? An electric motor converts electrical energy into rotary motion. By reversing the process and rotating a DC motor the other way, it becomes a dynamo, thereby producing electrical energy. With the drill firmly attached to the motor, Baylis began to turn it when suddenly it happened: "There was a bark of sound from the loudspeaker . . . someone, somewhere was discussing the strength of the pound against the deutschmark . . . never has the arcane jargon of the money market sounded so gloriously poetic."

It worked. Trevor Baylis's big idea—a product through which to broadcast educational programming to help mitigate the spread of AIDS in Africa—came to life in the form of a hand-wound, clockwork radio. Many years later, writing about Baylis's inspired idea, Matthew Bond of the *Times* wrote, "On paper that [a radio driven by clockwork] sounded akin to the everlasting light-bulb and the water-powered natural combustion engine. But in practice it actually works."

Although an inspired moment, which in Baylis's case led to the invention of the clockwork radio, may seem like a random act or in the category of accidental invention, in fact it was nothing of the sort. Baylis's story, like so many others who have experienced eureka moments, includes most all of the common precursors to creative insight: curiosity, domain expertise, sideways thinking, encounters with apparently irrelevant information, and even sleep. Consider what Baylis, like Archimedes, knew. He had working knowledge of the principles of electrical and mechanical engineering. He had the curiosity, much like that of Haüy, to want to solve the problem or at least to think about it. Recall that he chose not to change the channel to "less harrowing fare." However, it was not only his curiosity and his knowledge that inspired his creative insight; it was also the recognition of what was not possible because of the constraints placed on those living in the regions of Africa most vulnerable to AIDS. They did not have the money, infrastructure, and other resources to access educational programming even if it were available just miles away. Baylis arrived at his big idea, unknowingly yet naturally, using Toyoda's five whys. For some, this method of thinking transpires naturally; however, it is also a relatively easy task to replicate. After all, all that is required is that you ask the same question, Why? five times.

Consider how the five whys may apply in Baylis's case:

Question 1: Why is AIDS an epidemic in Africa? One reason given was related to the difficulty in transmitting information.

Question 2: Why is it difficult to transmit information? Not all Africans have access to working radios or televisions.

Question 3: Why don't they have access to radios or television? They have no way of powering them.

Question 4: Why do they have no way of powering them? In some areas, there is no electric grid.

Question 5 (the innovator's question): Why does a radio need an electric grid? The solution was introducing Trevor Baylis's hand-powered radio.

Launched in 1995, Trevor Baylis's award-winning clockwork radios sell around the world at the pace of 120,000 each month. Now a full-time inventor, Baylis has been awarded an OBE (Officer of the British Empire, a class of the British order of chivalry established by King George V in 1917). He has also won the Presidential Gold and Silver medals from the Institution of Mechanical Engineers and is a frequent visiting professor at many British universities.

Like Toyota Motor Company, Trevor Baylis does not have the world's largest R&D budget. In fact, he doesn't show up anywhere near the top one thousand R&D spenders, yet he has found a way to help solve a serious problem by nurturing his curiosity about the problem; recognizing the constraints placed on those in need; allowing his mind to "think without thinking," and asking the most important question, Why? five times. As Baylis describes creativity, "As long as you've got slightly more perception than the average wrapped loaf, you could invent something." The only thing I would add to Toyoda's five whys is a sixth *why* to ask yourself once you've generated the appropriate solution: Why not?

As we've learned, you cannot buy creative insight. Rather, it is the ability to identify and define problems that is a more significant precursor to creative insight. Therefore, if you have a choice of how to best allocate your R&D dollars, invest at least 10 percent of your budget into the development of creative problem-solving skills. Why 10 percent? Why not?

I suggest that the best place to start thinking about constraints is to reconsider which definition you choose to use for the word *problem*. The dictionary definition of *problem* provides three interpretations: "a state of difficulty that needs to be resolved," "a source of difficulty," and "a question raised for consideration or solution." Viewing problems not as sources of difficulty but as questions can have a profound effect on your capacity to create, as was the case of Baylis and his radio and Toyoda and his production system. A more psychologically tinged definition of a problem might be anytime you find yourself in a situation that is different from the situation you want to be in: you continue to place second in athletic tournaments, you've lost market share to a new entrant, or you can't seem to lose those last ten pounds.

Regardless of the situation, the recognition that you have a problem to solve typically arises from one of three sources: discomfort, frustration, or curiosity. In each of these moments, pay closer attention to how you feel, and try walking through the five whys to see if you can better define the source of the problem. Here is an example:

Question 1: Why can't I lose those last ten pounds? Because I eat out at lunch each day.

Question 2: Why do I eat out each day? Because I don't have time to make and take my lunch.

Question 3: Why don't I have time to make and take my lunch? Because I have to get up early to make a lunch to take to work.

Question 4: Why do I have to make it in the morning on my way out the door? Because the food won't be fresh if I make it earlier in the week.

Question 5: Why won't it be fresh? Because there is no such
thing as "prepackaged fresh food kits for those on the go."
Aha! A big idea is born.

As this example suggests, asking *why* once yields nothing more
than symptoms. For example, if you were to introduce an idea that
enabled a person to take lunch to work, you'd likely reinvent the
lunchbox. However, by focusing on the answer to the fifth question, you will be able to introduce a product that solves an unmet
need. In this way, fixing symptoms is like trying to treat pneumonia
with a tissue. Get to the root cause. Root causes beget big ideas.
Keep asking why.

Beyond self-inflicted problems, problems can also be given to
you by someone else. You might not have even known that a problem existed until the moment you were given the assignment to
find a solution to it—for example, sales are decreasing year-over-
year by 5 percent. The difference between an assigned problem and
a problem you have to decipher for yourself lies in the questions
you must ask. When you are assigned a problem, you must ask
why five times just to get to the root cause. Then you must also
ask: What is the current situation? What is the goal (what would
qualify as a solution)? What resources do I have available? What is
standing in the way of a solution? Someone other than you might
answer these questions. The problem may be identified by your
boss or by the customer, or you may identify the problem and have
to convince others that it is a problem and that you should be
allowed to try to solve it. However, no matter what definition you
are given, you have the opportunity to create your own definition
of the problem based on the information you are given. Much of
how you define the problem will be based on processes that are
going on largely or even entirely outside your awareness.

One of the most important features of problems is ambiguity.
The statement of the problem may be ambiguous, and therefore
people may disagree about exactly what problem needs to be
solved. Or it might not even be clear that a problem exists. To get

a sense of the ambiguity of problem solving, read this sentence: *John went to the bank.* This sentence is ambiguous insofar that it has more than one meaning. The word *bank* could mean either a financial institution or the edge of a river. Because the financial institution meaning is the more immediate inference, you likely interpreted the sentence as saying that John went to a financial institution. You then likely (subconsciously and immediately) began to think about things that are associated with that type of bank: cash, checks, loans, accounts, and so on. However, if "John went to the bank" was followed by, "He lost his footing and fell into the river," you would likely be momentarily confused. Your brain thinks: "River? What does a river have to do with a bank?" And therefore you are left momentarily confused since normally sentences occur in a context that disambiguates the meaning of individual words. But in this example, the disambiguating information follows the ambiguous word (*bank*) by almost a full sentence, so either interpretation is acceptable initially. It is only after reading the second sentence that you notice anything amiss if you made the financial institution interpretation. Although it may have surprised you to see the word *river* and you may have thought, "River? I wasn't thinking about a river," in fact, your brain actually was thinking about the "edge of a river" meaning of *bank* even though you were not aware of it.

Quite often we resolve ambiguity so automatically that we are unaware that ambiguity ever existed. (Most people are not even aware how ambiguous words can be. We are so skilled at resolving potential ambiguities that we don't realize that we are doing it. And it happens in a flash.) Becoming aware of the existence, or potential existence, of ambiguity, or a second meaning, makes creative solutions more readily available in our minds. The creative solution, that is, the eureka moment, comes when the ambiguity is recognized (often unconsciously) and resolved in a new way.

Why is being aware of ambiguity important to creativity? Because how the mind processes information determines the solution strategy you use or whether you choose to do anything at all.

This is best understood by understanding the basic processes of all cognition: memory processes, perceptual processes, and attentional processes. We discussed the role of memory earlier in the book in the context of sleep. Let's now turn to perception and attention.

Perception involves making sense of what comes through the senses. As is the case with perception, the same sensory experience can be perceived in different ways. Not only do different people perceive the same thing differently, but the same person can perceive the same thing differently from moment to moment. For example, using a classic illustration of testing perception, what do you see in Figure 7.1? Do you see the white vase or the two faces in profile? Regardless of which you see, you will eventually see both, and then, your mind will toggle back-and-forth uncontrollably from one image to the other. In fact, now that you've found both images in the single image, try to choose either the vase or the two faces and stare at the image for thirty seconds while trying

Figure 7.1. Now You See It, Now You Don't

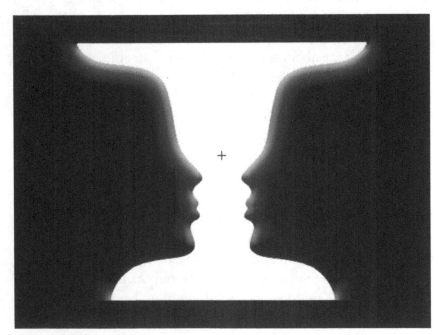

to discern only one of the two images and not the other. How did you do? If you are like most other people, although you may have chosen to try to focus only on the vase, your mind slipped into the image of the two faces now and then and vice versa.

It is virtually impossible to hold your attention on the single interpretation once you are aware of the alternate interpretation. And the same is true in reverse. Prior to recognizing that another alternative image exists, it was likely much more difficult for you to initially find the alternate image because you were so focused on the original image you saw.

Imagine the impact this phenomenon has on creativity and innovation. Once you have a known solution identified, you become fixated on it and are subsequently unable to see other possible solutions. This is a very human phenomenon and is something that occurs well beyond your conscious control. However, once you are shown alternatives, it is nearly impossible *not* to see other possibilities. This phenomenon is directly related to eureka moments insofar that it is often what we cannot see that is most important. However once we are exposed to it, the right solution or the big idea becomes blindingly obvious.

Although we'll explore this topic in detail in Chapter Nine on challenging conventions, one way you can replicate this phenomenon on a more deliberate basis is to focus on prevailing biases. It begins by asking yourself what the absolute truths about your business, product, or services are and then translating these biases into platforms for creative inspiration. Start by asking: "What if *x* were true? How would that change the way we solve the problem [or create new ideas]?" For example, imagine you are in the personal computer business, specifically focusing on laptop computers. The first step is to simply list the biases (or truths) associated with laptop computers: you need a keyboard to use them, screens flip up (and laptops have only one screen), batteries are required, software must be installed, you have to wait for them to boot up, they are expensive, and they are built to last a few years. Once you have exhausted all of the possible biases about the prevailing idea, then ask: "What if we were to change each of these truths in some way? What might be possible?" For example, What if laptops didn't have keyboards? How else could we make them respond to human commands? What if laptops had seven screens as opposed to one? What benefits would that offer to users? What if laptops didn't run on batteries? How else could we make them work? What if laptops didn't require software to operate? How would that change the interaction between software and hardware companies? What if laptops booted up like turning on a light (versus having to wait for them)? What if people were paid to use laptops versus having to buy them? How would that affect the features of a laptop? What if laptops were disposable? How would that affect the ways in which they are used?

Each of these questions will yield a wide assortment of ideas, from lunatic fringe to extremely practical. Look closely. Challenge the design of your environment. As one of my students, Jack Sheu, astutely observed, "Everything on earth is designed," from the chair in which you are sitting, to the book in your hands, to store layout, schools, museums, products, services, relationships. Everything is designed based on prevailing beliefs. Why are doors rectangular? Why do cars have four wheels? Why do we pay the same realtor's commission even though asking prices of homes differ? By identifying, defining, and challenging these beliefs (truths), you will be able to create the conditions for eureka moments to transpire more willingly.

As we'll discuss in Chapter Nine on conventions, this phenomenon of design bias both hindered and helped Sony engineers introducing the compact disc. At first, they couldn't see the opportunity; it made no sense to them at all. But after they received a hint from (of all things) a competitor (Philips), the idea became blindingly obvious.

Now that you've mastered the vase and two faces, try another perception exercise. What do you see in the image in Figure 7.2? Do you see a person's face or something else altogether? How about the one in Figure 7.3?

Figure 7.2. It's a Matter of Perception

Figure 7.3. It's All in How You Look at It

Like the vase and the two faces, regardless of which you saw first (the face or the word *liar*), you now likely see them both, making it virtually impossible to hold your attention on the single interpretation of either. However, in the absence of a known alternative, there is a moment when your perception is held constant: you are unable to see alternate solutions simply because of what you perceive the problem to be. This occurs during the split seconds that exist just prior to actually seeing the word *liar* as a second representation of the face. In fact, it happens so quickly that you are likely unable to recognize that it is happening at all. This is precisely why aha moments seem to occur with such a sudden burst of insight. There is not much standing in the way between "getting it" and "being completely lost." Changing perspective, whether physically or mentally, can change the interpretation of the problem.

What is also revealing about this second illustration is that because of your experience with the prior illustration of the vase and two faces, you were likely able to figure out the second illustration (the face and the word *liar*) simply because you knew to look for alternative solutions. This supports the case that you can learn to be more creative in your problem-solving abilities if you only try. In other words, once you were made aware that a trick was at play, you knew to look at a problem in multiple ways, and therefore you effectively become more adept at the second puzzle of the face and the word. This capacity to see multiple solutions to a problem is a learned skill. It just so happens to also occur naturally (and unconsciously). By making the unconscious conscious, you can give logic to your creative pursuits.

When it comes to solving problems, we have a tendency to offer solutions that fit with the problem as we see it or within a given rules set. For example, in the case of Trevor Baylis, you may have wondered why no consumer electronics company introduced the hand-powered radio before a stunt man living on an island in the middle of a river in England did. In fact, not only were the consumer electronics companies unable to see the opportunity, they refused to meet with the person who did see it: Baylis tried to get their attention on many occasions. The incumbents likely missed the opportunity because of how they perceived the problem. This is a case of not believing everything you are told. For example, if you were to believe the BBC narrator who explained that the problem of the AIDS epidemic in Africa was due to the lack of electricity, then all of your possible solutions would lead you to start thinking about how to create and install an electric grid in Africa. You would then likely be absolutely overwhelmed at the thought of creating the infrastructure necessary to wire Africa; the cost would be in billions! And so you would not only give up, but likely never even try to solve the problem beyond running the numbers on the cost of wiring the isolated areas of the continent. If instead you perceived the problem as Baylis did (by virtue of the five whys), you would have arrived at an entirely different solution: you don't need an electric grid to provide power; you only need energy.

In this regard, perception affects not only what we see but the solutions that are possible—or at least that we believe are possible. Those who are unable to solve problems or create new ideas often get stuck because of the way in which they have chosen to perceive and define the problem: they often don't ask enough whys and instead stop short of the root cause, and they end up fixing only a symptom. But once you are able to see the problem in one or more alternate ways or see it more deeply, you are then virtually unable not to see it both (or many) ways. This is the argument often made by those who promote immersion learning and travel abroad. Once you've walked a mile in the shoes of a person of another color, country of origin, or socioeconomic background, you are virtually unable not to consider his or her perspective just as you are unable not to see both the vase and the two faces. Broadening one's perception makes the big idea painfully obvious.

There are two ways to get around constraints: change how you solve the problem or change how you perceive the problem. Since perception requires very little in the way of additional resources (other than your willingness to see things a bit differently), I recommend you first attempt to change how you perceive the problem. Sometimes it boils down to a question of semantics. In order to illustrate, heed the linguistic mathematics of my three-year-old son, Charlie, who once convinced me to allow him to have a cookie for breakfast by simply repositioning how he (and I) chose to see the problem.

"Daddy?" Charlie said to me while pointing his sticky fingers to a half-eaten bag of Oreos, "Can I have a cookie?" "No, Charlie" I replied. "We don't eat cookies for breakfast." "But, Daddy, please, please," he importuned as he tugged on my shirt. "Can I have a cookie?" "What did Daddy just say?" I replied in a clichéd fatherly tenor. Knowing better than to answer my question, he came back at me with a declaration delivered with the confidence and poise of Winston Churchill: "Mommy said I could have a cookie for breakfast!"

Having heard this claim many times before, I went to my ace in the hole: logic that I believed was impenetrable: "Is that right? Okay. So go get Mommy, and let's see what she says," followed quickly by, "Daddy said no cookies for breakfast." Recognizing the rock and the hard place he had just gotten himself wedged in, Charlie retired for a few reflective minutes of play before returning to the kitchen with his second plan of attack, one that I never saw coming. "Daddy?" he said while pointing to the Oreos with puppy-dog eyes. "Those aren't cookies." A bit confused and even more suspicious, I looked at him and then at the bag and then at him, and then I responded with hesitation, "Yes . . . Charlie . . . they . . . are." "No, they're not," he retorted. "Yes, Charlie . . . *those* are cookies," I rebuffed. "No, Daddy," he insisted, "they are *not* cookies." Having no idea where he was headed with this logic, I ultimately succumbed and responded in agreement, "Okay, Charlie. You're right. They are *not* cookies!" And then the three-foot genius appeared. Knowing that he could eat anything but cookies for breakfast, Charlie replied with the assumptive close: "Okay. Those are not cookies, and so I can have one." I don't know where he gets it from. If a three year old can change perception, so can you. The question is, How do you do it?

In the business of innovation, perception is rarely changed through conversation. People believe through what they experience, not necessarily through what they see or hear. And therefore our focus is not on what people want but rather on what they are unable to do: constraints. These constraints provide the fodder with which to generate great ideas that solve problems. In order to manage the perception of constraints, in addition to challenging prevailing biases, we rely on two additional tactics: restating liabilities as assets and observation.

Restating liabilities as assets requires defining your disadvantages as advantages. It's the silver lining approach to innovation. For example, say you are working on a team in an organization that is responsible for creating a new category within your industry. This new category has the potential to reshape the industry and your organization's role in it. Although you and your colleagues are excited about the opportunity, it is an overwhelming task for the following reasons: you have a very small budget and access to resources versus the more established business units, you have tepid leadership support, and there is little existing research on the category since it is so cutting edge. Although interest in the project is high due to its potential, morale is low due to the reality often confronting corporate innovators.

So what do you do? Begin by restating negatives (liabilities) as positives (assets). A very small budget often equates to not being beholden to traditional and costly marketing research exercises like focus groups, quantitative surveys, and conjoint studies. Ironically, most of these methods are ill suited to innovation research anyway, so consider yourself lucky. Moreover, you have the advantage of being forced to learn about the efficacy of your ideas in more creative ways. Second, you have little leadership support. However, the upside of tepid sponsorship is that you will likely not have as many people looking over your shoulder and evaluating each decision made by the team. That means you have freedom, a critical precursor to creative insight and innovation. And third, since there is little existing research on the category in which you are focused (size of market, existing competitors, and so on), you have the luxury of defining the category as you would like it to be.

For example, as Tom Stat of IDEO observed, rather than measure itself based on conventional metrics, Porsche created a new metric, path accuracy, and then sought to own what it meant (how the car responds to its driver's demands, that is, how accurately the vehicle does what its driver wants it to do). Meanwhile, the rest of the industry continued to measure itself based on conventional metrics such as 0 to 60 miles per hour in x seconds, steering radius, miles per gallon, and so on. By creating its own metric, Porsche created a new place in the mind of automobile drivers by which to be measured, just as American Express created a new place in the mind of credit card holders with the feature, "Member Since . . ." Does it really matter how long you've been a loyal member of a credit card company? Likely not, but it works. Both Porsche and American Express exploited the luxury afforded to almost all innovators: defining the game as you would like it be played. In each of these cases, restating liabilities as assets serves a very important role in the pursuit of big ideas. Forcing the team to look on the bright side not only serves to build morale but in effect encourages new ways to solve problems.

The second innovation tactic we use to manage perception is observation. If you'd like a bit more instruction than that of my three-year-old son, consider the case of Shimano, the cycling industry's $1.4 billion components powerhouse. Although it may seem that there would be a significant difference between a three year old in want of a cookie and a billion-dollar business in want of a new customer, there really isn't. Resources are finite and desire infinite, and creativity is what closes the gap.

Shimano is a Japanese manufacturer of components for high-performance bicycles. It is the best and the biggest manufacturer of bicycle gearheads in the world. Its products include the greasy stuff that makes cycling fun: shifters, cranks, and derailleurs. Shimano maintains an enviable business. But a few years ago, it recognized a disturbing trend on the horizon: an increasing number of people aren't riding bikes. In the United States, although cycling enthusiasts have more than tripled in the past decade (this is Lance Armstrong's influence), the number of casual cyclists has dropped by 50 percent. This trend is most salient when you consider that in 1970, over 50 percent of kids rode their bikes to school; today, only 13 percent ride.

At first, one would think that Shimano wouldn't care so much about this drop in casual cycling because it built its business on cycling enthusiasts—those who follow the Tour de France and wear the funny clothes. However, in order to increase its business, it would be foolish not to consider the 160 million Americans who don't ride bikes versus the 25 million who do. The problem is figuring out how to get a nonrider to ride.

Regardless of the business you are in, the only way to get noncustomers to become customers is to start a new conversation. In order to do this and contrary to what some marketing strategists recommend, Shimano had to understand not what its customers' customers wanted (those who ride Trek, Raleigh, Giant); rather it had to understand just the opposite: what its customers' noncustomers want, in other words, what noncyclists care about. If you are a submanufacturer in any industry (components, ingredients, parts, and so on), this is a significant challenge primarily because you typically do not have day-to-day contact with end customers—in this case, bicycle riders. Your customers are original equipment manufacturers—the people who make and sell bikes. Therefore, the only way for Shimano to solve this riddle was to figure out why nonbicycle riders were not buying bikes; more important, they had to understand why people were choosing not to ride in the first place. (Notice that we're back to the root cause analysis provided by Toyoda's five whys.)

Shimano's mission was clear. In order to solve this riddle, it needed to change its perception. According to Shannon Bryant, project manager for Shimano American, the project team's initial perception was that people were riding less due to laziness and obesity. However, this was only one way to perceive the problem (like seeing only the vase and not the two faces). What the team discovered was something else entirely. By visiting the homes of over fifty nonriders and talking with them about everything from their childhood memories to their opinions about leisure, Shimano, along with its product design partners at IDEO, gained a new perspective. As Bryant recalled, "It was one of those eureka moments . . . we had never thought of it that way."

The way Bryant referred to was how nonriders perceived riding a bicycle: it wasn't an issue of laziness; rather it was an issue of memory. It was not that they didn't like to ride. In fact, they loved it. They spoke fondly about the simple pleasure it conjured up. The Shimano team suddenly realized that nonriders longed for their childhood memories of a bike ride, not the cycling industry's perception of what it meant to be a cyclist. Herein was the problem: over the past decade, the entire cycling industry had evolved into the opposite of what the majority of noncyclists wanted. The industry had become a shaved-legged, gearheaded, grease monkey business dominated by aloof cycle shop owners with ripped abs and piped calves, many of whom were more intimidating than the sauntering sales reps masquerading about Tiffany & Co. like members of the royal court. Dentists' offices are more inviting.

As for the products themselves, bicycles had evolved into five thousand dollar carbon contraptions more reminiscent of something found on the set of a James Bond flick than on the sidewalks of America's neighborhoods. An entirely new language had evolved as well: *getting yo-yoed* is not something the everyday cyclist would recognize, much less care to do. (*Getting yo-yoed* means not being able to hang on to the back of a group when riding in a pace line.) Ironically, noncyclists had been yo-yoed by the entire cycling industry. However, there's the catch: noncyclists weren't trying to hang on to the *industry*; they were trying to hang on to their *childhoods*.

David Webster, the project manager at IDEO who worked with Shimano on solving this problem recalled, "*That* was the biggest insight, because that is at odds with anything you could access within the cycling industry at the moment." Road bikes, racing bikes, hybrids, and recumbents did nothing to exhume childhood. Therefore, with IDEO at its side, Shimano created a new product prototype, the Coasting bike, that would cost less than four hundred dollars and weigh less than thirty pounds. Shimano's customers—Trek, Raleigh, and Giant—loved it. According to Chad Price, pavement-bike product manager at Trek Bicycle, the Coasting model "looks like it will be our number one bike by volume by the end of 2007."

How did IDEO get Shimano to change its perception (that is, to see both the vase and the two faces)? First, Ideo had Shimano live with its customers' noncustomers in order to see the world from the perspective of those who had the biggest problems with cycling and therefore opted out of the experience. Second, no one asked the noncyclists what they wanted in a bike; rather, they asked things such as: *Why did you use to ride a bike, and why don't you ride anymore?*

In the field of innovation, conversation can be as beneficial as observation as long as the questions are right. Answers are easy when the questions are right. Ask *why*, not *what*. And third, IDEO realized that it had to put Shimano and original equipment manufacturing executives in the shoes of noncyclists. In order to accomplish the feeling that noncyclists had expressed when they walk into the intimidating environment of a bike shop, IDEO sent the team of industry executives to cosmetics counters in department stores and asked them to buy fifty dollars' worth of cosmetics. As Trek's Price recalled, "I was genuinely uncomfortable. I didn't know what to ask for or where to start." Nothing is more compelling in changing one's perspective than in experiencing the actual emotions of the person whom you are attempting to understand. What must it *feel* like for a noncyclist to shop for a bike? Aha! It's like a gearhead buying cosmetics. Something must change. In fact, this experience led to the realization that not only did bicycle manufacturers need to change the product they were offering, they also needed to change the way it would be offered. Sales reps in bike shops had to go back to school for training in order to learn how to sell the new product to this new ("reborn") cyclist.

Changing perception is not easy, but I can guarantee that now that the cycling industry's leaders have seen the alternate option to what existed prior to this eureka moment, it will be virtually impossible for them not to see it in the future. Noncyclists are no longer thought of as simply "noncyclists." They are now viewed as a whole new market—one interested more in simplicity than in performance, more in fun than in winning, and more in childhood than in cycling. The challenge then became how to create a product in the form of a bicycle so that noncyclists could relive their childhood memories in the context of very different (and older) bodies. That equated to a bicycle that is easy to get on and off; a bicycle that has all of its gears enclosed and out of sight to eliminate the worry about getting a pant leg stuck in greasy gears; a bicycle whose handlebars allow its riders to sit upright; and, as a reminder of the "olden days," a bicycle stopped by simply pedaling backward.

Creating great ideas is easy once you have accomplished the even bigger challenge of answering, *Why do people behave the way they do?* This requires a change in perception. Once this change in perception is acquired, eureka moments occur almost instantly. How the mind processes information determines the solution strategy a person will use or whether he or she will choose to do anything at all in order to solve a problem. This involves three basic cognitive processes: memory, perceptual, and attentional processes. In the case of Shimano, we explored how a change in perception begat a great idea; however, the Shimano case involved memory as well as attentional processes. We've explored the role of memory previously in the book and will examine it further in Chapter Nine on challenging conventions, but now let's turn to the role of attentional processes in creative problem solving.

In his book *Guns, Germs, and Steel: The Fates of Human Societies*, Jared M. Diamond argues that it is the sheer quantity of available resources (plants suitable for agriculture, animals suitable for domestication, and so on) and the level of interaction between cultures that let some cultures produce more innovations and ultimately dominate other groups. This level of interaction is the same logic that holds for creative problem solving. The more information you have and the more varied that information is, the more likely it is that you will solve a problem. However, the

Figure 7.4. Who Am I?

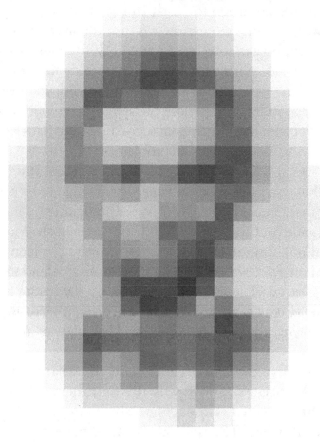

challenge we run into is in accessing information and deciphering whether the information we have is relevant to the problem at hand and how much of the apparently irrelevant information we should spend our time on trying to process. For example, what do you see in the image in Figure 7.4?

You may have seen a familiar face straight away. However, if you did not, try squinting. Or hold the book farther away from your eyes. Do you see him now? It's Abraham Lincoln.

When we try to solve problems, there is merit to the notion of focusing our attention by limiting extraneous information in order to see the picture more clearly. However, there is a darker side to focusing attention too early in the creative process. The problem with focusing too narrowly is that you may arrive at only one idea about how to solve the problem. While that idea may in fact be the big idea you are hoping for, chances are that it is not. In effect, you don't need a hundred ideas to succeed; you need only one great idea, and then variations on that idea. I'm not suggesting a silver bullet strategy; rather, I am suggesting that you seek variations to solving the fundamental problem.

Such was the case of Dyson vacuum cleaners: the vacuum cleaners that don't lose suction. James Dyson tinkered with 5,127 prototypes for four and a half years before launching his great idea that has made him the world's 746th richest person. Mind you, Dyson did not conjure up 5,127 different ways to clean carpet; he worked on 5,127 variations of a product that would solve the single biggest problem with existing products: vacuum cleaners lose suction. Like Dyson, the more problem-related ideas you are able to generate, the more likely you will generate an appropriate solution.

The cognitive capacity to generate many variations relies on attentional processes. This is why the right hemisphere of the brain is often credited (although grossly oversold) as the home of creative thought. The right hemisphere pays attention to a broader array of informational inputs than does the left hemisphere. However, creativity involves the entirety of the brain's processing power—both left and right hemispheres. The advantage of the right hemisphere is in how it interprets information; it's more liberal (that is, able to perceive and interpret information in multiple ways) and therefore is better equipped than the left hemisphere at considering multiple possibilities. Hence, we tend to attribute creativity to the right hemisphere, although we give it a bit too much credit.

Here is an exercise to illustrate how your entire brain, right and left hemispheres, interprets information in the attempt to solve a problem. Look only at these three words:

Pine
Crab
Tree

What one word that is not shown here do these three words share in common? That is, if you were to place the same missing word in front of or behind each of these three words, what word would work in all three cases?

If you got it, congratulations! You've just experienced a eureka moment (run naked at your own risk). However, if you are stumped, try thinking of a piece of fruit, and then look back at the three words again. Are you there yet? If not, the answer is *apple* (pine*apple*, crab*apple*, *apple* tree).

Using this as an illustration, let's consider what transpired. But first, a quick disclaimer: information processing in the brain is a highly complex activity. While a comprehensive scientific explanation of the actual processing that occurred in your brain during this simple exercise could fill the pages of this book, for our purposes, the following is a simplification of how your brain processed this problem leading up to and at the moment of insight.

When you saw the word *pine*, the left hemisphere of your brain likely focused on the word itself (see Figure 7.5). It likely did not consider other possibilities of what the word *pine* might mean.

Figure 7.5. How Brain Hemispheres Interpret Information

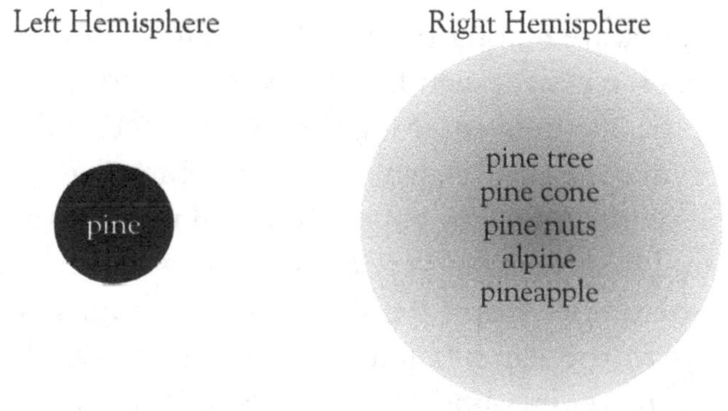

Left Hemisphere   Right Hemisphere

pine

pine tree
pine cone
pine nuts
alpine
pineapple

The same holds for the other two words: *crab* and *tree*. In each case, your left hemisphere translated these words literally based on your working knowledge of what the words mean to you. For example, *pine* may have translated as a type of wood, *crab* as a crustacean, and *tree* as a tall, leafy thing with branches. The right hemisphere of your brain interpreted these words much more broadly. For example, in your right hemisphere, the word *pine* also unconsciously signaled several possibilities for *pine*: *pine* as in "longing for something" or objects such as a pine tree, a pine cone, pine nuts, alpine, or a pineapple. The same holds for the words *crab* and *tree*. Your right hemisphere would have unconsciously activated *crab* not only as a crustacean, but perhaps also as "a grouchy personality" and *tree* not only as a tall, leafy thing with branches, but also as in "family tree" or "tree house." The notion of being a right-brained thinker does not equate to being more creative; rather it equates to being more liberal in the acceptance of alternatives. Both hemispheres are required in the act of creation.

The reason that eureka moments tend to transpire when we are not attempting consciously to solve the problem or to try to come up with a big idea is that in these moments, the left hemisphere is more "relaxed," thereby allowing the acceptance (consciously) of the "crazy alternatives" conjured up in the right hemisphere. Even the most distant clue could tip your mind into figuring out the problem. My advice is don't think so hard; take a break or go for a walk. Let your unconscious mind figure it out.

Edward Bowden, along with his research partner Mark Jung-Beeman, are among the notable neuroscientists who in recent years have made significant advances into the cognitive science of the aha moment using the aid of functional magnetic resonance imaging (fMRI), which is brain scanning technology. Through experiments using both behavioral measures and fMRI, Bowden and Jung-Beeman were among the first scientists in the world to isolate and observe the aha moment in captivity.

Similar to the *apple* example involving words that share a single word (compound remotes associates), Bowden and

Jung-Beeman also conducted inference experiments in which multiple answers could be possible. In the experiment shown in Figure 7.6, participants were shown three words on a screen: *glass, foot,* and *cry.* After the words were shown, the words were then removed, and a fixation cross was shown on the screen to ensure that people would continue to look at the center of the screen. Following the fixation cross, a related word (in this case, *cut*) or a word unrelated to any of the three words was shown. The time it took for the person to read aloud this fourth word was recorded. Bowden and Jung-Beeman discovered that people could read related words faster than unrelated words (this is referred to as priming). They could also read words that were only weakly related to the three words they had seen as fast as they could read a word strongly related to another single word (for example, *apple/ orange* or *doctor/nurse*). This means that although *cut* is not strongly related to *glass, foot,* and *cry,* it is as strongly activated (that is, the brain is thinking about it, but not necessarily at a conscious level) as a word closely associated with any one of the three words.

The small circles around the three words on the left in Figure 7.6 show how the left hemisphere narrowly defines each of the three words, while the larger circles illustrate how the right hemisphere more broadly defines each of the three words. Because the

Figure 7.6. Right Hemisphere Coding Increases the Likelihood of Semantic Overlap

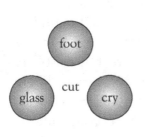

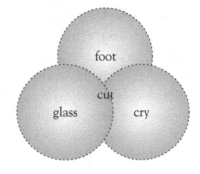

left hemisphere is more focused, only closely associated words are illuminated. Since the word *cut* is not closely associated with any of the three words shown (though you could argue that glass could be associated depending on the context), the word *cut* is left in the dark (not considered in the solution set). In the right hemisphere (the right illustration in the figure), the interpretation of the three words is wider but weaker so they illuminate more distantly associated words. Each word (*glass, foot,* and *cry*) weakly activates *cut* because glass can cut you, a foot can be cut, and you might cry if you were cut. Most important, the overlapping beams are additive, and so the word *cut*, even though it is not shown to participants (it's not on the screen as shown in the figure here; rather it comes and goes in the periphery in a split second), the word *cut* gets as much or more activation than a word strongly associated with only one of the three words. As a result, the solution comes from this convergence of information, not from activation evoked by any single word or the explicit word itself.

In a second experiment, participants were told a story in which the words were put into context. The story was about a person walking barefoot on a beach with *glass* scattered about, when he suddenly *cries* out in pain and grabs his *foot*. While hearing the story, participants were simultaneously shown words on the screen. In this experiment, the words were shown on either the left or right side of the screen, and people would read the words aloud. This target word was entered into the participants' field of vision by flashing the word in the far periphery of either their left or right eye. Because of the way the optic nerves connect to the eye, anything on the left side of the screen goes to the right hemisphere, and vice versa. Although the target word enters one hemisphere before the other, this information is then communicated around the brain through various connections and between hemispheres via the corpus callosum, the region of the brain responsible for interhemispheric communication, that is, cross-talk. Some scientists have suggested that the relative size of the corpus callosum may also be responsible for intuition. For example, the corpus callosum is often wider in the brains of women than in men, thus providing a more robust communication platform between brain hemispheres and explaining "women's intuition." Conversely, the relatively smaller size of the male corpus callosum also explains why women are often able to multitask better than men. It appears that men generally may be biologically predisposed (or at least relatively predisposed) to single-minded thinking, whereas women may be biologically predisposed to making connections between disparate pieces of information. In regard to the study, the target word was shown for only 180 milliseconds and then hidden from view in order to prevent processing in sensory memory. The reason is that in this short amount of time, a person is unable to move her eyes to fixate the word, and so the word becomes much like a passing hint—a flash of information—given first to only one hemisphere of the brain (much like that associated with the many historical eureka moments, such as Archimedes' observation of water running out of the tub and Newton's observation of an apple falling from the tree. They discovered that inference-related words were read more quickly than unrelated words and more quickly when shown to the right hemisphere. The right hemisphere also showed activation of the inference before the left hemisphere did.

In relation to creativity, the concept (for example, cut) is what connects all the disparate pieces of information into a sensible whole. In this way, a creative concept connects information that previously seemed unrelated. That connection is most likely to come from the overlapping beams of light (semantic fields) already available in the right hemisphere. In this way, the right hemisphere is not solely responsible for creativity; rather. it is responsible for suggesting alternate concepts that could possibly solve the problem.

In a third experiment, illustrated in Figure 7.7, Bowden and Jung-Beeman discovered that if a single word is shown first (for example, *foot* instead all three words: *foot, glass,* and *cry*) and then a strongly related target word is shown (say, *shoe*), the left

Figure 7.7. Priming in the Right versus the Left Hemispheres

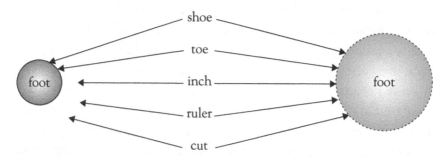

hemisphere shows more priming. When a more weakly related word (such as *ruler*) is shown in the left hemisphere, priming was lower. Because of the focus of the left hemisphere, only the most closely related words (*shoe, toe*) are illuminated, and therefore only the arrows from *shoe* and *toe* connect from the words to the left hemisphere circle while the more distantly related words (*inch, ruler,* and *cut*) are not considered by the left hemisphere. You may work with someone who suffers from this phenomenon: the myopic person whom you must continue to remind to see the big picture. Interestingly, this "extreme focus" is also evident in people who have experienced brain damage. In fact, individuals who have experienced damage to the right hemisphere are unable to understand jokes and metaphors. They become literal thinkers who fail (biologically) to see the bigger picture.

Also in the same experiment, when all three words (*foot, glass,* and *cry*) were introduced into the right hemisphere, priming was greater for all words shown. In the right hemisphere interpretation of *foot,* the arrows from all words (*shoe, toe, inch, ruler,* and *cut*) connect to the *foot* circle since all words are activated (considered) by the right hemisphere. This helps to explain why your best ideas come to you in the shower. This is a time that you are least likely to be focused on solving problems or it is a time you are least focused on thinking in general.

In another series of experiments directly related to the aha moment, people were shown three words (for example, *pine, crab,* and *tree*); within 750 milliseconds of having seen the first three words, a target word (*apple*) was then shown to the left or right visual hemifields. As before, this target word was entered into the participants' field of vision by flashing the word in the far periphery of either their left or right eye. The main findings were that the right and left hemispheres activated the eventual solution very quickly, but just as quickly, the left discarded the idea. In contrast, the right hemisphere held onto this information for at least the fifteen seconds people had to come up with a solution. The amount of activation in the right hemisphere was also found to correlate with the aha moment. The greater the activation (measured in speed of response), the stronger was the feeling of aha.

Bowden, Jung-Beeman, and John Kounios at Drexel University have further investigated these findings by looking at the brain during the creative moment. They have used the MRI scanner and electroencephalogram (EEG) to look at what areas of the brain act differently during insight and noninsight solutions to problems. Their two major findings are that the superior temporal gyrus of the right hemisphere, a spot in the brain roughly above your right ear, is more active during insight solutions than during noninsight solutions and that there is a neural signature (neural activity in a certain part of the brain and at a certain frequency) that occurs prior to problem presentation and predicts subsequent solution of the problem by sudden insight. Their findings suggest that important ideas—the creative ideas—may be lurking just below the threshold of awareness and that there appears to be a mind-set that is more conducive to creative moments.

What is most striking about the scientific findings on the aha moment is not only how the brain hemispheres interpret information, but how and when they choose (unconsciously) to use information. It appears that the right hemisphere makes several possible inferences early in the process of creative problem solving, and even more intriguing, it keeps these inferences available for the time when they might be needed. It also appears that information in the right hemisphere becomes active when a problem is presented and remains active until it is adopted or another idea is selected.

For example, recall Albert Einstein's aha experience while working at the patent office in Bern, Switzerland. It was in Bern that Einstein first made the mental connection between gravity and accelerated motion that eventually led to his general theory of relativity. As Einstein recalled, while he was lost in a daydream, "a breakthrough came suddenly one day" while thinking, "If a man falls freely he would not feel his weight." At the precise moment he made the connection between gravity and accelerated motion (a relationship likely consummated in his right hemisphere, his left hemisphere would have likely begun to work on proving the idea correct. In this way, ideas shift from one hemisphere to the other. We hold them unconsciously in our right hemisphere, like a mental unfinished business list, until we can reconcile (make sense of them) in the left.

Psychologist Colleen Seifert has proposed an index of failure, where the problem is marked as unsolved so when any information related to a solution is encountered, the problem is reactivated. In her theory, the activation might last for months or even years, as was the case of Einstein and his general theory of relativity. Recall that Einstein had the initial insight into the relationship between accelerated motion and gravity nearly a decade before this initial insight culminated in his ultimate solution: the general theory of relativity. Once the inference has finally been made, the activation in the right hemisphere simply fades away. Using the American pastime of baseball as a metaphor, once you've won the game (that is, figured out the riddle, come up with the big idea, or solved the problem), your brain no longer has the need to have a batter on deck (an alternate solution waiting in the wings to help you figure it out). Broadly speaking, the "light in the right" (hemisphere) goes out temporarily. Its job, for now, is done.

Ironically, in the moment that this learning happens, when questions become answers, you are immediately sent back to where you started. Now that you've found the answer that works, that answer then becomes a hammer looking for nails, and thus your challenge becomes attempting to unlearn what worked in the past for fear that you will miss the future once again. We will discuss this phenomenon of knowledge impairing creativity (functional fixedness) in Chapter Nine. In the interim, don't think so hard.

These and other experiments have much to teach us about becoming more conceptually creative. First and foremost, when you become stuck on a problem or are charged with trying to come up with the next big idea and someone advises you not to think so hard, heed this advice. Not thinking lessens focus in your left hemisphere, and, more important, the act of not thinking allows your right hemisphere to chime in with possible alternate solutions that beget flashes of sudden brilliance.

Second, as we've learned throughout this chapter, through perception and attention, once you become aware that there is a trick (a riddle) to problem solving, creative insight becomes more routine, more logical, and more controllable. For example, in Figure 7.8, which bar is bigger: the one at the top or the bottom?

The top bar may appear to be bigger than the bottom bar, but in fact, both are the same size. This illustrates how the visual system takes information into account, like the converging lines, to

Figure 7.8. Is There a Difference, or Is It an Illusion?

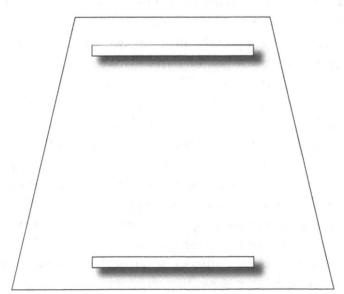

correctly interpret the size of an object based on the distance the object is from the viewer. In this illusion, the visual system is tricked because the converging lines make the brain think the top bar is farther away, and thus the top bar appears to be bigger. It is an illusion. Illusions are analogous to creativity insofar that the problem-solving system is tricked by what normally works. However, once you are aware of the trick, you can overcome it and reinterpret the problem. If the bars appeared to be the same to you when you first looked at the image, it is likely that you already knew that it was a trick question or you may be familiar with similar visual riddles, and so you moved the problem from your unconscious to your conscious. You tried to look for the trick.

Through your awareness that a problem may pose both relevant and irrelevant information, you become a better creative thinker insofar that you now know to look for, process, prioritize, weed out, include, and otherwise discard information that may or may not help you arrive at the right answer. The amazing thing is that it happens in a matter of milliseconds. Even more astounding, you can control it. You can make unconscious processing a conscious effort by paying attention to the reality that a trick may be involved requiring additional (or less) information to solve the problem.

The third lesson you should take away from this chapter is that contrary to urban legend, there is no such thing as a "right-brained" thinker. It is a myth. The right hemisphere is simply more liberal in its interpretation of information. Although the right hemisphere may generate more possibilities, it does not select one over another and therefore needs the left hemisphere. You use your entire brain in the creative process. The left hemisphere is critical to the creative process insofar that it provides the logic to ascertain the relevance or appropriateness of a possible solution. The application of this insight also applies to group creativity. For example, we see this same phenomenon transpire in group brainstorming sessions. Although it is true that diverse groups can generate more diverse ideas (like the right hemisphere does), at some point the group must select one idea to pursue. This often involves an entirely different set of questions (like the left hemisphere). This helps underscore why you should not rule out information too prematurely in an ideation process. Although the phrase *there's no such thing as a bad idea* is itself a bad idea, there is no such thing as bad information (at first). You never know what might work; therefore, it is best to consider information that on the surface may appear irrelevant. Give yourself time, consciously and unconsciously, to see if it makes sense or somehow finds its way into helping you solve the problem.

Most important, be aware that memory, perception, and attention are in a constant and unconscious waltz inside your head. The next time you get stuck on a problem or feel as if it's on the tip of your tongue, try not to think so hard; read something entirely unrelated to your problem, take a break, or go for a walk. This conscious lessening of focus in your left hemisphere will unconsciously allow your right hemisphere to think about it, and the answer may come rushing in.

Creativity is not only a function of resources; it is also a function of resourcefulness. What innovators lack in time and money, they make up for in perception and attention. In the right hands (and minds), innovation is the art of creative problem solving. And how you define a problem is largely derived based on how you choose to perceive it. Use constraints to your advantage, restate liabilities (disadvantages) as assets (advantages), and, most of all, just try to figure it out. Tinkering is half the battle. By identifying constraints (what is not possible and why it isn't possible), you will increase the likelihood of success in introducing creative solutions to work around those constraints. Once you've identified these constraints, then ask, What if some magic material, undiscovered technology, or nonexistent capabilities existed to help overcome these constraints? What would these nonexistent materials, technology, or capabilities have to be able to do? In lieu of these nonexistent materials, technology, or capabilities, ask what you can use in their place to solve this problem. This will help you link constraints to possibilities and increase your odds of finding creative solutions to existing problems even when currently available resources may be insufficient for solving the problem.

In order to learn how to link constraints to possibility, it is important to consider yet another precursor to creative insight: *connections*. One way in which to learn how to make unorthodox connections between seemingly distantly related domains is to consider analogous situations outside your industry, application, or category—what I call *thinking sideways* and what creativity scholar Edward de Bono originally referred to as "lateral thinking." To this, let's turn to following chapter.

Summary Points and Creative Exercises

- Constraints help inspire creativity.

- When there is a focused problem to solve and a sense of mission guides a team, limited resources (time, money) can provide just the right conditions for inspiring creative insight.

- When a broad-based charter and a sense of exploration guide the team, access to more resources (specifically, time) can create the appropriate conditions for inspiring creative insight.

- Increased research and development spending does not necessarily yield increases in sales or profits; in fact, there appears to be little if no correlation between spending and sales. How you think is more important than how much money you are given to think.

- There is no such thing as a right-brained or a left-brained human being. Both hemispheres play important roles in creative thinking.

- In order to think creatively in the presence of constraints, restate the constraints as opportunities, and start brainstorming by using the constraints to your advantage versus having them work against you.

8

DISTANTLY RELATED

Connections

Albert Einstein lost his mind. Actually, he didn't lose it; we did—like a sock in a dryer. Well, it wasn't technically lost; it simply went missing for several years following his death. In 1955, Princeton Hospital pathologist Thomas Stoltz Harvey performed an autopsy on Einstein's remains and, without Einstein's prior permission, removed his brain and kept it. He claimed to have taken the specimen in order to perform medical research on it. Subsequently Harvey lost his job and his medical license and became an operator of a plastics extruding machine. Although he took Einstein's brain, he didn't keep it to himself. He shared pieces of it with a few scientists: neuronauts interested in the biology of genius.

I refer to as neuronauts all those who are trained to pilot, navigate, or participate as crew members in the exploration of crevasses of the brain. Over the coming decades, adventures in neuronautical engineering will undoubtedly unlock many of the intractable mysteries of the mind, among them, the moment of creative insight (in fact, to some degree, it already has been unlocked). The increasing relevance of neuroscience to life's mysteries is evident in the considerable growth in membership of the Society for Neuroscience, a nonprofit organization whose membership includes basic scientists and physicians who study the brain and nervous system. The organization has grown from 500 members in 1969 to over 37,500 members today and is now the world's largest organization devoted to the study of the brain. From cognitive neuroscientists to cosmetic neurologists, pharmacologists, psychologists, and so-called neuromarketers (those who use brain science to design new products and advertising messages that best resonate with consumers), their interests remain the same: to understand how the brain functions in order to make advances in everything from medicine to marketing. As the Lewis and Clarks of the modern age, neuronauts map uncharted territories and stake claims to insights on brain development, learning and memory, sensation and perception, movement, stress, sleep, aging, and neurological and psychiatric disorders. The field also involves the study of molecules, genes, and cells responsible for the functions of the nervous system. One neuronaut of note, to whom Harvey gave a portion of Einstein's brain, is Marian C. Diamond, a researcher interested in the biology of genius who took one small step into a most peculiar place: the Brodman's area 39 portion (BA39) of Einstein's brain.

In 1985, Diamond and her colleagues reported that Einstein's BA39 had a higher proportion of glial cells to neurons than control subjects. (BA39 is often associated with semantic aphasia—the impairment of the ability to comprehend and produce language.) Glial cells are nonneuronal cells that are thought to provide support and nutrition for neurons, which are cells whose function is to process and transmit information—a process called synaptic transmission. What does Einstein's BA39 tell us about his creativity? In order to answer this question, it is helpful to take a look at Albert's younger years.

As a child, Einstein was mute: he didn't talk. Concerned about his silence, Einstein's parents took him to a pediatrician who, according to researchers, diagnosed him with developmental dyslexia, a condition that impairs reading and writing abilities and is also known to interfere with the processing of spoken language. Over a century ago, researchers discovered that people with developmental dyslexia may have abnormalities in the left angular gyrus region of the brain (BA39). In the case of Albert Einstein, it is possible that his loss of neurons was due to his dyslexia; however, Diamond attributed Einstein's loss of neurons in this area less to his dyslexia and more to his "connectivity." In other words, his brain was physically connected in a way such that he would process information using more disparate areas of his brain than the average person. Closer examination of photographs of Einstein's brain indicated an enlarged left inferior and undivided parietal lobe, unlike those of most other human beings. The parietal lobe is involved in the integration of information and is also involved in visuospatial processing. In lay terms, Einstein's abnormal left hemisphere may have been partially responsible for his highly specialized and superhuman right hemisphere, giving him a distinct advantage in spatial computations, a valuable asset in the creative process. In fact, Einstein himself believed that his creativity was dependent on spatial reasoning. Recall his daydream while working at the patent office in Bern of "a man falling." This visualization of movement through space was likely a common cognitive process that Einstein employed consciously or, more likely, unconsciously. It is believed that spatial reasoning enables the ability to integrate disparate sensory information (improves connectivity) and connectivity is highly correlated to creativity and innovation.

Kenneth M. Heilman, professor of neurology and health psychology at the University of Florida's College of Medicine, explains innovation as "the ability to understand and express novel orderly relationships." This requires high intelligence, domain-specific knowledge, and familiarity of innovation skills or methods. However, these three alone are insufficient in inspiring creative insight. The mystery is in how these three interact. What is it that enables the connections between disparate domains? As Heilman has expressed in his research, "Finding this thread might require the binding of different forms of knowledge, stored in separate cortical modules that have not been previously associated. Thus, creative innovation might require the coactivation and communication between regions of the brain that ordinarily are not strongly connected." Based on these findings, it may be that creative individuals like Einstein have alterations to specific brain regions as well as alterations of neurotransmitters that, as Heilman writes, enable "brains that are capable of storing extensive specialized knowledge" as well as special abilities in divergent thinking: the ability to identify multiple answers to the same question or multiple paths to the same destination (a hallmark of creative thinking).

The relationship between brain biology and creativity is most apparent among patients who have had their frontal lobes removed or injured. These patients are unable to perform divergent thinking: they are unable to break away from what they have been taught to believe or to access distantly related pieces of information. These findings confirm historical research in this area, specifically that of Charles Spearman, who in 1931, notes Heilman, suggested that "creativity results from bringing together two or more ideas that previously have been isolated."

Einstein's biological gift enabled his creativity. One could argue that his genius was not necessarily in creating novel ideas as much as it was in creating novel relationships between seemingly unrelated concepts (for example, between space and time). Aha moments then may occur among those who are biologically gifted to make unorthodox connections, such as those with dyslexia. However, the wonder of the human brain is that it can be manipulated. It is elastic. You can train it to make these types of connections. Moreover, should you practice this type of cross-domain thinking often enough, you can literally create new biological connections in your brain.

Aha moments often appear at the intersection of seemingly unrelated bits of information. Therefore, people who are able to make these connections, whether due to a biological gift or through a very deliberate process, are more skilled at conjuring up novel ideas on a continuous basis. Making unorthodox connections between disparate domains may be biologically demanding, but it is not impossible. Making connections, like breathing, occurs naturally, but again like breathing, it is something that you have control over. One way in which to learn to make unorthodox connections is to simply keep the unsolved problem activated in your mind even while you are not deliberately attempting to solve it. By keeping the problem at the top of your mind, you will be surprised at how relevant seemingly irrelevant information and experiences may be to helping you solve the problem. In order to illustrate, let's visit our naked scientist once again.

First, consider what Archimedes knew. He knew that gold and silver differ in density and that he could measure the weight of the king's crown. In fact, he even knew about the principle of water displacement from his work building boats for the king. One could argue that he had virtually everything that he needed to solve the problem, yet he was still at a loss for ideas. Why? This story captures the essence of conceptual creativity. While attempting to solve problems, we do initial work on the problem (try to figure it out), but often reach a dead end (an impasse), at which point, we have a choice: give up and abandon the search for a solution, or reinterpret some aspect of the problem and continue. In Archimedes case, the reinterpretation occurred while taking a bath. As in Archimedes' experience, this reinterpretation often appears to come about as the result of unconscious processing (that is, it "happens" at the moment when the solver is typically not overtly seeking a solution) and often involves making connections that were previously unseen. Following the reinterpretation, the solution seems to come suddenly (aha!) and appears clearly correct. Once Archimedes made the connection using water displacement to ascertain volume, the solution appeared to be blindingly obvious, yet only seconds earlier it had been a complete mystery. Is the Archimedes story typical? In many ways, it is.

Like Archimedes, most people attempting to solve problems have everything they need in order to figure them out: experience with the subject matter, knowledge of the situation and other similar situations, and access to information outside their own knowledge (it's a click away). Where most creative endeavors fail is in the inability to put all the disparate pieces together to formulate a coherent and relevant solution to the problem. By failing to make these hidden connections, we fail to get creative. This oversight (the unexplored connections between existing knowledge) is indeed what stumped Archimedes and is what often stumps scores of others who are challenged to figure it out. In our attempts at creative problem-solving, we are often blinded by what we cannot see: the space in between the lines, the connections between disparate activities, and the relevance of what we believe is intangible information. After all, how many of us would have made the connection between an apple falling out of a tree and universal gravitation or, as was the case with Archimedes, between designing boats and measuring crowns? And so, as is often the case, once we witness a great idea, we stand befuddled wondering, "Why didn't I think of that?"

The reason ideas seem so simplistically obvious once they are in front us is that we often possessed the knowledge and even the experience with the general idea before it appeared out of thin air. That's why insight, or the aha experience, feels so familiar to us once we understand. However, as was the case with Archimedes, creative solutions do not come out of thin air at all. Rather, they are based on existing knowledge and attempts to apply standard problem-solving methods.

Contrary to popular opinion, sudden acts of creativity appear to be much more logical constructs. They often emerge at the cross-hairs of a well-defined problem, significant depth of knowledge within a field, and the accidental or intentional introduction of information from outside the field. Here lies the trick. Without domain expertise, the accidental information would simply appear to be random. For example, if Archimedes had known nothing about density, weight, and boat building, he would have likely never come to the solution. He would have never experienced his famous eureka moment. Chance favors the prepared mind.

One of the most glorified contemporary examples of this misunderstanding—that previous knowledge is not as important as breaking the rules in the field of innovation—is the case of 3M's ubiquitous Post-It Notes. While the conception of the little stickies is legendary (it was an accident), this story hinders innovation by attributing too much weight to fate. On hearing this and other stories of accidental creativity, you may wonder, "Why should I try to solve the problem when it seems that great ideas occur by chance?" Here's why. Although there are endless examples of accidental inventions—Velcro, penicillin, the pacemaker—the precursors (events and knowledge) that gave rise to these ideas were not entirely random. Quite the contrary: they were conceived in controlled environments and by people who were working on problems somewhat related to the big idea. Even Art Fry himself, the famed "inventor" of Post-It Notes, has attempted to dispel the myth of accidental invention: "When Lewis and Clark discovered Yellowstone . . . they spent a year in preparation for the trip. The more you learn, the more you are able to see."

We fail to create when we are blinded by what we cannot see (connections). However, by remaining focused on the problem, applying domain expertise, and being willing to accept apparently irrelevant information as possibly helpful, you may be able to solve problems more often and experience aha moments more deliberately. As Fry describes the aha moment, "You can't predict it, but you can do the work that will lead you to those things." This is why remaining focused on the problem, doing the work (even when you seem to be at an impasse), and being open to seemingly irrelevant information matter. Moreover, there is some evidence to suggest that the act of taking a break (thinking without thinking) may also help to facilitate insight. In addition to the scientific research in this area are many anecdotal accounts of unplanned connections.

One such account came from a client of mine, an executive working for a large restaurant chain, who shared a story with me of unexplained innovation. At the end of the previous year, during an off-site strategy meeting, he and his team wrote down a list of problems they were seeking to solve and things they had hoped to accomplish in the following year. However, there was one small issue: they didn't have the budget to do anything. Nonetheless, he didn't want that to stifle their creativity, and so he published the list anyway, and each team kept it on the back burner in their respective functional areas. A year after that meeting, the team exhumed the list and discovered that every single item on it had found its way into the business. They were amazed. They had inadvertently innovated. Without a formal project or budget deployed against any of their action items, they had achieved 100 percent of what they wrote down. While this surprised the team, it would not surprise most cognitive psychologists. Here's what likely occurred.

When you put something in writing, beyond the obvious act of creating a physical unfinished business list, you also create a mental one. This unfinished mental list (for example, Archimedes' inability to measure volume or the restaurant chain's list of problems) is more likely to be resolved because it is now in the foreground versus the background of your mind. This represents much more than a practical exercise in creating to-do lists. Rather, it is a cognitive exercise in learning to be more conceptually creative. This phenomenon is known as *opportunistic assimilation*, an idea derived from the Gestalt school of psychology. Opportunistic assimilation works as follows. When you reach an impasse in an attempt to solve a problem, that problem is tagged (or kept in a state of higher activation). Subsequently any information encountered during the incubation period, that is, the time in which the problem is activated, is then assimilated into the problem itself. In lay terms, you try consciously or unconsciously to make the disparate pieces of information fit together, like puzzle pieces. You search for solutions. Archimedes searched for volume just as the restaurant chain executives searched for ways to get their ideas into the business. Through this phenomenon, you become suddenly brilliant when, one day, what may have been construed as irrelevant information (taking a bath) is now blindingly appropriate in helping to solve your problem. And thus, aha!

What is most important to note here is that it is the open question itself that facilitates assimilation. By maintaining and publishing that list of aspirations, the restaurant executives found a way to get creative without explicitly thinking about how to innovate. That they did it without funding is truly an act of creativity. Writing things down serves not only to focus your attention on the problem, but it also helps to keep your mind open to receiving future sensory information that you may not at first think is relevant. Recall the scrambled letter passage. You never really know what information your brain is using.

Beyond writing things down, yet another method for encouraging the ability to make connections is to foster independent thinking. This is based on the biological evidence that the frontal lobes are the areas of the cortex most important to creativity. This region of the brain is largely responsible for our ability to modulate the coactivation of disparate networks in the brain, thereby helping to form connections. One way in which to exercise this area is to foster independent thinking. Whether you are parenting a child or managing an employee, you might translate this as, "Let him or her figure it out alone." The search for the solution, including the many dead-ends and rabbit holes into which we fall, exercises divergent thinking, which in turn, fosters creativity.

The reason I believe we must be more thoughtful in our attempts at making unorthodox connections is that we have taken Adam Smith too literally. We have pushed the frontiers of the division of labor to the point of diminishing returns. In his seminal work, *The Wealth of Nations* (1776), Smith provides an example to illustrate his philosophy with the process of making pins. According to Smith, one person could make one pin in a single day. However, if the eighteen steps required to make a single pin were divided among ten people, together they could make forty-eight thousand pins in a single day. Increased specialization yields increased productivity.

With numbers like these, it should come as no surprise that earlier economic schools were abandoned as Smith's philosophy became the de facto standard, thereby paving the way for the field of classical economics. Well done, Adam. However, nearly 250 years later, I'm afraid we've taken the idea a little too far. We are standing on the threshold of a sea of minutia and are now at risk of losing sight of the big picture. Although there are certainly benefits to specialization, such as increased efficiency, these benefits come at the expense of a drain on our creative capacity: they eliminate the cross-pollination of ideas from one field to the next. Experts are valuable, but they tend to get stuck in single domain. As I often advise my clients, if someone claims that he or she is a specialist in innovation in a given field or industry, run! There is no such thing.

By definition, innovation is the business of cross-boundary thinking. Most great ideas are achieved not by experts working within fields but by generalists working across fields or by specialists who introduce ideas from one field into another field. Recall Henry Ford's creation of modern manufacturing. It was the result of three disparate ideas from three very different areas: meatpacking, the military, and cigarette manufacturing. Over the past several decades, this trend toward extreme specialization has transpired across industries and professions, thereby increasing productivity but at the expense of creativity.

Consider the field of biology. When Francis Crick and James Watson proposed the first acceptable model of the structure of DNA in their article, "The Molecular Structure of Nucleic Acids" (1953), the pair, along with Maurice Wilkins, not only won the Nobel Prize (1962), but they set in motion an entirely new field within classical biology: molecular biology. Molecular biology has since been divided into a number of subspecialties, including molecular genetics, bioinformatics, and computational biology (to say nothing of the related disciplines of biophysics, developmental biology, evolutionary biology, population genetics, and phylogenetics). In fact, they are all trying to answer the same two questions: Where do we come from? and Why are we here?

In marketing, similar subdivisions have occurred. We've reduced the field to advertising, brand and channel management, consumer behavior, customer relationship management, database marketing, direct marketing, market research, public relations, new product development, pricing, and sales management. And yet everyone in marketing is trying to answer the same two questions: Where do we find new customers? and How do we get them to buy from us?

Is it any wonder that society has lost sight of the big picture? We are no longer generalists exploring the boundaries of human ingenuity; rather, we are an expanding group of specialists running narrowly in search of the future. Certainly specialists are valuable in helping make sense of our increasingly complex world; for example, I'd rather have a brain surgeon do the job than a family practitioner. However, in order to foster creativity, we must attend to the big picture as much as the many small ones. There are two ways to manage becoming more creative in an increasingly specialized world.

The first has to do with team chemistry. For example, the world's premier management consulting firm, McKinsey & Company, works deliberately to balance its mix of specialists and generalists with the hope of achieving synergies between vertical (specialist) and horizontal (generalist) thinking. This is a viable option, but it introduces complexity in creative tasks. Specifically, although the logic may be true that a diverse team will likely generate a more diverse set of ideas, diverse teams have the additional challenge of social acceptance. Say a generalist on the team comes up with a great idea. The specialist on the team will often shoot down the idea based on the generalist's lack of knowledge (or more likely due to the generalist's lack of professional currency in the field). And so although the totality of the ideas may in fact be diverse, the ultimate ideas that are implemented are often less than creative. Nonetheless, it is an option. Should you pursue this option, recognize that you must work deliberately to manage the social reality of team-based creativity.

The second option is to learn to become an elastic thinker: to think broadly and deeply simultaneously, a highly attractive skill in the pursuit of creative production. One such elastic thinker was Charles Darwin. Although Darwin spent decades consumed by bird plumage, barnacles, and animal husbandry, his genius was in his ability to rise up from it all and arrive at a worldview about how it all fit together: species evolving from a common origin. In order to become elastic thinkers like Darwin, who studied medicine, theology, and geology, we must learn to become generalists once again: to think and live more broadly, encourage intellectual curiosity, and consume novel thoughts as much as we consume novel clothing. So, where to begin? For starters, we need to go back to "school"—not the institution but the mentality.

The word *school* has its origins in the Greek word *scholē* (meaning "leisure" or "serious activity without the pressure of necessity"). In ancient Greece, school was perceived as a luxury afforded to the sons of merchants who were allowed the opportunity to read, contemplate, and bask in knowledge from a variety of disciplines. *Scholē* also referred to the "time" in which people were allowed to dwell in possibility—encouraged not to think differently but to think broadly. As Aristotle observed, school is the "absence of the necessity of being occupied." This did not equate to "being without work"; rather it referred to "having the time to think," a luxury in today's fast-paced world. The good news is that we have history as a guide to reclaim the way things were. Once we thought more broadly because we lived more broadly. Beyond the ancient Greeks, how we in the Western world lived just two hundred years ago is rich in learning for how we can live more creatively today. And, no, I am not referring to the Industrial Revolution but to December 1783.

December 1783 was not a slow news month: at Fraunces Tavern in Manhattan, George Washington bade farewell to his officers because the American Revolutionary War had ended; in Maryland, Thomas Jefferson wrote a letter to George Rogers Clark soliciting his interest in leading an exploration of the West (Clark turned him down, although twenty years later his younger brother, William, accepted the offer); in Italy, an earthquake in Calabria left fifty thousand dead; and in England, twenty-four-year-old William Pitt the Younger assumed his post as the youngest prime minister who to this day has ever served in Britain.

Amid the flurry of breaking news stories, who knew that a clergyman in Berlin would trigger such vigorous debate with a seemingly innocuous question, "What is Enlightenment?" Referring to the philosophy that defined the period of time between the 1680s and the late eighteenth century, Johann Friedrich Zöllner attached this question to an essay he wrote for the December 1783 issue of the *Berlinische Monatschrifft* (*Berlin Monthly*), the leading Prussian journal of the Enlightenment. The magnitude of Zöllner's question is even more startling when you consider where it first appeared. It was not the title of his essay; rather it was a footnote to it. Due to its pint-sized appearance, it is safe to assume that even Zöllner did not appreciate the potency of his question. Or if he did, why would he bury it in fine print?

Zöllner penned his eminent afterthought in response to an anonymously published essay that appeared in an earlier edition of the journal. In it, Johann Erich Beister, the librarian of the royal library in Berlin, proposed that enlightened citizens should avoid having clergy preside at their weddings for fear that it would send a message that the marriage contract was somehow unique from other contracts since it was made with God himself while other contracts "are only made with men and are therefore less meaningful." Beister's intention was not to desecrate the sanctity of marriage; rather, he intended to suggest that all laws and contracts should receive equal respect. Zöllner was a clergyman, and he was agitated by this comment, so he wrote a letter to the editor (which happened to be Beister). In the footnote, Zöllner wrote: "What is Enlightenment? This question, which is almost as important as what is truth, should indeed be answered before one begins enlightening! And still I have never found it answered!"

In an age of religious controversy, scientific inquiry, and political dissent, Zöllner's terse question led to an abundance of answers. Within ten years after its publication, *enlightenment* had twenty-one different definitions. Among those in the choir of opinions was German philosopher Immanuel Kant. In the opening lines of his December 1784 essay, "Answer to the Question: What Is Enlightenment?" Kant wrote, "Enlightenment is man's emergence from his self-incurred immaturity. Immaturity is man's inability to use one's own understanding without the guidance of another. This immaturity is self-incurred if its cause is not lack of understanding, but lack of resolution and courage to use it without the guidance of another. The motto of enlightenment is therefore: *Sapere aude!* 'Have courage to use your own understanding!'"

Superstition, tyranny, and, mostly, religious dogma were the subject of Kant's commentary on immaturity. Therefore, like Kant and in an effort to divorce humanity from its shadowy past, intellectuals denounced the divinity of kings, elevated the physical sciences, and suggested that life on earth was as important as, if not more important than, life ever after. From healing to the heavens, this shift from the divine to the scientific marked a moment in history when we made the decision to think for ourselves. To put it simply, the Enlightenment was an era when we did a great deal of thinking about thinking. In fact, it is arguably the last time we as humans thought so deliberately about the process of thinking—until now.

Academics and the occasional lone innovator notwithstanding, the greatest challenge we have today is not that we have forgotten how to think; rather, we simply do not have the time to think, much less think differently. Even the world's richest man, Bill Gates, recognizes what a luxury thinking time has become. Gates's "Think Week," his annual sabbatical in which he reads incessantly and mulls over the future of technology away from the everyday chores of being the world's richest man, has become the stuff of legend. Because time has become an endangered species, how you think in those stolen moments of life will become increasingly important in your bid to remain relevant. However, before we get to these important lessons and in order to put the Enlightenment into perspective, it is helpful to understand the events that led up to and followed this thoughtful moment in history.

The Enlightenment was preceded by an era of cultural change: the Renaissance. The Renaissance, particularly the Italian Renaissance that spanned the end of the fourteenth century to the late sixteenth century, can effortlessly stake claim to countless artistic innovations. From the epic achievements of

Michelangelo, Niccolò Machiavelli, and Leonardo da Vinci to the construction of the Duomo in Florence and St. Peter's Basilica in Rome, the Italian Renaissance stands alone in the proliferation of art. On the other side of the Enlightenment, spanning the years between the late eighteenth and early nineteenth centuries, we experienced an embarrassment of invention riches during a period of time defined as the Industrial Revolution.

As significant as the Renaissance and the Industrial Revolution were and in spite of the contributions both made in the form of artistic and technological innovation, I believe it is what happened between these two periods—in the hundred years between art and technology—that allowed us to be so creatively prolific during and following the Industrial Revolution. While the Renaissance gave us art and the Industrial Revolution gave us technology, it was the Enlightenment that furnished us with the appropriate mind-set to innovate. The Enlightenment taught us how to think. From Johann Wolfgang Goethe's thoughts on evolution to Adam Smith's economics and Thomas Jefferson's inalienable rights, this era of thinking differently set the table for the innovation feast that fed the Industrial Revolution and has kept our creative cravings sated into the information age. It is my opinion that had we not divorced ourselves from the past, we would not have been able to create the future because we would not have seen it coming. After all, if only heaven knows, then what good is had by thinking? So what was it about the Enlightenment that cultivated conceptual creativity? What has changed over the past two hundred years that threatens our creative capacity? And what can we learn from this in the pursuit of the answer to the riddle, What inspires a great idea? There are three fundamental differences between how we lived during the Enlightenment and how we live today that hold the keys to understanding how to be more conceptually creative: we had more time to think, we lived more broadly, and we communicated more effectively. Let's consider each.

First, enlightened thinkers had time to kill. Because of growing religious tolerance and the rise of the scientific method, Europeans

were free to pursue intellectual pursuits without the fear of retri-
bution from the church that characterized earlier periods. Moreover, because of the conquest of the Americas, radical new ideas
such as capitalism began to make much more sense in the context
of global conquest. Therefore, those who proposed new ways of
thinking were given more freedom to do so.

The rock stars of the day were intellectual giants, among them
Adam Smith, Benjamin Franklin, David Hume, John Locke,
Joseph Priestley, Jean-Jacques Rousseau, Thomas Jefferson, and the
godfather of them all, Sir Isaac Newton. They had time to reflect,
contemplate, and consider. In contrast, even the most innovative organizations today spend no more than a small fraction of
their time really thinking about unsolved problems, attempting to
identify unmet needs, and challenging the prevailing success factors of existing categories. As individuals, time alludes us as well.
Given our lack of time, we focus our attention on those issues that
are most relevant to our immediate needs and interests. After all,
who has time to plant seeds when fighting fires? For example, ask
yourself: How much time do you dedicate to reading magazines
beyond your immediate areas of interest? How often do you attend
trade shows outside your industry? How frequently do you listen
to those who do not buy your products or services? When is the
last time you traveled to a place you've never been before or tasted
food that is new to you? Simply, when was the last time you did
something for the first time? Experiences such as these are often
the fodder for creative inspiration. However, each requires time.
One of the greatest challenges to creativity today is finding the
time to think. Therefore, in order to improve your creativity, you
must first revisit how to think about and allocate your time.

Time is like money: each of us finds different ways to spend
it. The challenge that most of us have today is finding the time
to think. In fact, what is most revealing about the U.S. Bureau of
Labor Statistics' American Time Use Survey is not necessarily how
we spend our time, but the fact that in 2003, the first year of the
survey, the overall response rate to the survey was only 57 percent.
What, you may be asking, was the reason respondents gave for not

completing the surveys? No time! The first challenge is to make the time to think. The second challenge is to figure out how to use this newly created time to enhance your creativity. Again we have much to learn from history in this regard.

During the Enlightenment, not only did people have more time to think, it was how they spent that time that is even more revealing. For example, in our schools today, students are burdened with the pressure to "get the grade" and "get involved" in extracurricular activities in order to "get rich." However, they must do it within the same time parameters. In exchange for the pursuit of achievement, they have little, if no, time to think, tinker, and get lost in their thoughts. As for enlightened experimentation (failure), there is certainly no time for that. It is true that students are taking more classes, working more jobs, and making more money than previous generations, but consider the trade-offs: holidays are near extinction, summer is officially dead, and winter break is on life support. Perhaps most troubling, because of increasing specialization in industry, students are encouraged to figure out what they want to do as early as possible and subsequently learn as much as they can about that discipline. We live more narrowly today than in the past and therefore think more narrowly. In order to think broadly, we must begin to live more broadly. And, more important, we must be willing to accept those who live and think broadly. Hire a dabbler—an enlightened thinker. Consider how things have changed. Several hundred years ago, one's résumé could read: chemist, financier, biologist, and economist, and no one would blink an eye. Words like *job hopper* didn't come around the watercooler until much later. Because of their diverse experiences and interests, the activist-entrepreneur-diplomats of the Enlightenment did not have to force themselves to think outside the box simply because they spent their lives living, working, and playing in at least a dozen different boxes.

Consider the work of one such enlightened dilettante, the chemist-financier-biologist-economist Antoine Lavoisier (1743–1794). In Lavoisier's short life (he lived only fifty-one years), he invented chemistry, named oxygen and hydrogen, introduced the metric system, and invented the first periodic table. And that was only at his day job. In addition, he was the administrator of a private tax collection company and chairman of the board of a bank. He lived broadly. Unfortunately, as fate would have it, Lavoisier also nurtured political interests, became prominent in the prerevolutionary French government, and was swiftly beheaded. Although he lost his head, you can't discount his creativity.

Then there was Benjamin Franklin (1706–1790): activist, author, diplomat, inventor, philosopher, printer, publisher, and scientist. Today we'd likely accuse Franklin of being indecisive in his career choices. "Ben, when are you going to settle down?" we would likely ask. However, consider Franklin's achievements. He invented bifocal glasses, the lightning rod, swim fins, the glass harmonica, and the Franklin stove. He published *Poor Richard's Almanac*, promoted colonial unity, founded the first American fire department, and created the first lending library. If that were not enough, he brokered the French alliance that helped make the American Revolution possible and then went on to serve as the postmaster general under the Continental Congress. He died an abolitionist. And along the way, he became fluent in five languages. And we wonder how Benjamin Franklin was so very good at thinking outside the box. Franklin lived broadly.

The only reason that history holds out Lavoisier and Franklin as outliers, lone geniuses in a sea of mediocrity, is that we believe you must find your interest and dedicate your entire life's work to it. If you want to be an accountant, than learn all that you can about accounting. But if you want to be an actor, then don't waste your time in accounting. Whatever you do, just don't jump around too much. In our advanced society, there is a fine line between wondering and wandering. Spend too much time moving around, and one is quickly deemed aimless by the silent majority. However, as my favorite "Life Is Good" T-shirt reads, "Not all those who wander are lost." Who said you couldn't be both?

Added to narrowcasting our minds, we are predisposed to consuming only the media that reinforce our previously held beliefs, political or otherwise; attending trade shows only within our industries; and investing in continuing education credits that further our specialization only in our chosen field. Intellectually, we no longer wander. And so we wonder, "Why didn't I think of that?" Although the depth and breadth of knowledge we possess today is the most advanced it has been in human history, in our collective effort to gain mastery over subjects, we risk narrowcasting our minds and stifling our collective creativity. On its current trajectory, while specialization may make society and organizations much more efficient, I believe that over the long term, it will have a negative influence on our ability to think creatively, innovate in a continuous fashion, and ultimately identify unique solutions to unsolved problems.

However, as always, we have history as a guide. How we lived in decades past holds many keys to unlocking creativity. Unlike today's theorists, the great thinkers of the Enlightenment were entrepreneurial philosopher-scientists, perpetually engaged in the process of discovery. Although they often had a depth of knowledge within a given field, they maintained innumerable interests outside their fields. As IDEO describes its ideal employees, "We like to hire T-shaped people." The figure T is a visual representation of a person's breadth of knowledge over many subjects and the simultaneous depth of understanding and experience in a given field. In fact, some at IDEO are more "F-shaped" and "E-shaped" (with broad interests and depth in, respectively, at least two or three fields). Innovators live broadly. By virtue of the way they spend their time, enlightened thinkers of the eighteenth and twenty-first centuries see problems more clearly, identify root causes more swiftly, and create solutions that are more relevant. Among the behavior of enlightened thinkers, they read broadly, dabble in all sorts of seemingly unrelated ventures, and are actively engaged in diverse social institutions and thus diverse conversations, all of which foster conceptual creativity.

We don't live this way today. In fact, according to the American Time Use Survey, Americans spend over half of their leisure time watching television (2.6 hours per day) and only 45 minutes a day socializing. Moreover, the time we spend socializing is often not allocated across broadly defined social networks; rather, it is spent in vertical niches, for example, attending industry trade shows, subscribing to magazines that reinforce our existing skills and knowledge versus widening the aperture of our minds, belonging to clubs whose other members live and act the way we do, and so on. Although these activities are certainly fun and engaging, by casting our experiences too narrowly, we risk impeding our collective capacity to create—to formulate novel combinations between seemingly unrelated bits of information, knowledge, and experience. It would behoove us all to live more broadly than we do now.

One signpost of the resurrection of broad-based living in the business community is a community called TED (Technology, Entertainment, and Design). The reason that the TED conference, a meeting held annually in Monterrey, California, has become a "can't miss" destination for many of today's leaders is that it provides a unique broad-based agenda, invites speakers from widely divergent disciplines, and encourages participants to search between the lines and find connections between domains that may not be obvious. From neuronauts to astronauts, poets to pop musicians, and Nobel Laureates to venture capitalists, TED fosters connectedness through a wildly divergent community. TED is the contemporary example of the nineteenth-century coffeehouse—a place in the social sphere that once promoted the cross-pollination of big ideas through dialogue, debate, and even media coverage. Sure, we have thousands of coffeehouses to choose from today, but what goes on inside them is entirely different from the way things were. Take a step inside penny universities.

During the Enlightenment, people communicated publicly through institutions that lent themselves to the discussion of broad-based topics. Among these institutions were academies, salons, secret societies, and coffeehouses. These institutions were instrumental in shaping public opinion, but they also played an instrumental role in broadening thinking by bringing together people of various backgrounds, interests, and affiliations. Perhaps the most significant of these institutions were coffeehouses, the so-called penny universities.

Coffeehouses first appeared in Constantinople (now Istanbul) in the sixteenth century and made their debut in Europe by 1645. Upon their arrival in Venice, clergy immediately denounced coffee as an infidel drink, but Pope Clement VIII promptly rejected these complaints, thereby making coffee an acceptable indulgence among Christians. Monarchs in German states, like the Italian clergy, also expressed concern over the introduction of coffee. However, their concern was due to economic reasoning more so than theological. Coffee had to be imported and, given its enormous popularity, had the potential to cause significant trade deficits. Therefore, German monarchs promoted herbal teas, which successfully held coffee at bay in some regions. Coffeehouses also received a cold reception by defenders of the British monarchy. They were viewed as "un-English" and chastised for thwarting the good English tradition of drinking toasts to the king (only ale would suffice). In fact, the English so feared coffee that pamphlets were issued warning men that if they spent too much time in coffeehouses, they would run the risk of infertility. Regardless of the attempts to stifle their growth, coffeehouses spread quickly throughout Europe, arriving in England by 1650, Germany by 1671, France by 1672, and Vienna by 1683. By the time Zöllner's famous question appeared in print, there were nearly a thousand coffeehouses in Paris alone. So why was the coffeehouse feared by some but beloved by many?

The coffeehouse was more than a drinking establishment. As Diderot wrote in his *Encyclopedia*, published between 1751 and 1772, coffeehouses were "manufacturers of ideas—good as well as bad." While this may sound familiar to our modern incarnation of the coffee shop, theirs were quite different indeed. Coffeehouses were not only frequented but glorified. Songs were written about them, and journalists covered them like crime scenes. Johann Sebastian Bach wrote a secular cantata for coffee in 1723—a story about a girl suffering from coffee addiction who considers kicking the habit in exchange for marriage but rejects all suitors who forbid her to drink it. Coffeehouse politicians were born giving birth to political spin. Newspapers were founded with the sole purpose of covering coffee-house culture, among them the *Tattler* and the *Spectator* (an idea that perhaps Starbucks should consider). These journals frequently accepted articles and essays from coffeehouse dwellers which would subsequently be read aloud at coffeehouses once published. Once monarchs understood the social currency of coffeehouses, they began to change their opinions of them. After all, just as antimonar-chical ideas were promoted through coffeehouses, so too could promonarchical ideas. So they used them.

Coffeehouses had broad appeal for a number of reasons. First, at a penny a cup (hence the nickname "penny universities"), they were cheap. No one had to buy rounds as was the case at the ale house. Second, they were a place to get an education. And third, coffeehouses became the regular meeting places of secret societ-ies, among them, the Royal Society of London, the Lunar Society of Birmingham, the Dilettante Society, the Hell Fire Club, the Ugly Club, and the Wednesday Society. In the 1770s, the Club of Honest Whigs met on Thursday nights in London. Its member-ship included Benjamin Franklin, Joseph Priestley, Richard Price, and others. They discussed everything from the latest develop-ments in electrical theory to prospects for liberty in Corsica. The real value of the coffeehouse, unlike today, is that they not only brought people together but encouraged the exchange of ideas in a public forum.

A second institution that helped foster connections was the secret society. Societies were often formed to discuss political issues, such as censorship and legal reform, and aristocratic privi-leges. Members of societies also used the institution as a safe venue in which to try out their ideas. Clergy would test out their ser-mons, editors would present stories, and scientists would discuss their emerging theories. One such society, the Wednesday Society, which flourished in the 1890s, had an enviable membership: coedi-tors of the *Berlin Monthly*, the Prussian Justice Department (whose members were in the throes of rewriting the Prussian Legal Code), the physicians of Frederick the Great, the academic tutor of the crown prince, and members of the Berlin clergy. Societies were more than social gatherings of diverse people and operated under a rules structure. First, all members were denoted by numbers, not names, to focus the presentations on the subject matter rather than who was presenting. Second, no specialized topics could be presented, and all subjects presented had to be deemed of interest to "the welfare of mankind." Third, everyone spoke once before anyone spoke a second time. This allowed all ideas to be received in an open format before debate. (Recall how disparate information leads to novel connections. This was inherent in the rules structure of the society.)

In addition to the secret societies were the Free Masons. Although the Masonic movement was founded by seventeenth-century English stone masons, the guild opened its membership as well to artisans, aristocrats, and even women, a liberal idea at the time, as a way of funding services for the families of guild members (recall: necessity and invention).

Flash-forward a few hundred years, and there are whispers of enlightened societies, although they do not wield the influence that they once did. The closest thing we have to the society today is the university, although the role of the university is also changing in terms of where knowledge resides. For example, in 1970, if you were asked, "Who are the most knowledgeable people on the planet?" you would likely have identified people such as university professors, research scientists, and the occasional well-intentioned journalist. Today the most knowledgeable people on the planet have just recently learned to drive. They are the millennials, those born between 1982 and 1993. Over the next decade, 80 million retiring baby boomers will be replaced by 75 million millennials in the workforce. As Neil Howe and William Strauss suggest in their book *Millennials Rising,* "The Millennial Generation will entirely recast the image of youth from downbeat and alienated to upbeat and engaged—with potentially seismic consequences for America."

Unlike those born before humans adopted the same middle name (@), millennials have not suffered the hardship of having to read, remember, and recall information for book reports, bar mitzvahs, and best man speeches with the same rigor and difficulty of prior generations. To millennials, the world is a click away. Why memorize anything when you can Google everything? What millennials lack in wisdom, they make up for in knowledge. The only difference between knowledge circa 1970 and millennial knowledge is where it is stored: rather than keep it in their heads, millennial keep it at their fingertips. Why clutter the storage capacity of the mind when you've got a terabyte under your thumb? Here's why.

Recall how knowledge stored in long-term memory interacts with novel experiences and unrelated information in order to create the conditions for epiphany. Although our next-generation leaders may be able to navigate information more readily than previous generations, this begs the question: Will they be able to create with the same capacity? While walking across campus, I continue to be amazed at how they communicate. With MP3 player earbuds permanently affixed to their heads, their faces buried in the glow of their cell phones, and their thumbs pounding out text messages to friends they've never met off-line, they walk and talk. Millennials don't remember a time before computers, cell phones, or the Internet. Parallel processing and multitasking are not only capabilities of this generation; they are a way of life. What concerns me most about this newest generation of emerging leaders is their relationship with knowledge and the pursuit of it. My concern can be summarized by the response I received from one of my students who, in answering my question about his favorite new product, replied, "My favorite new product is Wikipedia [the online user-generated encyclopedia].""Why?" I asked. "Because," he answered, "you don't have to think anymore." The worst part of it was that the rest of the class laughed in hesitant agreement. Clearly he was not alone.

Today the most wired people are the most knowledgeable people. This, however, does not make them the most creative. In fact,

I would argue that they risk losing their creative capacity by not exercising their memory and attention skills. Yet with advances in technology, this generation also has a unique advantage in studying the way we think. There is renewed interest in thinking about thinking (with one subtle difference). Philosophers remain, but their titles have changed. We now call them cognitive neuroscientists. Fully armed (and sometimes dangerous) with advanced technology in the form of skin sensors, functional MRI machines, and EEGs, today's philosophers and psychologists are shedding new light on creativity. What is most promising is that their findings underscore the need to continue to pursue knowledge, exercise memory, and not give up on thinking just yet. In pursuit of creativity, continue to exercise your memory, attention, and perception skills even in an age where information is just a click away. Don't give up on thinking just yet. In the spirit of the issues explored in this chapter, read broadly, seek out relationships with people different from you, go to a trade show that you've never been to before and that you know nothing about, or take a class in a subject that you think is completely irrelevant to your work. Thinking outside the box is not that difficult if you live outside it.

This brings us to the role of the proverbial box (that is, convention) as it relates to inspired thought. As it turns out, the box may be more useful to creativity than some may lead you to believe. To this precursor to eureka we turn in the following chapter.

Summary Points and Creative Exercises

- Making unorthodox connections between disparate domains may be biologically demanding, but it is not impossible. Making connections, like breathing, occurs naturally, and again like breathing, it is something that you have control over.

- In order to learn to make unorthodox connections, keep the unsolved problem activated in your mind even while you are not deliberately attempting to solve it. As you encounter new experiences, try to make that information relevant to solving your problem.

- Increasing specialization (expertise) may improve productivity as an individual and as a group, but it may also hinder creativity. Spend time learning about things you know nothing about as much as you spend time learning more about what you already know.

- Just as you take a vacation, take time away to think. It appears to have worked for Bill Gates, who has an annual Think Week, and it may work for you. Create a list of unsolved problems, and then schedule a time and place to go in order to simply think. Take along books, magazines, articles, and other information sources that may provide inspiration for helping you think things through.

9

DIAMETRICALLY OPPOSED

Conventions

Abbott and Costello. Martin and Lewis. Beavis and Butthead. There is something implicitly funny about the juxtaposition of opposites. They make us laugh. This occurs because, when paired, opposites jar us into processing unrelated ideas as single concepts. The union of opposites, much like the relationship between the setup and punch line of a good joke, is therefore humorous. For example, consider "the world's funniest joke," based on a joke contest orchestrated by Richard Wiseman at the University of Hertfordshire:

> A couple of New Jersey hunters are out in the woods when one of them falls to the ground. He doesn't seem to be breathing; his eyes are rolled back in his head. The other guy whips out his cell phone and calls the emergency services. He gasps to the operator: "My friend is dead! What can I do?"

Up to this point, there is no humor to be found. In fact, this is anything *but* funny. However, consider what happens once we add the punch line:

> The operator, in a calm, soothing voice says: "Just take it easy. I can help. First, let's make sure he's dead." There is a silence; then a shot is heard. The guy's voice comes back on the line. He says: "Okay. Now what?"

This disassociation between setup and punch line causes laughter. Without it, there would be no humor. Rather deliberately, the setup is designed to send your mind in one direction, while the punch line is designed to send it in the opposite direction. When setup and punch line meet, humor is created.

Beyond the science of a good joke is a more revealing phenomenon: once you've heard the joke, it is no longer funny. Sure, it may be fun to share (if you can remember it), but to hear it again, the humor is lost. This happens because you've already made the connection, and you know what's coming. The setup and punch line are no longer two opposing ideas, but rather a cohesive whole. Once you get it, a rule is installed in your mind. Herein is the dark side of learning to create unorthodox connections, a previously discussed precursor to creative insight. Once you've made a new connection, you run the risk of becoming trapped by the law of the way things work. What was once open in your mind as an unanswered question has now been resolved—whether as the punch line to a joke or the appropriate solution to a problem—and therefore you are no longer as curious about the problem because you've "got the answer." This explains why we have a hard time imagining a world without cars, computers, or disposable diapers. These once crazy ideas are now commonplace. The unorthodox is now conventional. The impossible is now possible.

Over time as you learn new things—jokes, tasks, expertise in a job—your experiences create conventions, or beliefs, in your mind about the way things should work. The difficulty with conventions is that we are often not aware of the biases we carry around in our minds. For example, see if you can figure out the following riddle: "Last year a man in the United States married twenty different women. All of them are still living. He has not divorced any of them or has broken the law. How is this possible?" At first, you probably asked, "How can a man legally be married to twenty different women at the same time?" And therefore, your initial attempts to solve the problem may have led to answers such as *he was a fundamentalist Mormon* or some other rationale that would help you get around the idea that it is illegal to be married to more than one woman. However, here is where conventions, those deeply held beliefs, interfere with the ability to solve problems. The difficulty in finding the correct answer to this question is based on a person's beliefs about the word *married*. The word, in fact, has two meanings: "to get married" and "to perform the marriage ceremony." In this case, the answer to the question involves the second definition: the man is a minister.

Beliefs can help or hinder the creative process. As we'll explore in Chapter Ten on creative codes, heuristics, or rules of thumb, can help make creativity more logical and manageable, but if they are applied incorrectly, they can hinder creative insight. In keeping with the idea that once you learn something, it is hard to forget, if you were to hear the riddle again about the minister, you would invariably remember the correct answer just as you would see the punch line coming from a known joke. Your belief about what the answer should be can help solve the problem, but it also has the effect of eliminating spontaneity. Once you know the punch line, the humor is lost. The challenge with beliefs when we are attempting to solve a problem is that we hold them over all sorts of things: what new products should look like, how to eliminate poverty, and even whether you "look good in those jeans." Beliefs abound! Adding to the challenge of beliefs is that even though you may succeed at identifying and defining prevailing beliefs in one area (for example, knowing both definitions of the word *married*), this recognition does not necessarily transfer to the ability to other areas. In other words, just as we have beliefs about what the word *marry* means, so too do we have beliefs about the meaning of many other things: words, people, places, and so on.

In order to illustrate the complexity and pervasive nature of beliefs, try another riddle: "A father and his son are in an automobile and have an accident. The father is killed, and the son is rushed to the hospital. A surgeon is called in to perform an intricate operation. When the operation is successfully completed, the surgeon looks at the boy's face for the first time and says, 'Why that's my son!' How could that be?"

If you are having difficulty figuring out this riddle, it is not necessarily your "fault" per se; rather, it is the result of your life's experiences that form the foundation of your belief system. The challenge with beliefs is that they tend to strengthen over time based on these experiences. The answer to this riddle is that the surgeon is a woman and the boy's mother. The word *surgeon* is more strongly associated with male than female just as the word *married* in your mind was likely more strongly associated with "getting married." Moreover, the mention of father and son early in the setup of the riddle also activates the association with males. As a result, these powerful associations combine to bias you unconsciously toward the assumption that the surgeon is a male. Moreover, although you successfully challenged your beliefs about the word *married*, you may (or may not) have then been stumped by yet another word: *surgeon*. Now consider how bias can change depending on context and experience. In a more contemporary context, where it is not uncommon for children to have same-sex parents and where female surgeons and male nurses abound, the surgeon riddle is much easier to figure out. However, consider its context in the 1970s, when there were far fewer female surgeons. (In fact, in the United States, the number of female physicians increased tenfold between 1970 and 2001.)

Bias, informed by experience, culture, society, and memory, helps to explain why researchers and entrepreneurs are often more creative in their theories and experimentation early in their careers. Not only do they maintain some level of idealism in their thoughts, they are not yet set in their ways. Recall that Isaac Newton was only twenty-three years old when he conjured up universal gravitation, Albert Einstein was twenty-eight when he conducted his famous "thought experiment," and Bill Gates was only twenty-six when he licensed QDOS to IBM. Today's Internet, biotech, and hedge fund billionaires are really nothing new. Young people have always created the future, in part, due to their inexperience. Experience begets conventions, and although conventions beget success, they also hinder the next big idea. Furthermore, success is a double-edged sword. The irony of success is that once you've accomplished something, the exploration often ends. In this way, success can stymie creativity. After all, you know what works, so why try something new? Moreover, as we grow older or gain more experience within a given subject, conventions become more difficult to break. Although we cannot turn back the clock, we can turn back our beliefs and challenge convention. You may recall that earlier in the book, I suggested that you not throw out the box just yet. Now is the time to think about the box.

Conventions create artificial boundaries in our minds—the proverbial box. By learning to identify, challenge, twist, turn, and otherwise reconstruct this box, you can create the conditions to inspire creative thought. One way in which to challenge conventions is to learn how to think in opposites. The difficulty for many of us, particularly those of us who were born and raised in the West, is that thinking in opposites (unless you happen to be trained as an attorney) is not part of our culture. In fact, to a large degree we are taught to think in absolutes: black or white; Republican or Democrat; paper or plastic. Therefore, anything other than categorical thinking not only appears foreign to us but is often construed as hysterically funny.

Thinking in opposites is a precursor to creative insight insofar that aha moments often come about as the result of a disruptive shift in how we normally process information, thereby causing us to see problems or situations in a different form: back to front, upside down, inside out. In this way, the act of thinking in opposites is a highly desired cognitive skill when attempting to solve a problem or create a new idea.

The study of opposites is referred to as dialectics. The general idea is that by studying contradictions, we are better equipped to arrive at the most creative solution. The process of a dialectic is to state a thesis, develop a contradictory antithesis, and then combine and resolve the two in order to arrive at a coherent synthesis. For example, the following questions are designed in a dialectical debate: *Do people spend more money because they are unhappy? Or are people unhappy because they spend more money?* Those who agree with the first question—that people spend to fill a void—might suggest that these same people "get a hobby" in order to solve the perceived problem of emptiness. Those who agree with the second question—that people are unhappy because they are broke—might suggest "creating a budget" in order to solve the perceived problem of financial irresponsibility. Independently, the two solutions differ widely; more important, neither alone is really all that creative in solving the fundamental problem. The fact is that you're broke and unhappy. Here is where thinking in opposites can help to find a creative solution that is likely superior to those conceived by considering only a single perspective.

By examining both sides of the issue (thinking in opposites), you quickly arrive at a more holistic solution that fills both the emotional void (by "getting a hobby") and provides fiscal responsibility (by "creating a budget"). This notion of both-and versus either-or is the central premise of opposites thinking. It is also this type of thinking that helps to break down conventions. In this example, you likely had an opinion about the original question of the root cause of the person's problem. For most of us raised in the West, life is a series of trade-offs based on our beliefs: if you lower taxes, you must cut programs; if it's good for you, it must taste bad; and if it sounds too good to be true, it is. In the West, we don't encourage "middle thinking" (harmony); rather we promote "having an opinion" (pick a side). However, those who create the future are able to find ways to introduce ideas based on both-and thinking (for example, "Tastes great. Less filling") versus either-or thinking (you can be either a big fish in a small pond or a small fish in a big pond). There is a third way: there are very big fish living in very big ponds (many of whom are, or are related to, those who have previously challenged convention in their respective fields).

The concept of opposites thinking has been a topic of fierce debate for thousands of years. Over three thousand years ago, roughly around the time that Archimedes ran naked through the streets of Syracuse, the pre-Socratic Greek philosopher Heraclitus, whose ideas have influenced generations of thought leaders, including Socrates, Plato, Aristotle, Nietzsche, Heidegger, Whitehead, Kant, Jung, Engels, Marx, and even Chairman Mao Zedong, proposed the idea that all change comes about through contradictions. Heraclitus referred to the idea of opposites thinking as Becoming, in which opposites are interrelated. He wrote: "Opposition brings concord. Out of discord comes the fairest harmony," and, "By cosmic rule, as day yields night, so winter summer, war peace, plenty famine. All things change." Although both Plato and Aristotle were influenced by Heraclitus, his influence affected them only insofar that they disagreed with him. Plato believed that each thing had one definition, one purpose, a single existence. Aristotle went so far as to express his opposition in his "law of noncontradiction." Socrates, however, evolved Heraclitus's idea into his Socratic method of questioning (teaching) that you are likely familiar with from your school days. Outside Greece, not only were others "opposed to the idea of opposites" (itself rich in irony), they violently opposed it, among them, the medieval philosopher Avicenna who wrote, "Anyone who denies the law of non-contradiction should be beaten and burned until he admits that to be beaten is not the same as not to be beaten, and to be burned is not the same as not to be burned."

Although Heraclitus's thoughts were novel to the Western world, the notion of opposites has a long history in the East. In Asia, yin and yang date back three thousand years to the *I Ching* and to Taoist master Lao Tzu, who flourished twenty-five hundred years ago. Taoism contends that change is the only constant. According to Taoist philosophy, "Gradual change leads to a sudden change of form." The idea of opposites can also be found in the history of the Aztecs in Mexico, the Lakotas in North America, and the Dogon people of Mali in Africa. Although the theory of opposites remains relevant in the East, it is not part of the Western tradition. Blame Aristotle for the Western tradition of "either-or" versus "both-and."

Some argue that the demise of opposites thinking in the West may have come about when St. Thomas adopted Aristotle's doctrine, thereby making noncontradiction the central thesis of medieval religion. Others claim that because Western philosophy failed to recognize that progress comes through the conflict of opposing forces, we were not entirely prepared to grasp the unprecedented changes that came rushing in during the nineteenth century. However, this same argument has been made of Eastern philosophy. Eastern philosophy recognized change as a constant, but it viewed it as cyclical rather than an evolutionary process, and therefore the advances of the nineteenth century were as disruptive to those in the East. After all, the nineteenth century was not only an age of contradiction that forced an evolutionary change; it was a revolutionary time. The Industrial Revolution changed everything in a noncyclical disruptive lurch forward. It is worth noting that as the Industrial Revolution began, Western philosophers (among them, Kant and Hegel), like Wall Street analysts chasing headlines, resurrected the idea of dialectics as something worth "reconsidering." After all, how else could such a dramatic change come into being? We needed a sound philosophy to help explain it.

Dialectics is not wasted on philosophy alone. Wherever conventions exist, thinking in opposites is a relevant tool to help generate creative insight. This includes government, industry, organizations, and even individuals, including you and me. In the pursuit of creative insight, thinking in opposites provides the opportunity to break free from previously formed conventions (beliefs) about what works and what doesn't, what is possible and what isn't, and what is and what could be. In order to illustrate how conventions can blind us to possibility, consider how opposites thinking helped consumer electronics giant Sony break free of its beliefs about the products it sold.

In the 1970s, Sony temporarily abandoned a very important project, the development of the compact disk, because no one there could imagine putting eighteen hours of music on a single CD. Where did the eighteen-hour figure come from? A twelve-inch CD, of course—the same shape and diameter of the existing format: LP record albums. Philips, the Dutch electronics giant, had a different point of view based on its willingness to challenge prevailing conventions about recorded music. In the spirit of discussing worldwide audio standards, Philips sent a team to Japan to meet with Sony engineers. Unaware that Sony had already halted its work on the CD, Philips researchers shared its prototype of the CD with Sony. Philips's prototype was roughly the size of today's CDs: approximately five inches. Where did Philips get *its* sizing? Its researchers asked music conductor Herbert von Karajan what he thought would be the appropriate capacity. His response was, "If you can't get Beethoven's Ninth on one side, it is not long enough." Five inches would do just fine.

Sony, like many other would-be innovators in search of the next aha moment, had been trapped not by possibility but by the past, the single greatest competitor to the future. It was stuck not only in time but also in space. Its researchers were focused on the size of the product (the space to fill) and therefore couldn't see the concept of the product (the time desired). Therefore, Sony concluded, "How could you possibly price a CD with eighteen hours of music on it and actually expect consumers to buy it?" For Sony, the business case never added up, and therefore the project was brought to a screeching halt. It took nothing more than a glimpse of what could be (Philips's prototype built around time, not space), and suddenly Sony's program was reinvigorated. Sony got lucky: Philips had already thought differently about what the CD could be.

There is no reason that the Sony engineers could not have arrived at the same conclusion themselves. Had they challenged the prevailing conventions about LP records (convention about size: they must be twelve inches in diameter; convention about content: you must fill the entire space available with music; convention about space: they must have two sides), they may have arrived at the concept of the CD much more quickly. What this case also illustrates is how even the most fleeting thoughts or experiences can dramatically shift perception. For example, as soon as the Sony engineers saw the prototype and experienced a blinding glimpse of the obvious, their point of view about the commercial viability of the compact disk changed immediately. In that moment, they broke free of their beliefs and suddenly saw possibility.

In his 1962 book *The Structure of Scientific Revolutions*, philosopher and science historian Thomas Kuhn advanced the notion that science evolves in a nonlinear fashion and therefore all science textbooks that are written linearly are wrong. He contends that you cannot simply add to the knowledge that already exists, as if adding photos to a family album. At some point, new books need to be written.

While the human race has evolved, the greatest leaps in human progress tend to come directly after a disruptive shift occurs within a domain. For example, Galileo's seventeenth-century telescope and his observation of falling objects flew directly in the face of Aristotle's theories about the nature of heavenly bodies, just as Philips's conceptualization of the CD contradicted the conventional notion of space in favor of time. Galileo and Philips challenged convention.

Scientifically, the phenomenon that hinders creative thought is referred to as *functional fixedness*—a cognitive bias that limits a person's perception of an object's utility based on its traditional use. Functional fixedness is a common barrier to creativity leading to legendary quips such as that of the cofounder of Digital Equipment Corporation, Ken Olsen, who observed in 1977, "There is no reason for any individual to have a computer in his home." In fairness to Olsen, circa 1977, computers were half the size of most people's living rooms. Nonetheless, he was functionally fixated. The object of his fixation was the existing computer, a large system used by large organizations. Yet again, it is what Olsen could not see—alternative uses for the computer—that blinded him the most. In hindsight, his comment sounds ridiculous, even humorous. However, in reality, many of us fall into this thought trap on a daily basis. We just don't realize it until we break free of our fixation. All new ideas are guilty until proven innocent. As it turns out, the more experience a person has working within a field, for a company, or within an industry, the more likely that person is to become fixated on what solutions are available. In the field of creativity, functional fixedness is one of the primary barriers to the creation of novelty.

The concept of functional fixedness was first advanced by Gestalt psychologists, who emphasized holistic information processing: that the whole is separate from the sum of its parts. Maier's two-string problem is a widely used illustration of functional fixedness. In this problem, the subject is in a room with two strings tied to the ceiling, both strings of equal length. The objective is to tie the ends of the two strings together. The problem is that although the strings are long enough to be tied together, they are short enough that a person is unable to grasp one string, walk over to the other string, and tie the two together (Figure 9.1). Scattered around the room are a number of objects: a plate, some books, a chair, a pair of pliers, an extension cord, and a book of matches.

To resolve the problem, the real source of the problem must be located. The fundamental source of the problem can be viewed as one of the following: the string is too short, my arms are too short, the end of one string won't stay anchored in place while I get the other string, or the string won't come to me. Depending on what objects are located around the room, any one of these problem sources can be resolved by, for example, using an object such as the extension cord to lengthen one of the strings or using an object (such as a chair, for example) to lengthen one's arms and so on. If the only object in the room were a pair of pliers, then the solutions become much more limited, because this object cannot be used to resolve all of the possible problem sources (assuming the pliers are not large enough to extend the person's reach enough). About 60 percent of the participants in this study failed to find a solution within a ten-minute time limit because they saw the pliers only as the traditional tool they are, not recognizing that

Figure 9.1. The Two-String Problem

Source: From http://psy.ucsd.edu/~mckenzie/Problem%20Solving.pdf.

the pliers could be used as a pendulum bob, swinging at the end of one of the two strings, thus resolving the "string won't come to me" problem source.

   Most of us have difficulty in seeing the pair of pliers in the example as anything other than a tool, as that is what we have always been taught they are. Through force of habit, we are fixated by the fact that the object's function is that of a pair of pliers. If we can overcome this fixedness, then we can see that they have many other uses. The pair of pliers could be used as a weight (paper-weight, pendulum weight, weapon, fishing sinker), an electricity conductor (emergency fuse, car jump start kit), and so on. The reason that overcoming functional fixedness is so important is that because innovation consists of finding new uses for knowledge we already have, we need to try to get past the barrier that a particular bit of knowledge has only the use it was originally intended for.

There is one additional insight provided by the two-string problem. Recall the hint Philips provided to the Sony engineers; as soon as those engineers saw the prototype—the hint—they were immediately liberated from their fixation with twelve inches and eighteen hours. This phenomenon is also captured by the two-string problem. In this case, the experimenter created a hint by "apparently accidentally" brushing across one of the strings in order to set it into a swinging motion, which soon after clued in the participants to devise a way to get the string to swing. This small but relevant hint broke the convention that the pliers could be more than a tool. They could be used as a weight. Once this hint was provided, performance in solving the problem improved. In fact, after the hint was provided, only 23 percent of participants remained stymied in solving this riddle.

Like Sony's sudden realization that it needed to change its perspective and think in opposites, so too did Henry Ford conceive his big idea in an act of backward thinking. Recall Ford's conceptual transfer of the assembly line from the meatpacking industry to the automobile industry. The question is, How did he come up with the idea in the first place? What Ford did not see is what is most revealing about his epiphany: he did not see an assembly line for what it was—a line for assembling things. Rather he saw the line as a tool in the context of mass production. In fact, he didn't see "assembly" at all. While touring the meatpacking plants in Chicago, Ford saw a "disassembly" line. After all, meatpackers don't assemble livestock; they butcher it. As William Klann, head of Ford's engine department, recalled of the infamous visit to Swift's Chicago meatpacking plant, "If they can kill pigs and cows that way, we can build cars that way." Ford's big idea came by thinking in opposites. Aha! Rather than "cut things up" (livestock), he would put things together (automobiles). Ford thought backward.

It is worth noting that the notion of backward thinking may help to explain why many creative people are commonly diagnosed with learning disabilities. For example, among the world's most creative people diagnosed with dyslexia and other learning disabilities were Alexander Graham Bell, Richard Branson, Thomas Edison, Leonardo da Vinci, John Lennon, Charles Schwab, and Ted Turner. In the field of business, one could argue that those with dyslexia are afforded a creative advantage by being able to see the world in unorthodox ways, something many companies spend a lot of money attempting to master. Like many other icons, mavericks, and geniuses, Henry Ford was also dyslexic. It may be that Ford's dyslexia led to one of his most significant aha moments: the introduction of the assembly line in automobile manufacturing. Recall that Swift disassembled animals, and Ford assembled cars. How did Ford conjure up the idea to visit Swift's plant in the first place? Of note, Upton Sinclair's 1906 book, *The Jungle*, which vividly exposed Swift's bloody slaughterhouse experience in gruesome detail, was published just two years before the introduction of mass production at Ford and the subsequent introduction of the Model T in 1908. Who knew that Upton Sinclair's *meme* (a term coined by zoologist and evolutionary scientist Richard Dawkins in 1976 to describe "a unit of cultural information transferable from one mind to another") would find a home in the mind of Henry Ford?

Although we know that thinking in opposites is a frequent precursor to creative insight, why do some people have a predisposition to this way of thinking while others have a tendency to become fixated? Is it biological? Is it learned behavior? Or is it influenced by sociocultural experiences? The odds are that it is a combination of all three. Having advised organizations around the world on innovation, I believe that culture plays a significant role in a person's approach to creative tasks. For example, the differences between creativity in the East and creativity in the West can be observed and traced back to respective histories, philosophies, values, and even family structures. By way of example, consider the differences between how the Japanese and Westerners approach innovation.

Western creativity is based on individual freedom. Westerners, particularly Americans, admire those who live on the frontier, push the envelope, and take chances. Japanese creativity is based on harmony. The Japanese ideal is *ii ko* ("a good child"). Words often used to describe *ii ko* include *otonashii* ("mild"), *sunao* ("obedient"), *akarui* ("bright eyed"), *genki* ("spirited"), *hakihaki* ("prompt"), and *oriko* ("smart"). In China, a related concept is that of *xiao* ("filial piety"). Although *xiao* is taught to young children, it is intended to be exercised by the adult children of aging parents. *Xiao* emphasizes financial support, the production of offspring, and the preservation of the family name. In both Japan and China, it is best to be "a good child" than to "go West young man." In terms of objectives, Westerners prefer fuzzy targets that allow for personal freedom and BHAGs ("big hairy audacious goals"), while the Japanese prefer open-ended targets that promote conformity and avoid public embarrassment. This is largely based on Zen, in which the only goal is enlightenment. Solutions are decadent. In fact, the Western notion of eureka that refers to scientific discovery is echoed in Japan as *satori*, which means "personal enlightenment."

In the West, we seek to stand out from the crowd. Spontaneous creativity is encouraged. In Japan, the authors of unique ideas are frequently ignored, distrusted, and even mocked by their peers. Although intuition, based on Zen meditation, plays a central role in the creative process, running naked with inspiration is highly frowned on. In the West, the fastest way to a desired destination is in the form of a straight line. In Japan, it is a circle—always and forever in a perpetual ebb and flow between the past, the present, and the future. Perhaps the most telling difference between Western and Eastern creativity philosophies is the difference in worldview. In the West, things are measured as either right or wrong. There is often one best way to do just about anything. Westerners are an objective people. Japan is a polyocular society: all things can be seen from multiple perspectives. The Japanese believe in wholeness: more perspectives on a problem or an opportunity invariably lead to a better outcome. In fact, prior to Westernization, there was no word for *objectivity* in the Japanese language. The Japanese have since coined words to conceptualize Western ideology: the objective perspective is known as *kyakkanteki* ("the guest's point of view"), whereas the subjective perspective is known as *shukanteki* ("the host's point of view").

These differences in philosophy, virtues, and values not only have a dramatic effect on creativity; they have an effect on how we perceive the world around us. Intrigued by these differences, University of Michigan psychologist Richard Nisbett organized an international team to study the cognitive differences between Easterners and Westerners. In one of their experiments, Nisbett asked Japanese participants at Kyoto University and American participants at the University of Michigan to view an animated underwater scene (Figure 9.2). After viewing, participants were then asked to recall what they saw. The American subjects focused on the biggest, brightest fish; the Japanese subjects made 70 percent more comments about the scene's background: the plant life, rocks, the snail, the frog, air bubbles, and so on (see Figures 9.3 and 9.4).

Figure 9.2. Animated Underwater Scene Shown to American and Japanese Subjects

Source: Richard Nisbett, *The Geography of Thought: How Asians and Westerners Think Differently ... and Why* (New York: Free Press, 2003).

Figure 9.3. Japanese Subjects' Recall of the Original Background, No Background, and a Novel Background

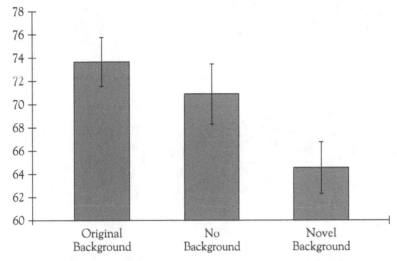

Source: Nisbett, *The Geography of Thought.*

Figure 9.4. American Subjects' Recall of the Original Background, No Background, and a Novel Background

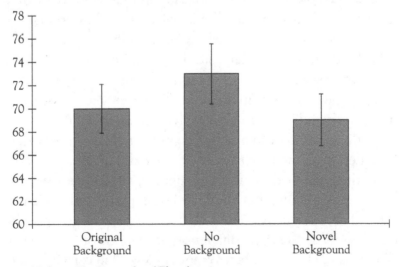

Source: Nisbett, *The Geography of Thought.*

Figure 9.5. Which Two of These Go Together?

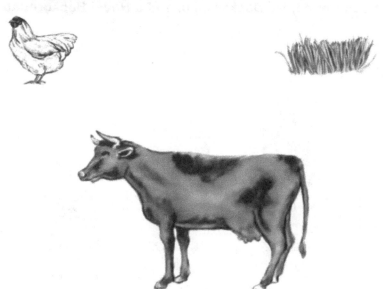

Source: Nisbett, *The Geography of Thought.*

In yet another experiment, participants were shown a picture of a cow (Figure 9.5) and asked to pair it with either a chicken or a patch of grass. (You may wish to try this yourself. What would you pair with the cow?) The researchers found that Westerners linked the cow to the chicken (classifiable objects) and Easterners paired cow with the patch of grass (field-oriented relationship).

Nisbett's findings underscore the nature of Eastern thought: viewing objects within a context versus fixating on a single object or thinking categorically as in the West. This is very much in keeping with Eastern and Western philosophy, values, and culture. In the East, individuals exist in a web of complex relationships, whereas Westerners focus more on the idea of self and individual objectives.

As these and other findings suggest, while the world may be flat economically, it is anything but flat culturally. We think differently based largely on how we live, what we value, and whom we admire. Whether these differences are genetic or learned is still up for debate. Here is Nisbett's point of view: "I'm certainly not an essentialist in that I think that these differences are genetic . . . and I'm not an essentialist in that I think these things aren't changeable. We don't know at what point these differences become ingrained, and we don't know how fixed they are in being ingrained." Although Nisbett's findings may spark controversy in some circles, as he puts it, "Universalism is a kind of religion. It wasn't just that I had a deep intellectual conviction; it was really a religion for me that we were all the same. It was very important. But if we are really different, we ought to know that. Otherwise, we can attribute difference to the other person being a jerk, or to them belonging to a group that's inferior in some way."

So, the question is: Who is right when it comes to creativity? Is it better to think like a Westerner or an Easterner? Here is where the puzzle gets a bit more complicated. Looking at cognitive process alone is insufficient outside of social context. For example, I would argue that Eastern cognitive biases provide the natural framework for creativity since they tend to consider information in a field-oriented fashion (that is, within a context), whereas Western cognitive biases tend to fixate on categorical thinking, which can limit unorthodox connections and reinforce conventions or beliefs that may limit creativity. Yet what Westerners lack in field orientation, they more than make up for in enthusiasm, passion, and entrepreneurial zeal to make ideas happen. And what Easterners lack in the social acceptance of novelty, they make up for in their willingness to consider multiple perspectives. Western idealism with Eastern holism is the ideal combination for creative inspiration and creative production: the translation of ideas into tangible products, services, and so on.

In the pursuit of the great idea, it seems that the greatest obstacle to creativity and insight depends largely on your point of view and beliefs about what is possible. In order to remedy these obstacles to innovation, it is important to get the diagnosis right. Given the Western predisposition to think categorically, Westerners must work to break free of conventional and myopic definitions of what things do and why they exist (for example, a hammer can do more than drive a nail). In a business context, this might include things such as questioning who your competitors really are (the obvious set or unconventional substitutes, for example, Quicken accounting software's belief that its competitors are not only accountants but the personal check register and a pencil), what products you really sell (versus what people are really buying when they buy your products, for example, does Disney really sell pricey tickets to a glorified amusement park, or is it selling a rite of passage?), and what industries you believe you compete in (versus how you define the industry, for example, McDonald's refers to itself as a "quick service restaurant" while consumers call it "fast food").

The divergence between self-belief and what others believe can hinder creativity insofar that we perceive ourselves as offering something other than what people are buying. In these ways, Westerners tend to define things too narrowly or group them incorrectly. Westerners also tend to ignore the unobvious competitors that may not seem to be in the same category but truly are. Therefore, Westerners need to challenge convention by exploring the opposite point of view. Easterners, who are naturally predisposed to consider opposites, must work to build the social networks and political and personal equity in order to nurture the confidence to share their unique points of view—to stand out from the crowd. Contrary to some claims that Easterners are not creative, the fact is that they are not outwardly creative. They need only a bit more provocation or the opportunity to introduce something unique without being laughed out of the room. Saving face is paramount, although this belief is itself being challenged in some parts of the Eastern world.

In Japan, *soozoo* ("creativity") has become the new national mantra. The Japanese are learning to manage this tension between novelty and face-saving through what are called creativity circles: five-person teams that are often deployed in product development settings to come up with the next big idea. The challenge, however, is that Japan does not have a tradition of innovation. You are likely familiar with Japanese brands such as Sony; however, the country as a whole historically derived its ideas from China, Korea, and India, and in the past hundred years, its ideas have come from the United States and Europe. Much like the Italians' nineteenth-century reverence for the art of the knock-off, so too do the Japanese have a long history of admiration for imitation. Creativity circles are intended to help change this way of thinking. Recognizing that they cannot continue to copy that which is created elsewhere in the world—largely due to the reduction in trade barriers; increases in tourism and travel outside the country; access to products widely available through unorthodox channels (online), and so on—creativity circles meet not to discuss how to knock off existing ideas; rather, they meet to discuss problems with existing products as well as to brainstorm new ideas. In order to manage the cultural conflict with creativity, Japanese business leaders are fostering confidence among their teams to bring new ideas forward by borrowing a page from the American playbook: they've appointed team leaders. These leaders are typically noted scientists who are given control over their own budgets and the autonomy to recruit their own teams. And so, the question is: Who is more creative: Eastern or Western thinkers? The answer: neither.

Both Easterners and Westerners maintain the capacity to create. The difference is that while Westerners may be more willing to publicly challenge prevailing conventions in the pursuit of novelty, Easterners will find a way to disrupt the apple cart and create new wealth while saving face at the same time. What Westerners have in spades—the willingness to take a measured risk—Easterners more than compensate for by being the best in the world at perfecting new ideas. In the pursuit of innovation, both are needed to succeed.

Given these insights into how Easterners and Westerns think differently, think back to that historic meeting between Philips and Sony and the story of the compact disk. Imagine how differently they must have perceived the world prior to changing it. Perhaps now it may be clearer why new entrants often have a much easier go at challenging convention in the pursuit of novel ideas. They are not beholden to the past or fixated on the present. They are simply looking for a better way to solve a problem.

Flash-forward a few decades from that meeting between Philips and Sony, and notice that it took a computer manufacturer named after a piece of fruit (not a consumer electronics company) to once again challenge convention and create the next generation of music. But if history is any guide, Apple will not be the company to create the next frontier in the music industry. The future always favors the outsider. I wouldn't be surprised if the next disruptive shift in music comes from someone as divergent as a magazine publisher or a telecommunications company. After all, who understands subscription services of information, media, and entertainment and their respective business models better than these folks? Of course, this opinion stands on the supersized assumption that these respective groups are in touch with their latent capabilities as much as the products they sell—no doubt, a big assumption and, in fact, a convention.

As history continues to teach us, the single greatest competitor to creating a desired future is a comfortable past insofar that the past, both success and failure, begets conventions or beliefs about what works and what doesn't, what is valued and what isn't, and what is sacred and what should be challenged. Whether that past was informed by cultural upbringing or prior success really doesn't matter. The point is that the greatest barrier to creating the future is in recognizing when, why, and how conventions can help or hinder creative insight. As you approach the leveling-off point of the learning curve, you must continue to challenge that which is familiar, comfortable, and commonplace. In fact, turn everything you know to be true upside down, shake it vigorously, and whatever comes out, bet on it. A client of mine, a successfully serial entrepreneur, once suggested, "Trends are misleading. The big ideas are always in the countertrend."

Having considered the four commonly occurring precursors to eureka—curiosity, constraints, connections, and conventions—this brings us to the ultimate prize of *The Riddle:* the creative code. By bringing together these disparate precursors into a manageable framework, the creative code is a method by which you can learn to manage the chaos of creativity in a deliberate and organized fashion.

Summary Points and Creative Exercises

- Conventions are commonly held beliefs about the way things work. Seek to challenge them in order to inspire new ideas.

- Dialectics is the study of opposites. Aha moments often come about by considering the problem in reverse.

- Heuristics, or rules of thumb, are loaded with assumptions that may have historic relevance but can hinder innovation. In order to challenge convention, write down the generally accepted rules of thumb relevant to your problem. Then seek to challenge each of these by thinking of the opposite of each.

- Creativity is influenced by the cultural context in which each of us was raised. Those from the East tend to be field oriented: they consider a broad array of information when solving problems. Those from the West tend to be goal oriented: focused on specific targets and ways in which to solve specific problems. Where Easterners are challenged to take calculated risks (what many Westerners do naturally), Westerners are challenged to think more broadly (what many Easterners do naturally). Neither way of thinking is superior. Both are required for successful innovation.

10

SUDDENLY BRILLIANT

Codes

What do grandmaster chess players, the 1960s sitcom *Gilligan's Island*, serial entrepreneur Stelios Haji-Ioannou, and improvisational theater share in common? Codes. Creativity codes are frameworks on which innovators generate new ideas (mostly, ideas that work). As you've come to appreciate by now, creative insight is not necessarily the result of random events. Based on experience identifying constraints, making unorthodox connections, and challenging prevailing conventions, innovators ultimately develop over time an almost automatic ability to generate new ideas by using a set of creative frameworks for interpreting the world around them. They use codes.

Creative codes arise as the result of years of experience working, successfully and unsuccessfully, within a given field. These codes are the stuff on which intuition, or gut instinct, is created. You've likely experienced your own creative code at work. Think about it this way. Have you ever had an idea that just felt right? You didn't necessarily know why it was a good idea or the right solution to the problem, but you knew that it would work. You likely felt that way because the idea fit your creative code. It fit the framework that you have used many times in the past, either consciously or unconsciously, to solve a problem. Therefore, the new idea, as crazy as it may seem, makes sense to you. It's as if you have seen it before.

Once you are aware of something, it seems to pop up all over the place. For example, my wife and I recently purchased a new Honda minivan, and suddenly it appeared that minivans were everywhere. Why does this occur? *Convergence of the relevant.*

Minivans are now relevant in our lives, and therefore we notice them. This phenomenon is related to heuristics in decision making. General rules of thumb come into being through experience making good, and sometimes bad, decisions.

Creative codes work much the same way. They come into being through an awareness of what works to inspire you and also through an empathetic interest in what is most relevant to your intended audience (child, customer, fan, player, student). In fact, you are likely operating from a creative code at this very moment—one that you've developed over years of experience. It is important, however, to recognize the difference between fixation and a creative code. Although both are the products of experience, creative codes are agnostic to objects. In other words, they are not necessarily fixated on any particular thing or its utility, for example, that hammers are made to hit nails into wood; rather, creative codes are focused on capabilities, for example, what a hammer allows you to do. We'll address this difference in more detail in this chapter, but in the interim, know that experience can affect creativity in two ways: (1) it can lead to fixation (an obstacle to creativity), and (2) it can help foster the development of a creative code (a framework for managing creativity). In both cases, experience is involved.

Some creativity literature refers to the "ten-year rule." It is based on the suggestion that in order to master a skill and ultimately make a creative contribution to a given field (a masterpiece), one must have experience in that field for a minimum of ten years. This includes everything from playing the cello to hitting a golf ball to mastering music composition. Although this may certainly be true in terms of mastering a skill, the logic doesn't quite hold up in the context of conceptual creativity. There are countless cases of new entrants to a category or industry that entirely change the rules of the game or make the discovery of a lifetime, often with little or no experience in the field.

Consider the case of Roger Bacon. While scientists scoffed at his suggestion that refraction defects of the eye could be corrected, the thirteenth-century English Franciscan monk ignored them and ultimately invented eyeglasses. Remember Trevor Baylis, the underwater stunt man who invented the clockwork radio. And perhaps the most stunning testament to the creative contributions of new entrants is the fact that the preeminent work in biology, *On the Origin of Species by Means of Natural Selection*, was written not by a biologist but rather by the exact opposite: Charles Darwin was an ordained minister. Most stunning in Darwin's case is the fact that his scientific observations aboard the *Beagle* and in the Galápagos largely contradicted his own religious beliefs about creation. Not only was Darwin a new entrant in the field of biology, although one who eventually committed his life to it, one could argue that for some period of time, he was a likely opponent to the mere suggestion of an alternate view to creationism. The evidence must have been compelling. It is important to note, however, that while Darwin spent years thinking about his evidence before arriving at his big idea, the codiscoverer of natural selection, Alfred Wallace, is said to have arrived at his idea on the subject while bedridden with malaria. However, it is important to examine Wallace's bedridden epiphany a bit more closely. Wallace, like Darwin, had a background studying variations in nature, specifically, the wildlife of South America and Asia, and he supplied birds to Darwin for his studies. Perhaps the most significant advantage Wallace had was the time he spent in bed not thinking (thinking on an unconscious level) about the implications of his research. Wallace eventually sought Darwin's assistance in publishing his own ideas when, in 1858, he sent Darwin his theory that virtually mimicked the ideas Darwin had developed over several years.

Although the theory of the ten-year rule is certainly relevant to skill mastery or even scientific discovery, it is an entirely different thing to create a novel and relevant solution to an existing problem. Simply, there is a difference between skill and imagination. For example, learning to master the game of chess (a skill) and creating a successful new product (applied imagination) both involve creative inspiration; however, they are the products of different ways of thinking. For example, while mastering a skill such as playing chess often involves intense memorization, creating something new, such as imagining a new product, often involves intense forgetting about the rules of the game, about how things are typically done, and about what people say they need versus what they really want. Nevertheless, although skill mastery and imagination are different, both reveal insights into epiphany. In order to illustrate the difference between the two, let's consider examples of each, beginning with skill mastery (playing chess) and then moving on to the creation of a new product (producing new TV shows).

Psychologists have a longstanding relationship with chess because it provides a unique environment, devoid of luck, in which to study problem solving. The first known studies of the game were conducted by Alfred Binet in 1894. Binet, who is best known for his intelligence tests, studied blindfolded chess players in order to investigate memory processes. To the average person, playing chess blindfolded is virtually impossible; however, even while blindfolded, many masters can win consecutive games with relative ease. Reuben Fine, a distinguished master chess player during the 1930s and author of *The Psychology of the Chess Player*, claimed that any master should be able to play at least a single game blindfolded. The question is, What do masters do differently than amateurs? Although attempts have been made at correlating all sorts of factors to chess mastery, including physiological differences, the evidence suggests only a single factor: chess masters know more than amateurs do.

Based on their experience playing the game and studying the games of historically famous matches, the average grandmaster can recall between 50,000 and 100,000 patterns and moves. Although this may sound like an impossible amount of information, the average adult can recognize over 20,000 words in his or her native language. In his 1894 experiment, Binet concluded that blindfolded grandmasters won based on knowledge and experience, imagination, and memory. However, by surveying players regarding their blindfolded play, Binet's original hypothesis, that chess requires strong visual memory, was wrong. Although the blindfolded masters did respond that they had a general abstract view of the board in their mind during play, they did not rely on visual memory as much as they relied on verbal memory. In fact, one master player, Goetz, was able to recall all 336 moves he made while playing ten blindfolded games simultaneously.

Following Binet, Dutch psychologist Adriaan de Groot, himself a master, explored the minds of chess players in his 1965 book, *Thought and Choice in Chess*. Regarded as the first psychological exploration into the minds of chess players, De Groot studied players of differing abilities, from world champions to experts to class (lower-ranked) players. In one study, he exposed players to a board that illustrated a position from a game. In the study, players were allowed to look at the board for only three to four seconds before it was taken from sight. When asked to reconstruct what they had seen, De Groot discovered that top players (grandmasters and masters) were able to recall 93 percent of the pieces, experts 72 percent, and class players 51 percent. De Groot concluded that top players were able to recall more pieces not due to perceptual abilities (reconstructing what they had seen—visual memory) but due to their experience (reconstructing what they knew to be legal positions: those allowed under the rules governing the game). They had developed a code, that is, a framework, of tens of thousands of positions that they had played themselves or had seen in previous matches between other players and in books.

This finding was confirmed by a 1973 study in which players were shown legal positions as well as random positions and asked to recall them in much the same format as De Groot's study. In all legal positions, recall performance was directly related to the player's chess rating. The higher a player's rating was, the higher his or her recall of the board and vice versa. However, when shown random positions, that is, not legal chess positions, all players, from grandmasters to class players, did approximately the same, further dispelling the belief that grandmasters have more advanced visual memories. The researchers concluded that high-ranked players employed an encoding system whereby they were chunking positions together for future recall. As De Groot discovered, masters were not recalling visual relationships; they were recalling functional relationships, an idea that is often confused in the field of human performance where so much emphasis is placed on "seeing your objective." Rather than seeing individual chess pieces and their respective positions, advanced players see relationships between pieces and positions; that is, they see concepts. For example, as Mark Jeays suggests in "A Brief Survey of Psychological Studies of Chess," "Where a bishop was pinning a knight to its queen would be remembered in terms of the pin *relationship*, rather than by recalling the bishop to be at g5, the knight at f6, and the queen at d8." As Jeays points out, "Even a mediocre player would be able to encode the six pieces comprising a castled king and rook, fianchettoed bishop, and three surrounding pawns as a set, while a beginner would be forced to remember these separately." Because of the challenge of remembering each of these positions separately, most amateur chess players are unable to see beyond the next five moves in a game. This encoding conducted by high-ranked chess players is the result of experience playing the game. Their creative capacity, in this case, their skill, is mostly enhanced by one thing: their knowledge of previous games. Thus, we have the ten-year rule.

Although much of the psychology literature on creativity contends that one must spend at least ten years studying within a given field before achieving mastery over the domain, I believe it is possible to generate new creative codes without spending a decade to formulate them. These codes are not intended to master a subject or skill; they are intended to create something new—to exploit the imagination—based on a logical framework. In order to create these codes, it is important to recognize the difference between skill mastery and novelty creation. If you are solely seeking to solve a problem that has a known solution using your skill of the game (for example, by conjuring up an appropriate chess position to counter an opponent's move), category, or industry, then experience and memory will always win. Thus, computers now dominate the game. This is much like the imitation-ideal of the Italian Renaissance: creative genius is measured by the ability to replicate the masters. However, if you are seeking to be inspired to create a new idea, you need to create an alternate code based not only on memory and experience but also on imagination. Like grandmaster chess players' use of memory in problem solving, other everyday geniuses deploy creative codes in the context of idea creation. In order to illustrate how creativity codes work in the context of idea creation versus skill mastery, let's consider a few individuals who have used these codes to amass great wealth, beginning with a man who became the world's most prolific television producer: Aaron Spelling.

I know what you're thinking. *Aaron Spelling? Wasn't he that guy who produced all that bubble-gum pop television in the 1980s?* That's the guy. He was a creative genius. Aaron Spelling nearly single-handedly created 1970s pop culture (and the 1980s and a large part of the 1990s). Seasoned couch potatoes would likely agree that Spelling was the most prolific television producer in the history of the medium. He produced over 50 television series, 10 theatrical films, and 150 made-for-TV movies, making him *The Guinness Book of World Records*' most prolific producer of television drama. According to the *Guinness* calculations, Spelling had produced 3,842 hours of television as of 1999, enough to fill three and a half years of prime-time television seven nights a week without a single rerun. In addition, he wrote over one hundred scripts and was awarded two Emmys. He managed to bag two Lifetime Achievement Awards: one from the People's Choice Awards and the other from the National Association of Television Program Executives. In addition, in his lifetime, the National Association for the Advancement of Colored People bestowed five awards on him.

Among the shows that Spelling produced are *The Mod Squad, The Rookies, Burke's Law, The Love Boat, Fantasy Island, Starsky and Hutch, The Boy in the Plastic Bubble, Hotel, Charlie's Angels, Hart* to *Hart*, *Charmed*, *Twin Peaks*, *Dynasty*, *The Colbys*, *T.J. Hooker*, *Beverly Hills 90210*, *Melrose Place*, and the HBO miniseries *And the Band Played On*. Love him or loathe him, at one point, Spelling's creations represented six of the top ten shows on ABC, causing critics to rebrand the network "Aaron's Broadcasting Company." According to dictionary.com's first entry under *producer*, a producer is "a person who produces." Spelling certainly lived up to his title in a sea of production mediocrity. For Spelling, television was an outlet for his creativity and, to some degree, his insecurity.

From an early age, Spelling was driven by a lack of confidence, a reticence that he managed through writing. As he puts it, "I was a frail and sickly child . . . a poor Jewish kid growing up in Texas." He was bullied. However, he wouldn't *be* bullied. As Spelling puts it, "I had a new weapon to use to combat the bullies, storytelling. Whenever they would try to pick a fight I would just tell them a story and not finish it. I'd tell them I'd finish it the next day and they let me go home. I'd run like hell before they changed their minds." *To be continued* was not lost on Spelling's childhood. Although Spelling was prolific in his creativity, he was not necessarily unique. In fact, to some degree, he was largely predictable. However, his predictability was like that of the guest rooms at the Ritz-Carlton: a desired predictability. And that is what made him great. When he was behind the camera, audiences knew what they were getting, and they and Hollywood studios couldn't get enough of it. Television viewers wanted to escape, and they knew that Spelling would help them get to their desired destination. He was intuitively aligned with what his viewers wanted. How did he know what they wanted?

One of the benefits of living in one of the largest homes in southern California is that tour buses have the house on their permanent itineraries. And so when rubbernecking tourists would descend from the many coaches parked in front of Spelling's sprawling Holmby Hills mansion, he would walk out and talk with them rather than hiding behind the gates. Mostly he listened. What is most revealing about Spelling's "mobile focus groups" is the question that he chose to ask: "Why do you watch television?" As Spelling advised aspiring writers under his tutelage, "Pick several shows, and study them. Learn why they're a success or why they're a failure. And then go on to develop characters." The invariable answer Spelling heard from his mobile focus groups about why they watch TV was "to escape." As Spelling recalled, "I can't tell you how many good ideas I've stolen from those tour buses. You see, you can't get a gauge on what the American public likes by listening to the Beverly Hills and Bel Air crowd. They won't admit to watching *Melrose Place*. If you listen to them, the only show they watch is *60 Minutes*." Spelling knew better.

Aaron Spelling is a classic case of a conceptual thinker. He had the ability to connect existing problems with relevant solutions for a specific audience. His conceptual capabilities were not random but were designed on a simple code, a formula that we'll explore in a moment and one that you'll likely recognize. He learned this code through years of experience working as a struggling actor and eventually as a successful writer, director, and producer. His code rarely let him down. In fact, it made him outrageously wealthy, although even in the lap of luxury, he never let go of his childhood insecurity. In a way, his insecurity played an instrumental role in his motivation to "get creative" throughout his entire life.

In 1943, on his eighteenth birthday, Spelling joined the U.S. Air Force, which he served as a field correspondent—a writer. While working in Germany, he was shot in his left hand and knee. The military surgeons wanted to amputate his fingers, but he told them he was a pianist (yet another "story"), so they sewed him up. Upon returning to the United States, he enrolled at Southern Methodist University on the GI Bill and after graduating eventually made his way to Hollywood, where his insecurity followed him. In 1955, as a young writer, he was so afraid that he would lose his best ideas that he used to store them in his refrigerator when he left his apartment in fear of a potential fire.

Spelling originally attributed his creative capacity to pipe smoking: "Whenever I looked at pictures of writers in Hollywood,"

Spelling recalls, "they were always smoking a pipe. So, I started pipe smoking when I moved here. I figured it would help make you a better writer. I also learned that smoking a pipe is the greatest crutch a writer has in the world. The producer asks you a story question and you take your time, load your pipe, and light it. By the time you've finished, you've thought of an answer for him." On the need for a continuous stream of creative inspiration, he said, "As often happens, eventually the material runs out and original work is commissioned." Eventually all new ideas grow long in the tooth. Novel ideas for products, services, and businesses that were once successful are shamelessly imitated, forcing all those who created them to go back to the proverbial drawing board. Great ideas are never lonely. However, for Spelling, going back to the drawing board was a welcome task. In fact, the blank slate created Spelling's first big break in Hollywood.

Alan Ladd, the most famous Hollywood actor at the time, had caught wind of Spelling's promising talent and asked Spelling to read a script and give him notes on it. Ladd didn't like the script, and Spelling had no idea how to give notes to Ladd, America's number one box office attraction. And so rather than give notes on the script, the young Spelling went home, threw the script away, and rewrote the entire thing. On reading the rewrite, Ladd called the network back and said, "I'm going to do it, and my producer's name is Aaron Spelling." From that moment forward, Spelling adhered to a set of principles, a code that inspired his future creative works. Spelling reflected about his work on the *Dick Powell Show*: "Before we started production, I got this great idea about having cameos by famous guest stars to round out the show. It was the first show to use multiple guest stars. Much later we did it again on the *Love Boat, Fantasy Island*, and *Hotel*. Viewers love seeing their favorite stars pop in and out of the show." This became an integral component of Spelling's creative code.

Just as people can have codes, so too can products. If products defy their underlying code, they won't work. For example, as Spelling once commented on the genre of westerns, "You can't make fun of a Western. Western fans just won't stand for it." It goes against the code of a western. Therefore, Spelling steered clear from attempting to do so. Of note, a creative code need not be shared by everyone. For example, Spelling's code, which, among other things, excluded making fun of westerns, was in fact the very thing that led to one of Mel Brooks's biggest hits, *Blazing Saddles,* in which Brooks pokes fun at the genre. Like Spelling, Brooks operated under an equally successfully, yet entirely different, creative code.

Like Brooks's introduction of humor into subjects where humor was not often present (westerns, quasi-historical documentaries, and so on), Spelling's code—three stories and the appearance of multiple guest stars—became his calling card. Although it was more than his signature, it was a model that he knew, through years of experience, worked. And although this code worked for Spelling, one of Spelling's heroes, another prolific writer, operated under an entirely different code. Rod Serling was the legendary producer of the most successful television anthology in history, *The Twilight Zone.* Intrigued by the notion of continuous creativity (the ability to generate ideas not as an event, but as an ongoing process), Spelling himself once asked Serling, "How can you write so many scripts for the *Twilight Zone?*" "Simple," Serling responded, "I don't need a third act to explain anything. All I have to do is say, 'And that's the way it was in the Twilight Zone,' and I'm home free."

Sterling, like Spelling, understood the power of maintaining a creative code. It is important to note here that it is not necessary that a creative code be shared by others or even be known to others in order for it to be useful in sparking creative insight. It must be relevant only to you and your intended audience; otherwise, all that you end up with is art—unique objects admired for their beauty but not necessarily relevant. Although this is certainly not a bad by-product of maintaining a creative code, in some applications, such as business, relevance to an intended audience is required. Moreover, creative codes do not necessarily have to be entirely unique, but they must work in the context in which you use them or be unique to the time in which they are used.

Spelling's code was partially derived from memories of his youth, specifically his love of anthologies of stories by O. Henry, the pen name for American writer William Sydney Porter (1862–1910). Porter's surprise twist endings—his code—caused audiences to reconsider the entire plot due to some last-minute introduction of information. In fact, Porter's code became so famous in Hollywood that they became branded "O. Henry endings." Since Porter's invention, endless Hollywood directors have adopted his code. Most famous among those who have used the O. Henry ending was Alfred Hitchcock in his direction of Robert Bloch's pulp thriller, *Psycho* (1959). Right up until the end of the film, the audience is deliberately sent down a path whereby they believe that Bates and his overbearing mother coexist in a perpetual state of fits, fights, and squabbles. It is not until the final scene, where Hitchcock allows the audience to see Anthony Perkins's character, Norman Bates, dressed as Bates's mother in a multiple-personality, freaky, psychotic sort of existence that truth is revealed to the viewer. At that very moment, viewers suddenly, and screamingly, experience severe psychological whiplash as they move from just starting to begin to think, "That was a good scary movie," to "Oh, my God! Bates *is* his mother! Hitchcock is a genius—creepy, twisted, and evil—but nonetheless, a genius!" That *everything I thought I knew I no longer know* feeling was the essence of Porter's code. The intention of the O. Henry ending is to turn all assumptions upside down and rethink the entire storyline based on this small yet disruptive introduction of withheld information. Porter's code worked beautifully in *Psycho,* just as it worked in M. Night Shyamalan's *Sixth Sense* when the audience suddenly realizes that Bruce Willis's character is a ghost, not a living human being.

Spelling was inspired by Porter's anthologies (his code) and his clever twists and turns. However, he did not simply copy Porter's technique; he adapted it for his viewers and expanded on it using three stories and guest stars to round it out. Early in his career, Spelling recognized and admired the simplicity and flexibility that this creative tool (code) provided the creator. Creative codes provide the structure on which to generate and manage ideas—to give ideas shape and form, make ideas work, and, mostly, inspire new ideas. After all, when one walks around life with a framework with which to interpret the world, opportunities become that much more obvious.

You may be wondering, Doesn't the idea of a code contradict the notion of challenging convention? Not necessarily. Creative codes are frameworks, that is, ways of structuring information, that free the mind to fill in possibly creative details. Coming up with the framework is often the big creative moment that allows smaller creative moments to occur. Just as the best money managers maintain parameters on when to invest and, more important, in what to invest, when you know what to look for by maintaining a code, aha moments become more commonplace. Once you've discovered a code that works, aha moments are not as emotionally charged simply because opportunities become more obvious to you. Such was the case of Spelling's greatest achievement: a story about three women—Sabrina Duncan, played by Kate Jackson; Jill Munroe, played by Farrah Fawcett-Majors; and Kelly Garrett, played by Jaclyn Smith—and their boss, Charlie, played by John Forsythe.

The show always began with the same dialogue: "Once upon a time there were three beautiful girls who went to the police academy, and they were each assigned very hazardous duties. But I took them away from all that and now they work for me. My name is Charlie." In its original manifestation, *Charlie's Angels* was a cop show unlike any other: women carried the show. This was unheard of in Hollywood when it began. When Spelling arrived in Hollywood, the rule of thumb was that no actress could carry an hour-long show. She could lead in a sitcom, but executives were convinced that viewers would not buy into a drama unless it had male leads. (One wonders what fed ABC's belief about male leads considering that at the time, in the 1960s, ABC's ratings were hemorrhaging in its pursuit of CBS and NBC, causing comedian Milton Berle to quip, "Put the Vietnam War on ABC. It'll be over in thirteen weeks.")

So where did the idea for *Charlie's Angels* come from? As Spelling recalls, "Len Goldberg and I were brainstorming in our office one day—looking for something new for Kate Jackson—since *The Rookies* was coming to an end and we didn't want to lose her. We thought, *Why not do something outrageous—a cop show with women—only women.* We came up with something we called facetiously the *Alley Cats*—about three karate-chopping, leather-attired, female detectives named Alley, Lee, and Catherine and pitched it to ABC's Barry Diller and Michael Eisner. "That's the worst idea I've ever heard," said Michael, and Barry added, "You guys should be ashamed of yourselves." Anyway, we changed the entire concept of the karate-chopping, leather-attired, and also dropped the name the *Alley Cats.*" However, it didn't end there.

As Spelling continues,

Michael Eisner called us a few months later to discuss a problem. [A problem: music to an innovator's ears!] In order to get Natalie Wood and Robert Wagner to agree to star together in our ABC TV film *The Affair*, we had agreed to jointly-develop a TV series with Wagner and Wood that they would co-own with us. ABC had set aside $25,000 to develop a pilot but we had never come up with the right property. Michael had called because a deadline was about to expire. And if we didn't submit something, ABC would have to forfeit the $25,000. "Why don't we write a script for *Charlie's Angels*," we said.

Michael gave up fighting. The deadline was looming, and he'd rather have a script he didn't like than no script at all. So we went to Bob Wagner and told him the concept for the show, and he responded just like Barry and Michael. "That's the worst idea I've ever heard," he laughed. "But what do I know about TV production. You guys are the experts. Go do it." So the *Charlie's Angels* script got written. But Michael and Barry's tastes didn't change overnight. When it arrived, they passed. *Charlie's Angels* sat on the ABC shelf gathering dust. A year later, a new programming head took over at ABC. He was looking for new shows to put on the air to get ABC out of third place. He went through the development reports and called me after reading the description for our show and said, "That thing you have about these three girls. You still want to make it? Let's do it." Finally, our pilot was ordered. It's funny how we came up with the final title. Len [Goldberg, Spelling's production partner] and I were brainstorming in my office and Kate joined us. She saw a picture I had on the wall of three angels, "Maybe you could call them the Angels." Originally, it was going to become *Harry's Angels*, but at the time ABC had another show—*Harry O.* So we became *Charlie's Angels*. ABC tested our pilot with sample viewers. Most people don't know this, but *Charlie's Angels* was one of the *worst testing* pilots in the history of ABC. The average score on good pilots is 60 and *Charlie's* was way, way, way below that. ABC was convinced they had a real loser on their hands, so they didn't put the show on the schedule, but they aired the pilot of *Charlie's Angels* in June. There was no promotion of the show and certainly no big stars in the cast, but the show attracted a huge 59 share—comparable to the kinds of crowds only attracted by mega-events like the Super Bowl. The show was a national phenomenon. Men turned in to see the young ladies and women tuned in for the exact same reason."

Spelling's code, which worked again, had these components. First, challenge convention. It turned out that women leads can carry entire shows. In fact, not only can they carry entire shows, they can even do it while playing very male roles—detectives in this case. Second, create the show around three storylines (there were three actors and therefore three stories). And third, use guest stars to appeal to a broad audience and expand the reach of the show. Among those who appeared over the long run of the series were all cast members of yet another one of Spelling's creative masterpieces, the *Love Boat* (for which Spelling used the same code).

Spelling, Serling, Porter, Hitchcock, and other legends have long understood the importance of creative codes in the pursuit of continuous innovation. Once you've figured out the code, the variations on the theme are nearly endless. As long as the newly introduced ideas that are created based on a given code are relevant (for example, they help viewers escape), the idea will not only be welcome, but the predictability of the idea itself will likely be overlooked (or at the very least, it will be accepted). In fact, in the entertainment industry, codes have become so predictable that a former graduate student in computational psychology at the University of Chicago wrote a computer program to predict the outcome of sitcoms by comparing elements of their plots with other plots stored in its memory, an algorithm similar to those that have found success among master chess players.

Daniel Goldstein created the software program "Structuralist Gilligan" as an assignment for a class on artificial intelligence in response to his professor's request to write a software program with "cocktail party appeal." By watching a few hundred sitcoms, including the popular late-1960s television show *Gilligan's Island,* a story of seven shipwrecked castaways stranded on a desert island, and reading hundreds of plot synopses, Goldstein, like Spelling, Hitchcock, and others, discovered predictable plots, techniques, and methods that make sitcoms work. Inspired by Russian literary critic Vladimir Propp, Goldstein then mapped out narrative paths for the sitcoms. This example from *Gilligan's Island* illustrates Goldstein's code:

> *Initiating event*—Enter the danger indicator: the water level surrounding the island rises above the danger level on the professor's water-height measuring stick, an invention he conjured up in order to determine whether the stranded crew are at risk of drowning should the island sink.
>
> *Conflict*—A belief that there is danger: the professor concludes the island is sinking.

Action—Take action against danger: everyone relocates to a dry part of the island.

Resolution—The danger indicator is false. As it turns out, Gilligan moved the measuring stick when fishing, so the stick position, not the water level, had changed.

If you have ever watched the show, this example likely just elicited a small smile on your face. This was the *Gilligan's Island* code (with a hint of an O. Henry ending).

Every show revolved and ultimately resolved around Gilligan's misadventures. Goldstein's experience and knowledge from studying these storylines, like master chess players studying historical matches, helped inform his code, which has since evolved into what he refers to as "structure school improvisation."

When he graduated from the University of Chicago, Goldstein pursued a career in theater as an actor, dancer, singer, writer, and director. He studied advanced improvisation at the world-famous Second City theater company (best known for spawning *Saturday Night Live* and training scores of famous comedians and actors) and also performed at ImprovOlympic and the Annoyance Theater, both institutions of master improvisation. Based on his graduate school experiences, Goldstein developed a form of improvisation called structuralist improvisation. He says that this improvisation "enables actors to create solid, coherent stories in real time which please not only the audience, but the actors as well." The structure contains all of the elements relevant to theatrical improvisation: plot, relationship networks, scene lengths, stage design, blocking, stage movement, and other factors that deliver on the goal of pleasing the audience.

According to Goldstein, "To improvise well, we must have a feeling for the overall structure of what we are trying to create. Will it last for five minutes or an hour? In short-form, the structure is given to us in the form of the rules. In much long-form, rules and structure are abandoned and anything goes. Often, such improvisations do not tell a story. Perhaps because of this, they fail to satisfy the actors and audience. In Structured Improvisation, we study the structure of an art form before improvising in it."

Like Spelling's code and O. Henry endings, Goldstein's structured improvisation provides the framework to generate novel ideas on a continuous basis while maintaining a logical storyline for the audience. His code is not explicitly apparent to the audience, merely implied in the performance itself. You know something is going on that is holding things together, but you are not quite sure what it is. As Goldstein suggests, "By studying structures, we can learn to improvise pieces that flow so smoothly they seem scripted. Audiences look on in amazement at Structured Improvisation, knowing that something is guiding the beauty of the creation, but unable to say what it is." That *something* that guides long-form improvisational theater is the same thing that guides most other acts of creativity in art, science, and business. It is a code—a framework on which to create new ideas.

Just as Archimedes' eureka moment did not come out of thin air, neither does the humor associated with improvised theater. It is based on knowledge of the improvisation form along with heuristics that inspire creativity. This is the basis of all creative codes, including Goldstein's. His code of structured improvisation eventually led to the creation of the world's most widely produced structured long-form show, *SITCOM*. Having extended runs in thirteen cities and four countries, *SITCOM* looks like a prime-time television show. It has two half-hour episodes including commercials, jokes, theme music, and even improvised scenery made of fifty-six modular building blocks. The content for the show is derived based on suggestions from the studio audience. Although the show appears to be entirely improvised, it is created based on rules that guide it. These elements of improvisation are commonly found in short-form improvisation but rarely in long-form, thereby causing conventional long-form productions to get lost in subplots that never resolve and leave the audience wondering where they are and how they got there. In order to create the conditions for creativity that fuel outstanding improvisation theater, master improvisers rely on principles. According to Goldstein, these principles include information acceptance, history development, and line-for-line dialogue. Let's consider each of these starting with information acceptance.

My brother, Alan, an actor, once advised me on rule number one of improvisation: *never say no*. As Alan puts it, "The word or concept of *no* stops the flow of the scene in its tracks. If an idea is created and offered by another actor, you have to go with it. You must find a way to make it work and make it work immediately. For example, if you and I were on stage and I said to you: *I haven't seen you wear that hat in a long time,* the worst response you could give me is: *It's not a hat. It's a bird.* In improvisation, this is the equivalent of saying no. It immediately stops the flow of the scene, and the audience will be left unsatisfied."

Goldstein refers to this as the acceptance of information: whatever is said is true. In this example, by denying the existence of a hat, the scene is killed (worse yet, in improvisation theater, denial is an insult to your stage partner's setup about the hat). Go with the hat idea, and build on it. Alan suggests, "A response should move the dialogue forward. Keeping with this example, in response to my comment, *I haven't seen you wear that hat in a long time,* the actor should respond with something like, *Remember the look in that guy's eyes when I took it. Only in Tijuana!*" This is information acceptance or, as my brother puts it, *not saying no*. It also involves a second concept that is integral to improvisation code: history development. In these simple two lines of dialogue, you know much more than the fact that one person is wearing a hat and another person is admiring that hat. The response, *Remember the look in that guy's eyes when I took it. Only in Tijuana!* adds instant history to the scene. You now know much more about the two: they are likely friends, have traveled together to Mexico, and got involved in some questionable activities while in Tijuana. Adding history gives the dialogue somewhere to go. It provides a robust platform for creative inspiration—for the creation of new ideas.

In addition to information acceptance and history development is a concept called *line-for-line dialogue*, a hallmark of master improvisation. It has two steps: an actor says a line, and then the responding actor bases his or her comment on the last thing the stage partner said and so on in a back-and-forth game (line for line).

Using the hat example, the actor's response to the last line— *Only in Tijuana!*—might be, *Does your mother still own that brothel there?* At this point, the other actor responds, *She sold it to a guy that opened a hat shop*, and the dialogue would continue. Eventually the humor will come. As Goldstein puts it, "Never try to be funny or tell jokes on stage. Humor will arise naturally out of tight relationships and solid, simple plots."

Trying to be funny during improvisation is the equivalent of trying to come up with a great idea during a brainstorming session. Without the proper framework, it just doesn't work. You may get a few cheap laughs or generate a few good ideas, but you will not likely produce bellyaching laughter or brilliant insights. However, if you adhere to a creative code, a framework on which to base your ideas, your likelihood of success will increase. Creative codes are not lost on grandmaster chess players, Hollywood producers, and actors. They are the same framework that encourage creative improvisation in business and have made more than one serial entrepreneur fabulously wealthy, among them, a Greek-born British entrepreneur known by a single name: Stelios.

Stelios Haji-Ioannou is the founder and owner of easyGroup, a private holding company that creates new ventures and owns the brand named easy. Born in Athens, Greece, in 1967, Stelios moved to London in the early 1980s, where he studied at the London School of Economics and earned a degree from the City University Business School in shipping trade and economics. He is a classic serial entrepreneur, moving from industry to industry and category to category, creating new wealth for himself and his stockholders along the way. He is best known for founding (at the ripe old age of twenty-eight) the single largest European discount airline, easyJet, PLC. easyJet was floated on the London Stock Exchange in 2000, although Stelios remains its single largest stockholder. Stelios has established more than seventeen new ventures, including Stelmar Shipping, which he founded at the age of twenty-five, took public on the New York Stock Exchange in 2001, and sold to OSG Shipping Group for $1.3 billion in 2005.

Like Spelling, Stelios is a producer, though a producer of new businesses versus new TV shows. Other easyGroup companies are easyCar, a low-cost car rental company with over two thousand locations globally; easyCruise, cruise ships for young people; easyBus, low-cost transportation between airports and city centers; and easyHotel, low-cost accommodations in city centers. In addition, easyGroup companies are engaged in such diverse activities as Internet cafés, online price comparisons, personal finance, movie theaters, male toiletries, online recruiting, pizza delivery, music downloads, mobile telephony, and even wristwatches. To the casual observer, these may appear to be completely unrelated ventures. However, to Stelios, they are exactly the same.

Herein is Stelios's creative code. Each of these businesses shares common elements, and each of these elements creates the conditions under which Stelios derives creative inspiration. Stelios's code is built on a framework designed around simplicity, although it's not that straightforward. Just like Aaron Spelling's use of "beautiful people" in nearly all of his productions, on the surface it may appear that the name *easy* is the tie that binds Stelios's ventures. However, becoming a billionaire is not quite that simple.

Stelios's billions have been derived from his creative code, which comprises the following factors: (1) deliver great value (where there is a large gap between price and product), (2) take on the big boys (in industries where they dominate), and (3) create for the many, not the few. This is Stelios's creative code, one that is agnostic to industry or category. In practice, his code involves industries and businesses whose value equation is out of equilibrium (where he can deliver "great value," as at movie theaters); where dominant and lethargic industry incumbents exist (and he can "take on the big boys," as in insurance); and where he can make an appeal to a broad base of customers through simple solutions (create products for "the many not the few," such as easy-Internet cafés). It is this code, and not only the name *easy*, that is the basis for Stelios's creativity. This code allows Stelios and endless other serial entrepreneurs to find inspiration for new ideas using a logical framework.

The benefit of identifying and defining a creative code that works for you is the ability to generate great ideas in a more deliberate fashion—to give logic to creativity. In this regard, creative codes are built on the primary themes of this book: nurturing curiosity, identifying constraints, challenging prevailing conventions (assumptions), and making unorthodox connections (forcing a confluence of disparate information). Together these precursors to creative insight are instrumental in the production of a creative code. In order to begin designing a creative code for yourself or for a given situation, follow these steps:

1. *Understand intimately how the game is played.* This is where curiosity comes into play. For example, much like Spelling's insight into what makes TV shows work or Stelios's understanding of how the "big boys operate" within a given industry, you'll want to explore these factors as well within your industry, category, or context. For Spelling, this entailed an awareness of what he knew worked in the past. This came about through his appreciation and knowledge of storytelling techniques (for example, O. Henry endings) as well as through his own experiences. These insights will serve as the basis for the conventions (or rules of the game) that you can then seek to challenge within your field, industry, or other context. Like investing, although past performance is no predicator of future performance, there may be timeless elements that you can use (for example, three storylines and three guest stars remains a proven model). In fact, awareness of these elements is what enabled Spelling to produce shows for teenagers well into his later years. As Spelling put it, "I don't think anyone questioned

Mark Twain's age when he wrote *Tom Sawyer* or *Huckleberry Finn* or George Bernard Shaw when he wrote *Pygmalion*. If you have an imagination, what does age have to do with it?" Yet another example of how to identify these conventions is what we learned from Stelios. He is a classic example of why you do not need to spend ten years studying or participating in an industry in order to make a novel contribution. Although he did not spend ten years in each of his businesses, he does understand them. He intimately understood how the airline industry operates—its economics (or lack thereof), its operations, and so on—before going into the business. Write down these success factors. This list will set out those conventions (beliefs), as well as the principles or rules of the game. You'll come back to this list, but for now, move on to the second step.

2. *Understand what your audience desires—what they want but are unable to articulate.* This is your list of constraints. It requires exploring the question, *Why?* You must determine why they buy (or choose not to buy) as much as what they want. Depending on your business, this may entail why they watch, ride, consume, participate, attend, belong, and so on. As you did previously with your list of conventions, write down these factors. This list will likely identify motivating factors (for example, "I watch TV to escape") as well as constraints ("I use the TV as a virtual babysitter because I can't afford a nanny").

3. *Explore and define those macrofactors that, should they collide, could provide the basis for a new idea or a solution to a given problem.* This list will become the fodder for formulating unorthodox connections between disparate pieces of information. This could likely be the most important material for the creative code insofar that the more random the connections you are able to make, the more likely you will generate ideas of value. Therefore, in order to construct this list, consider information from a broad array of sources. (Recall the information in Chapter Eight on making unorthodox connections.) You are essentially seeking to create an opinion about how disparate information—trends, needs, technologies,

lifestyles, categories, industries, materials, time, space, and so on—might change things when forced to a point of confluence. Recall our naked scientist, Archimedes: his big idea came at the crosshairs of the confluence of information about shipbuilding, personal hygiene (taking a bath), and formulas for measurement. Who knew? There is no such thing as bad information; however, insufficient information could lead to ho-hum ideas. Try to trace your thoughts. Pay attention to thoughts that seem to arise randomly and may at first appear unrelated. Why did you think that? At that moment?

4. *Once you have these lists complete, begin to design candidate creative codes.* Take one item from your list of constraints (for example, "I can't afford it [travel, eating out, going to the movies, and so on"]), one input from your list of conventions (for example, "affordable luxury," which sounds like an oxymoron and therefore is perfect), and one input from your list of connections (for example, yield management plus inventory-rich businesses), and you have basis for a creative code. Yield management is a concept used in businesses such as airlines and hotels to manage inventory, using price to drive demand as needed. By creating the connection between the concept of yield management, something Stelios knows well from running Europe's largest discount airline, with inventory-rich businesses (seats in an Internet café), the connection creates the opportunity to apply pricing to Internet café rentals: during peak hours, it costs more; during slow times, it costs less.

Each of these factors—curiosity, constraints, conventions, and connections—is the basis of a creative code. In this case, they are the basis for the formulation of Stelios's code: "How can I [curiosity = "economic model"] deliver great value in air travel [constraint = "I can't afford it"] for the many, not the few [challenged convention = "affordable luxury"] in industries dominated by the big boys [connections = "yield management + inventory-rich businesses"]? Once this code is in place, you will begin to see why and how Stelios has come up with so many profitable ideas.

There is logic to creativity. Stelios, like many other consummate innovators, operates using a creative formula—a code. By nurturing curiosity, identifying constraints, challenging conventional wisdom, and forcing connections between seemingly unrelated pieces of information, you too will eventually begin to formulate your own code. Like Stelios, Spelling's code consisted of similar elements: constraints ("I watch TV to escape"), challenged conventions ("Women leads in TV drama"), and connections (anthology formats + guest stars).

In order to get started right now, put the precursors to Eureka to work by reviewing your own experiences and answer the following questions:

1. What unanswered questions most interest you, that is, what problems would you like to attempt to solve?

2. What are the existing constraints, that is, what is hindering the ability to solve the problem and how can you look at these constraints in new ways? Recall the role of perception.

3. Given the problem you've identified and the respective constraints, how can you challenge conventional wisdom about the problem and your constraints?

4. What analogies exist where a similar problem was solved (perhaps outside your category, industry, or area of expertise), and what other unorthodox connections can you make about the problem, seemingly irrelevant bits of information, and possible solutions?

This is the solution to the riddle. By thinking more deliberately about how you perceive problems, how you choose to use constraints to your advantage, how you manage seemingly irrelevant information and its confluence with your past experiences and knowledge, and how you choose to challenge prevailing conventions about the world around you, you will become inspired.

Summary Points and Creative Exercises

- Creative codes are frameworks on which successful innovators generate ideas. They differ from conventions insofar as they are not specific to any specific problem. Rather, they can be applied across problem sets.

- Creative codes are popular mechanisms often used among the best in the creative community of filmmakers, television producers, publishing houses, improvisational theater companies, and serial entrepreneurs.

- Creative codes provide the platform on which to generate ideas on a continuous, rather than accidental, basis.

Epilogue: And So It Is with All Things New

As you have ascertained by now, I believe we all have the capacity to create, including those who claim they are "not creative." I also believe that conceptual creativity can be learned. Nevertheless, you likely know people who have declared that they are just not creative. If so, and should you wish to help one of these people begin to apply the lessons in this book, I suggest you start by discussing three specific words before you begin your teaching of the principles found in this book: innovation, failure, and success.

First, ironically, the word *innovation*, because it means so many different things to so many different people, is one of the greatest impediments to the successful application of conceptual creativity. Therefore, my advice to you is this: if you want to succeed at innovation and want to help others learn to succeed at innovation, don't innovate. Instead, solve problems. By focusing on problem solving rather than on the creation of unique things, you will increase your odds of success in the pursuit of innovation. Redefining how you think about the word itself is perhaps the simplest and most important thing you can do to improve your creative capacity. For those who claim not to be creative, ask them: "When was the last time you solved a problem? How did you solve it?" That was an act of creativity. Become a problem solver, not an innovator.

The second word that I encourage you to consider is *failure*. In regard to failure, it is important to remember that failure in the context of innovation not only encompasses a willingness to take chances; it also plays an instrumental role statistically insofar that it reduces the number of possible solutions to an existing problem (assuming you learn from what didn't work). What is most important to understand about failure is the *attribution* of failure: Why did it fail? Often we think that failure was due not to the idea itself but to the execution of the idea or some other force beyond our control that led to its demise. Although this may very well be true, such an attribution might be a barrier to future success because we perseverate on the solution thinking it is our execution that is at fault for the failure. Therefore, when things go wrong (as they will, or you're not trying hard enough), stop and ask why. And when things go right (as they will), ask, Where did the idea come from? What was I doing just prior to having the big idea? Based on these answers, what can you do in the future to recreate the conditions for creativity to flourish? Keep track of why and what led to these ideas as deliberately as you track the ideas themselves. Write them down, and then study this information trail. You will likely begin to observe a pattern beyond the happy accident. This has the potential to help define your creative code. Use it.

This brings me to the final word: *success*. Like *innovation* and *failure*, success may also stifle your ability and that of others to create on a continuous basis. Here's why. Although failure reduces the number of possible solutions, success ends the search for a solution. Ironically, once the journey ends, curiosity is often shelved as the new idea moves into the generally accepted category of great ideas. However, be mindful of what happens almost immediately following success. Success begets a new set of rules that, once again, blind us to new opportunities. Moreover, success creates a new frame of reference as the great ideas become revered by many in lieu of anything better. For example, just because Apple, Starbucks, and Google have succeeded with their innovations does not mean that their ideas are the best ideas. It only means that their ideas are the best ideas at the moment. Sustainable success, like democracy, is not a destination; it is an aspiration. And so in order to succeed at innovation, think of success not as a place but as a process. And don't forget to look in the rear-view mirror now and then. It has all been done before.

The one thing I can tell you with complete certainty is that once the next big idea comes along, few will remember, but history will remind us: "What has been will be again, what has been done will be done again; there is nothing new under the sun. It was here already, long ago; it was here before our time. There is no remembrance of men of old, and even those who are yet to come will not be remembered by those who follow." And so it is with all things new.

Notes

Introduction

Edward de Bono is the author of *Lateral Thinking* (New York: HarperCollins, 1973) and one of the world's leading scholars on creativity.

Stage-Gate is a popular process for managing new product development within organizations, developed by Robert G. Cooper and Scott J. Edgett. See www .prod-dev.com.

Statistics on dental floss, over-the-counter pain relievers, and running shoes were reported by W. Michael Cox, "Productivity Should Be Higher Still," in Federal Reserve Bank of Dallas, *The Right Stuff: America's Move to Mass Customization* (Dallas: Federal Reserve Bank of Dallas, 1998), p. 6. The five brands of running shoes on the market in 1970 can be found at www .sneakerhead.com.

For more on Kleenex's Anti-Viral Tissues, see http://www.kleenex.com/au/ range/anti-viral/.

The quotation attributed to Carlos Pellicer (1898–1977) can be found in *Vuelo*, a publication of Mexicana Airlines, Feb. 2007, p. 86.

Chapter One

Robert Sternberg's quotation on the relationship between anxiety and creativity is from Robert J. Sternberg and Todd I. Lubart, "Investing in Creativity," *Psychological Inquiry*, 1993, 4, 229.

Information on LifeStraw is from "Design for a Better Planet," *Smithsonian*, May 2007, p. 38.

Ford Motor Company's $400 million flop, the Edsel, is reported at http://www .edsel.com/anecdote.htm.

Ralph Nader, *Unsafe at Any Speed* (New York: Grossman Publishers, 1965). Andrew Hargadon's quote on Henry Ford is from his book *How Breakthroughs Happen: The Surprising Truth About How Companies Innovate* (Boston: Harvard Business School Press, 2003), p. 46.

Comments on Henry Ford's modern automobile manufacturing plant from Hargadon, *How Breakthroughs Happen*.

Chapter Two

Information on Zeus's Muses and sources of creative insight according to the ancients is from Robert Weisberg's *Creativity: Understanding Innovation in Problem Solving, Science, Invention, and the Arts* (Hoboken, N.J.: Wiley, 2006), pp. 90–91.

Plato's quote on divine inspiration is from Margaret Boden's *The Creative Mind: Myths and Mechanisms* (New York: Basic Books, 1990), p. 4.

Plato's quote on madness is from George Becker, citing Plato's *Phaedrus* and the Seventh and Eighth Letters: "The Association of Creativity and Psychopathology," *Creativity Research Journal*, 2001, *13*(1), 45–53.

Joyce Johnson's book *Minor Characters: A Beat Memoir* (New York: Penguin, 1999) is an award-winning memoir of the 1950s and her relationship with Jack Kerouac.

Herb Caen coined the word *beatnik* on April 2, 1958. His column appeared in the *San Francisco Chronicle* six months after the launch of the Russian *Sputnik*. In response, Allen Ginsberg wrote to the *New York Times:* "If beatniks and not illuminated Beat poets overrun this country, they will have been created not by Kerouac but by industries of mass communication which continue to brainwash man." http://www.richmondreview.co.uk/features/campbe01.html.

Harriet Beecher Stowe's quote on her inspiration for *Uncle Tom's Cabin* was reported by G. S. Balakrishnan in "The Creative Gene," *Financial Daily*, July 26, 2001.

Sigmund Freud's analysis of Leonardo da Vinci's Mona Lisa can be found at http://www.studiolo.org/Mona/MONASV12.htm.

Graham Wallas published his stages of creativity model in *The Art of Thought* (Orlando, Fla.: Harcourt, 1926).

Teresa Amabile, *The Social Psychology of Creativity* (New York: Springer-Verlag, 1983).

Honda's comment is from Gene Landrum, *Profiles of Genius* (New York: Prometheus Books, 1993), p. 186.

Chapter Three

For a thorough analysis of the Cambridge University mind game, see http://www.mrc-cbu.cam.ac.uk/~mattd/Cmabrigde/.

For more on top-down and bottom-up processing (knowledge of grammar, syntax, and context, that is, certain words cannot appear in just any position in a grammatically correct sentence), see David E. Rumelhart, "Toward an Interactive Model of Reading," in R. B. Ruddell, M. R. Ruddell, and H. Singer (eds.), *Theoretical Models and Processes of Reading*, 4th ed. (Newark, Del.: International Reading Association, 1994).

The original demonstration of the effect of letter randomization is attributed to Graham Rawlinson. He wrote a letter to *New Scientist* (May 29, 1999, p. 55) in response to K. Saberi and D. R. Perrot "Cognitive Restoration of Reversed Speech," *Nature*, 1999, 398, (16) on the effect of reversing short chunks of speech. In his letter, Graham says: "This reminds me of my PhD at Nottingham University (1976), which showed that randomising letters in the middle of words had little or no effect on the ability of skilled readers to understand the text" (http://www.newscientist.com/article.ns?id=mg16221887.600).

Carlos Fuentes's remarks on the fear of losing his love of writing were made in an interview with Blanca Granados in *Vuelo*, a publication of Mexicana Airlines, Oct. 2006, p. 108.

Sarah Breedlove Walker and her Walker method of hair care is documented by Ethlie Ann Vare and Greg Ptacek in their book *Mothers of Invention: From the Bra to the Bomb: Forgotten Women and Their Unforgettable Ideas* (New York: Quill/Morrow, 1987), p. 69.

Commentary on the moments of insight of Sir Isaac Newton, Friedrich August Kekulé von Stradonitz, Albert Einstein, and Paul McCartney were described by Dan Falk in his article, "Eureka! Where Great Ideas Come From," *University of Toronto Magazine*, autumn 2005, http://www.magazine.utoronto.ca/05autumn/eureka.asp#moments.

Statistics on the Beatles' "Yesterday" being performed 7 million times in the twentieth century and being the most recorded song in history are from the performance rights organization BMI (Broadcast Music Incorporated). Some sources claim that Irving Berlin's "White Christmas," originally recorded by Bing Crosby, has more cover versions. See http://en.wikipedia.org/wiki/Yesterday_(song).

Chapter Four

For the origination of the idea for *Fantasy Island*, see A. Spelling and J. Graham, *Aaron Spelling: A Prime-Time Life*, 2nd ed. (San Bruno, Calif.: Audio Literature, 1996).

For the study on how sleep interacts with learning, see U. Wagner and others, "Sleep Inspires Insight," *Nature*, Jan. 22, 2004, pp. 352–354. The studies on brain activity in rats and the number reduction task are from the same source.

The statistics on the study linking insight and problem solving are from Robert Stickgold and Matthew Walker's review of it in "To Sleep, Perchance to Gain Creative Insight," *Trends in Cognitive Sciences*, 2004, 8, 191–192.

Meat Loaf is the stage name of rock singer Michael Lee Aday, known for his hit album *Bat out of Hell*. "Let me sleep on it and I'll give you my answer in the morning" is from the song "Paradise by the Dashboard Light" written by Jim Steinman and performed by Meat Loaf. http://en.wikipedia.org/wiki/Meat_Loaf.

Chapter Five

The Fantasy Island fee of fifty thousand dollars is reported by http://en.wikipedia
.org/wiki/Fantasy_Island.

For the analysis of Robert Schumann, see R. Weisberg, *Creativity: Understanding
Innovation in Problem Solving, Science, Invention, and the Arts* (Hoboken, N.J.:
Wiley, 2006).

The quote attributed to Edward Bowden is from an e-mail he sent to me on
February 5, 2007.

The study of scuba divers and memory leading to insights on context-dependent
memory in two natural environments, land and underwater, is from
D. R. Godden and A. D. Baddeley, "Context-Dependent Memory in Two
Natural Environments: On Land and Underwater," *British Journal of Psychology*, 1975, 66, 325–331.

The studies and findings on mood-dependent memory are attributed to Eric
Eich, "Searching for Mood Dependent Memory," *Psychological Science*, 1995,
6, 67–75, and S. M. Smith and E. Vela, "Environmental Context-Dependent
Memory: A Review and Meta-Analysis," *Psychonomic Bulletin and Review*,
2001, 8, 203–220.

Dr. NakaMats' quote is from http://www.brainsturbator.com/site/comments/
yoshiro_nakamatsu_we_salute_you/.

The Pentagon's investment in research ($20 million) studying smart drugs
was reported by Melissa Healy, "Total Recall? 'Smart' Pills Make Headway,"
Orlando Sentinel, Mar. 2, 2005.

For more on cosmetic neurology, see A. Chatterjee, "Cosmetic Neurology: The
Controversy over Enhancing Movement, Mentation, and Mood," *Neurology*,
2004, 63, 968–974.

Cy Young's 512 wins and 313 losses are documented by Gene Landrum, *Profiles
of Genius* (New York: Prometheus Books, 1993).

For the Babe Ruth commentary, see http://www.turtletrader.com/babe-ruth.html.

Mao Zedong's quote is from his May 1963 piece, "Where Do Correct Ideas
Come From?" in his *Four Essays on Philosophy* (Honolulu: University Press
of the Pacific, 2001). The quote is from a passage Mao wrote in "Draft Decision on the Central Committee of the Chinese Communist Party on Certain
Problems in Our Present Rural Work," which was created under the direction of Mao. 1968 Foreign Language Press Edition. See http://www.etext.org/
Politics/MIM/wim/oncorrect.html.

Chapter Six

Teri Pall's interview with *Inventor's Digest* regarding her cordless phone and
Stephanie Kwolek's invention of Kevlar are documented by Ethlie Ann Vare
and Greg Ptack in *Patently Female* (Hoboken, N.J.: Wiley, 2002), pp. 21–22
(cordless phone) and pp. 7–8 (Kevlar).

The history of braille is from P. Kimbrough, "How Braille Began," which can be found at http://www.brailler.com/braillehx.htm.

A. Gopnik, A. Meltzoff, and P. Kuhl, *Scientist in the Crib* (New York: Harper-Collins, 2000), http://www.berkeley.edu/news/media/releases/99legacy/8-10-1999.html.

Steve Jurvetson's quotation on childlike thinking is from a Q&A with *Fortune Magazine*, June 28, 2006, about "issues, people, and values that matter now." See http://money.cnn.com/2006/06/27/magazines/fortune/attendeeanswer.fortune/index.htm.

For more on metacognitive skills, J. Flavell, "Metacognitive Aspects of Problem-Solving," in L. Resnick (ed.), *The Nature of Intelligence* (Mahwah, N.J.: Erlbaum, 1976), argued that metacognition explains why children of different ages deal with learning tasks in different ways: as children get older, they develop new strategies for thinking. Research studies seem to confirm this conclusion; as children get older they demonstrate more awareness of their thinking processes. See O. K. Duell, "Metacognitive Skills," in G. Phye and T. Andre (eds.), *Cognitive Classroom Learning* (Orlando, Fla.: Academic Press, 1986).

Historians Robert Friedel and Paul Israel document the twenty-two inventions of the incandescent light bulb and Edison's acquisition of the U.S. and Canadian patents on the electric light bulb for five thousand dollars and his patent in 1880 in their book, *Edison's Electric Light: Biography of an Invention* (New Brunswick, N.J.: Rutgers University Press, 1987).

Lewis Latimer's light bulb story is from P. C. Sluby, *The Inventive Spirit of African Americans* (New York: Publishers, 2004).

P&G CEO A. G. Lafley's quotation can be found at http://www.allbusiness.com/retail-trade/food-stores/4251276-1.html.

Hargadon's quote is from his book *How Breakthroughs Happen: The Surprising Truth About How Companies Innovate* (Boston: Harvard Business School Press, 2003), p. 46. The quote from Mina Edison's diary is also in Hargadon's book. The history of the Leica A, a 35 mm camera, can be read about at: http://images.google.com/imgres?imgurl=http://www.cameraquest.com/jpg6/Leica_A_3.jpg&imgrefurl=http://www.cameraquest.com/leicaa.htm&h=346&w=224&sz=14&hl=en&start=4&tbnid=Np1RoOzbmZQRcM:&tbnh=116&tbnw=75&prev=/images percent3Fq percent3Dleica percent2B1925 percent26svnum percent3D10 percent26hl percent3Den percent26lr percent3D percent26sa percent3DG. The history of Canon and its 35 mm camera can be read about at http://www.canon.com/camera-museum/.

The history of Diner's Club can be read about at http://www.dinersclubnewsroom.com/anniversary.cfm. The history of American Express can be read about at http://home3.americanexpress.com/corp/os/history.asp.

The history of Code-a-Phone Corporation and its telephone answering machines can be read about at http://home.adelphia.net/~dgudas/code-a-phone.htm. The history of Panasonic and its telephone answering machines can be read about at http://panasonic.net/history/corporate/h_pre.html.

For more on Louis Braille, see C. M. Mellor, *Louis Braille: A Touch of Genius* (Boston: National Braille Press, 2006). The Keller quote is also from this book.

The 1926 study that cites tenacity of purpose is C. Cox, *Genetic Studies of Genius, Vol. 2: The Early Mental Traits of Three Hundred Geniuses* (Stanford, Calif.: Stanford University Press, 1926). The 1952 and 1984 studies of eminent scientists that cite driving absorption are A. Roe, "A Psychologist Examines Sixty-Four Eminent Scientists," *Scientific American*, 1952, *187*, 21–25, and D. K. Simonton, *Genius, Creativity, and Leadership* (Cambridge, Mass.: Harvard University Press, 1984). The reference to a 1993 biographical study of seven creative geniuses citing "intense involvement in their work" is from H. Gardner, *Creating Minds* (New York: Basic Books, 1993).

Chapter Seven

Statistics on Israel's annual water supply are provided by Yedidya Atlas in "Israel's Water Basics" (1999). http://www.freeman.org/m_online/nov99/atlas.htm. Atlas is a senior correspondent and commentator for Arutz-7 Israel National Radio. He also serves on the advisory committee of the Freeman Center for Strategic Studies.

For more on water and the Middle East, read geologist Martin Sherman's *The Politics of Water in the Middle East* (New York: Macmillan, 1999).

Data on upcoming global water shortages and the need for increases in global food production are from the United Nations Food and Agricultural Organization: http://www.netafim.com/img/new_sys/media1/4/449_5602.pdf.

The Aharon Wiener quotation is from R. Popkin, *Technology of Necessity* (Westport, Conn.: Praeger, 1971), p. 66.

The Nakamatsu quotations are from an interview with Chic Thompson, recorded on Apr. 29, 1990, in Pittsburgh, Pennsylvania, at the Duquesne Club.

The study of workplace creativity and time is from Teresa Amabile, Constance N. Hadley, and Steven J. Kramer, "Creativity Under the Gun," *Harvard Business Review*, 2002, 80(8), 52–61.

Research on R&D spending in relation to sales growth, gross profit, and total shareholder returns was conducted by Booz Allen Hamilton and reported in B. Jaruzelski, K. Dehoff, and R. Bordia, "The Booz Allen Hamilton Global Innovation 1000: Money Isn't Everything," *Strategy+Business*, winter 2005, 1–16. The Global Innovation 1000 spent $384 billion on R&D in 2004, representing a 6.5 percent growth from 1999. In 2002, the rate jumped 11 percent. The top two thousand corporate R&D spenders spent $410 billion—only $26 billion, or 6.8 percent more than the top one thousand—so this list includes 80 to 90 percent of the total population of largest R&D spenders and likely 60 percent of global R&D, including government spending. This list is publicly traded companies only (not private) and includes only those that disclose R&D spending (therefore, financial services firms are not included). Looked at as a percentage of sales to eliminate company size issues (for example, Intel, number 12 on the list, spends on R&D eighty times that of the much smaller Cymer, number 766 on the list, but both have an R&D-to-sales ratio of 14 percent of sales; Ford, number 3, spends 130 times as much as Nissin Kogyo, number 790, but both have a ratio of 4.3 percent. And since some industries have a much higher percentage of sales (pharmaceuticals is intrinsically higher than utilities, for example), you can index across industries to normalize the comparisons. For example, Toyota, holding the number 5 spot, is a benchmark for the industry, although it is only the third highest spender in the auto industry. The company's focus on product and process excellence has resulted in the shortest development cycle time in the industry, the leadership position in hybrid technology, and a market value (in October 2005) greater than that of the next three largest vehicle manufacturers (by market cap) combined ($167 billion versus $160 billion).

Trevor Baylis's quotes are from his book, *Clock This: My Life as an Inventor* (London: Headline Book Publishing, 1999).

The statistics on people living with AIDS and deaths attributed to AIDS are reported by the nonprofit organization CARE at http://www.care.org/campaigns/hiv.asp?source=170740260000&WT.srch=1.

Matthew Bond's quotation can be found in Baylis, *Clock This*, p. 240.

The story of James Dyson and statistics on his success were cited by Hannah Clark in her article "James Dyson Cleans Up," *Forbes*, Aug. 1, 2006. http://www.forbes.com/2006/08/01/leadership-facetime-dyson-cx_hc_0801dyson.html.

For the aha studies, see: M. Jung-Beeman and others, "Neural Activity Observed in People Solving Verbal Problems with Insight," *Public Library of Science—Biology*, 2004, *2*, 500–510. E. M. Bowden and M. Jung-Beeman, "Aha! Insight Experience Correlates with Solution Activation in the Right Hemisphere," *Psychonomic Bulletin and Review*, 2003, *10*, 730–737. M. Jung-Beeman and E. M. Bowden, "The Right Hemisphere Maintains Solution-Related Activation for Yet-to-Be Solved Insight Problems," *Memory and Cognition*, 2000, *28*, 1231–1241. M. J. Beeman, E. M. Bowden, and M. A. Gernsbacher, "Right and Left Hemisphere Cooperation for Drawing Predictive and Coherence Inferences During Normal Story Comprehension," *Brain and Language*, 2000, *71*, 310–336. E. M. Bowden and M. J. Beeman, "Getting the Right Idea: Right Hemisphere Contributions to Solving Insight Problems," *Psychological Science*, 1998, *9*, 435–440.

For demonstrating that hints we are not even aware of can influence are thinking, see E. M. Bowden, "The Effect of Reportable and Unreportable Hints on Anagram Solution and the Aha! Experience," *Consciousness and Cognition*, 1997, *6*, 545–573. The statistics and quotes on Shimano's Cruising bicycle were cited by Catherine Fredman, "Executive Secrets," *Hemispheres*, Feb. 2007, pp. 82–87.

J. Diamond, *Guns, Germs, and Steel: The Fates of Human Societies* (New York: Norton, 2005).

Discussion of the differences in the corpus callosum in men and women is attributed to de C. Lacoste-Utamsing and R. L. Holloway, "Sexual Dimorphism in the Human Corpus Callosum," *Science*, 1982, *216*, 1431–1432.

The failure index is discussed in J. W. Schooler and S. Dougal "Why Creativity Is Not Like the Proverbial Typing Monkey," *Psychological Inquiry*, 1999, *10*, 351–356. Schooler and Dougal discuss the work of C. M. Seifert and others, "Demystification of Cognitive Insight: Opportunistic Assimilation and the Prepared-Mind Perspective," in R. J. Sternberg and J. E. Davidson (eds.), *The Nature of Insight*. Cambridge, Mass.: MIT Press, 1995.

Chapter Eight

For more on Einstein's brain, see M. Paterniti, *Driving Mr. Albert: A Trip Across America with Einstein's Brain* (New York: Dial Press, 2001).

For more on losing Albert Einstein's brain and Marian C. Diamond's analysis of the Brodmann's area 39 portion, see F. Balzac, "Exploring the Brain's Role in Creativity," *Neuropsychiatry Reviews*, 2006, *7*(1), 19–20. http://www.neuropsychiatryreviews.com/may06/einstein.html

Membership size data and organization mission for the Society for Neuroscience are from the society's Web site: http://apu.sfn.org/index.cfm?pagename=about_SfN. M. C. Diamond, A. B. Scheibel, G. M. Murphy Jr., and T. Harvey, "On the Brain of a Scientist: Albert Einstein," *Experimental Neurology*, 1985, 88, 198–204.

The discussion of Albert Einstein's brain is from Balzac, "Exploring the Brain's Role in Creativity."

For Heilman's comments, see K. M. Heilman, S. E. Nadeau, and D. O. Beversdorf, "Creative Innovation: Possible Brain Mechanisms," *Neurocase*, 2003, *9*, 369–379.

Art Fry's comments on creative insight are from an article that ran on MSNBC.com on Apr. 27, 2004, entitled, "Behind Eureka! Plenty of Preparation: Accidental Inventions? They Are More Myth Than Reality."

For more on opportunistic assimilation, you may wish to read the abstract "Incubation in Problem Solving as a Context Effect," by Rachel Seabrook (Oxford Brookes University) and Zoltan Dienes (Sussex University) at http://www.lifesci.sussex.ac.uk/home/Zoltan_Dienes/Seabrook percent20& percent20 Dienes percent2003.pdf.

J. Watson and F. Crick, "The Molecular Structure of Nucleic Acids: A Structure for Deoxyribose Nucleic Acid," *Nature*, 1953, *171*(4356), 737–738.

The definition of *scholē* is from P. Madow, *Recreation in America* (New York: Wilson, 1965), p. 31.

The Aristotle quote on school is from M. Mead, "The Patterns of Leisure in Contemporary American Culture," in E. Larrabee and R. Meyersoh (eds.), *Mass Leisure* (New York: Free Press, 1958), pp. 11–12.

Thomas Jefferson's letter to George Rogers Clark is referenced at "American Journeys: Eyewitness Accounts of Early American Exploration and Settlement," http://www.americanjourneys.org/lewisclark.asp.

The earthquake in Calabria, Italy, that left fifty thousand dead was reported in "Italy's Earthquake History," BBC News, Oct. 31, 2002, http://news.bbc .co.uk/1/hi/world/europe/2381585.stm.

For Beister's quote, see N. Hinske and M. Albrecht (eds.), *Was ist Aufklärung? Beiträge aus der Berlinische Monatsschrift*, 4th ed. (Darmstadt: Wissenschaftliche Buchgesellschaft, 1990).

Johann Friedrich Zöllner's question that changed the world, "What is Enlightenment?" was posed in the December 1783 issue of the *Berlin Monthly*. This fact is from James Schmidt, *The Modern Scholar: The Enlightenment* (audiobook).

That there are twenty-one different definitions of *Enlightenment* is from Schmidt, *The Modern Scholar*.

Immanuel Kant's response to Zöllner's question is from Kant, "Beantwortung der Frage: Was ist Aufklarung," which 'can be found in H. Reiss (ed.), *Kant's Political Writings* (Cambridge: Cambridge University Press 1970), p. 54. James Schmidt recounts Kant's response to Zöllner's question in his article, "The Question of Enlightenment: Kant, Mendelssohn, and the Mittwochsgesellschaft," *Journal of the History of Ideas*, 1989, 50, 269–291.

Time studies information can be found at the U.S. Department of Labor Bureau of Labor Statistics press release on the "American Time Use Survey" 2005 results, July 27, 2006, at http://www.bls.gov/news.release/pdf/atus.pdf.

Antoine Lavoisier's accomplishments are from his biography at http://en.wikipedia .org/wiki/Antoine_Lavoisier.

Benjamin Franklin's accomplishments from his biography are listed at http:// en.wikipedia.org/wiki/Benjamin_franklin.

N. Howe and W. Strauss, *Millennials Rising: The Next Great Generation* (New York: Random House, 2000).

Chapter Nine

"The world's funniest joke" was a study conducted by Richard Wiseman of the University of Hertfordshire in 2002. Wiseman created a Web site and solicited people to submit and rate over ten thousand jokes for research into differences between culture and demographics. The experiment was conducted in the United Kingdom. Forty thousand people submitted jokes, and nearly

2 million votes were cast. The author of the winning joke was Gurpal Gosall of Manchester, England. http://en.wikipedia.org/wiki/World%27s_funniest_joke.

The growth in the number of female physicians in the United States is from a presentation given by Dixie Mills, M.D., FACS, Department of Surgery, Maine Medical Center, Sept. 19, 2003. http://www.womensurgeons.org/aws_library/pub_resources.htm.

Heraclitus's quotation is reported in "Heraclitus: The Complete Fragments: Translation and Commentary and the Greek Text," translated by William Harris, fragment 98; http://community.middlebury.edu/~harris/Philosophy/heraclitus.pdf.

Avicenna's quotation on Aristotle's "law of noncontradiction" can be found at http://en.wikipedia.org/wiki/Law_of_non-contradiction.

"Gradual change leads to a sudden change of form (hua)" can be found in Stephen Karcher, *Ta Chuan: The Great Treatise* (New York: St. Martin's Press, 2000), p. 53.

The story of Sony and Philips and the development of the compact disk is cited by Joel Barker in *Paradigms: The Business of Discovering the Future* (New York: Harperbusiness, 1993).

The nonlinear progression of science is suggested by Thomas Kuhn in *The Structure of Scientific Revolutions*, 3rd ed. (Chicago: University of Chicago Press, 1996), p. vii.

DEC's founder Ken Olsen's quotation on computers and the home is available at http://en.wikipedia.org/wiki/Ken_Olsen.

The results of Maier's two-string problem in 1931 are reported by R. E. Landrum, "Maier's (1931) Two-String Problem Revisited: Evidence for Spontaneous Transfer?" *Psychological Reports*, 1990, 67, 1079–1088.

William Klann's comment after touring Swift's Chicago meatpacking plant is in A. Hargadon, *How Breakthroughs Happen: The Surprising Truth About How Companies Innovate* (Boston: Harvard Business School Press, 2003), p. 43.

A definition of Richard Dawkins's *meme* can be found at http://en.wikipedia.org/wiki/Memes.

The information on Western versus Japanese philosophies of innovation and creativity is from P. Herbig, *Innovation Japanese Style: A Cultural and Historical Perspective* (Westport, Conn.: Quorum Books, 1995).

The definition of *ii ko* ("a good child") is from H. Stevenson, *Child Development and Education in Japan* (New York: Freeman, 1986).

Principles of the Chinese concept of *xiao* are from A. Kinney, *Chinese Views of Childhood* (Honolulu: University of Hawaii Press, 1995).

Richard Nisbett's images are from his book *The Geography of Thought: How Asians and Westerners Think Differently . . . and Why* (New York: Free Press, 2003).

For information on creativity circles, see P. Herbig and L. Jacobs, "Creative Problem-Solving Styles in the USA and Japan," *International Marketing Review*, 1996, 13(2), 63–71.

Chapter Ten

The material on Darwin and Wallace can be found at http://links.jstor.org/
    sici?sici=0021-8510(198101)15%3A1%3C17%3ACAESCR%3E2.0.CO%
    3B2-T.

Statistics on master chess players learning between 50,000 and 100,000 moves
    are from Mark Jeays, "A Brief Survey of Psychological Studies of Chess"
    (http://jeays.net/files/psychchess.htm), which references P. Saariluoma, *Chess
    Players' Thinking: A Cognitive Psychological Approach* (London: Routledge,
    1995).

That the average adult can recognize over twenty thousand words in his or her
    native language is from R. W. Weisberg, *Creativity* (Hoboken, N.J.: Wiley,
    2006).

For information on Alfred Binet's studies, see http://www.psychology.sbc.edu/
    Alfred%20Binet.htm.

Statistics on Goetz's recall of 336 moves over ten simultaneously played games
    is from M. Jeays, "A Brief Survey of Psychological Studies," which references
    D. H. Holding, *The Psychology of Chess Skill* (Mahwah, N.J.: Erlbaum, 1985).

A. D. de Groot, *Thought and Choice in Chess* (The Hague: Mouton, 1965). The
    1973 study is found in H. A. Simon and K. J. Gilmartin, "A Simulation of
    Memory for Chess Positions," *Cognitive Psychology*, 1973, *5*, 29–46.

Algebraic notation is commonly used to describe the position of chess pieces.
    The letters *a* to *g* represent the columns, and the numbers 1 to 8 represent the
    ranks. Therefore, a1 is the lower left-hand square, from white's viewpoint.

Aaron Spelling's *Guinness Book of World Records* entry is published by NNDB's
    "Tracking the Entire World" biography on Spelling: http://www.nndb.com/
    people/950/000022884/.

All of Spelling's quotes are from A. Spelling and J. Graham, *Aaron Spelling:
    A Prime-Time Life*, 2nd ed. (San Bruno, Calif.: Audio Literature, 1996).

The introductory dialogue and the list of guest stars on *Charlie's Angels* are from
    http://www.thrillingdetective.com/angels.html.

"Structure School Improvisation" is from an interview with Daniel Goldstein:
    J. Rigby, "Virtual TV," *University of Chicago Magazine*, Dec. 1994. http://
    magazine.uchicago.edu/9412/Feat1.html. Goldstein's quote on how to impro-
    vise well is at http://www.dangoldstein.com/creative.html.

Stelios's biography is from http://en.wikipedia.org/wiki/Stelios_Haji-Ioannou.
    easyGroup information can be found at http://www.easy.com/about/index.
    html.

Epilogue

"There is nothing new under the sun." Ecclesiastes 1:9–14.

Further Reading

Amabile, T. M. *Creativity in Context*. Boulder, Colo.: Westview Press, 1996.

Amabile, T. M. "How to Kill Creativity." *Harvard Business Review*, 1998, 76(5), pp. 76–87.

Boden, M. A. *The Creative Mind: Myths and Mechanisms*. New York: Routledge, 2004.

Csikszentmihalyi, M. *Creativity: Flow and the Psychology of Discovery and Invention*. New York: HarperCollins, 1997.

De Bono, E. *Lateral Thinking: Creativity Step-by-Step*. New York: HarperCollins, 1973.

Guilford, J. P. *The Nature of Human Intelligence*. New York: McGraw-Hill, 1967.

Razeghi, A. *Hope: How Triumphant Leaders Create the Future*. San Francisco: Jossey-Bass, 2006.

Simonton, D. K. *Origins of Genius: Darwinian Perspectives on Creativity*. New York: Oxford University Press, 1999.

Smith, S. M., Blakenship, S. E. "Incubation and the Persistence of Fixation in Problem Solving." *American Journal of Psychology*, 1991, 104, 61–87.

Spearman, C. *Creative Mind*. New York: Appleton-Century Crofts, 1931.

Sternberg, R. J., Lubart, T. I. "The Concept of Creativity: Prospects and Paradigms." In R. J. Sternberg (ed.), *Handbook of Creativity*. Cambridge: Cambridge University Press, 1999.

Torrance, E. P. *Torrance Tests of Creative Thinking*. Bensenville, Ill.: Scholastic Testing Service, 1974.

Wallas, G. *Art of Thought*. Orlando, Fla.: Harcourt, 1926.

Weisberg, R. W. *Creativity: Beyond the Myth of Genius*. New York: Freeman, 1993.

Weisberg R. W. "Genius and Madness: A Quasi-Experimental Test of the Hypothesis That Manic-Depression Increases Creativity." *Psychological Science*, 1994, 5, 361–367.

Acknowledgments

I am grateful to all those, past and present, who have helped shape the ideas found between the covers of this book. Most notably, I thank Edward Bowden for his guidance, creativity, and depth of knowledge. We met as strangers, and through this project and our mutual interest in the origin of ideas, we have become friends. Also, I thank Robert Weisberg of Temple University, Teresa Amabile of Harvard University, Edward de Bono of the University of Malta, and Mark Jung-Beeman of Northwestern University for their generosity, their lifelong dedication to researching and promoting creativity, and allowing me to stand on their shoulders. Thanks also to my wife, Cindy, an abundant source of inspiration to me and all those around her. I thank my son Charlie for his insights on how to persuade his father to allow him to eat cookies for breakfast, and my newborn son, Matthew, for his unencumbered point of view. Thanks to my brother, Alan, for his insights on the art of improvisation. Also, thanks to my community of creative friends: Salvador Alva, Adriana Garza, Eduardo de la Garza, and Ernesto Sanchez of PepsiCo; Carlos Cruz and the students and faculty of Tecnológico de Monterrey; Tom Stat and the creative mojo of IDEO; and Urs Eberhard, Maureen Hubbs, Neil Hart, John Ward, Chuck Templeton, Jonathan Greenblatt, and Paul Sestak. Also thanks to the team at Jossey-Bass for their professionalism and commitment to big ideas and the written word: Susan Williams, Rob Brandt, Mary Garrett, Beverly Miller, and Carolyn Miller Carlstroem. Finally, I thank my students at Northwestern University for their wide-eyed idealism, endless enthusiasm, and wanting to do well by doing good.

The Author

Andrew Razeghi is an adjunct associate professor at the Kellogg School of Management at Northwestern University, where he teaches course work on innovation. As founder of StrategyLab, Inc., he works with organizations seeking growth through the creation and introduction of new ideas. His clients include Aurora Healthcare, Brinker International, Carlson Restaurants, Cytec Engineered Materials, Darden Restaurants, GE, GlaxoSmithKline, the Houston Texans, Intermatic, Novartis, PepsiCo, Treehouse Foods, and World Kitchen. In addition to his consulting work, Razeghi is a popular speaker on growth strategy and innovation. He is vice chairman of the Wright Centers of Innovation Review Panel at the National Academy of Sciences in Washington, D.C., and he serves as an adviser to Americans for Informed Democracy, a nonpartisan organization whose mission is to promote global awareness among next-generation leaders. He also is a faculty adviser to Unitus, a worldwide leader in scaling innovative solutions to global poverty. Prior to joining Kellogg, Razeghi taught the capstone M.B.A. course at the Graduate School of Business at Loyola University and was among the first American professors to teach free market economics at the Prague School of Economics in Prague, Czech Republic, shortly after the fall of communism. He is the author of the best-selling book *Hope: How Triumphant Leaders Create the Future* (Jossey-Bass) and has written many articles on creativity, innovation, and leadership. He earned his undergraduate degree in international business from Bradley University and his M.B.A. from Loyola University. For more information, visit The Andrew Razeghi Companies, LLC at www.andrewrazeghi.com. To book Razeghi as a speaker, contact info@andrewrazeghi.com.

Index